Better, Faster, Lighter Java™

Other Java™ resources from O'Reilly

Related titles

Java™ in a Nutshell

Head First Java™

Head First EJB™

Programming Jakarta Struts

Tomcat: The Definitive Guide

Learning Java™

Java™ Extreme Programming
Cookbook

Java™ Servlet and JSP™
Cookbook™

Hardcore Java™

JavaServer™ Pages

**Java Books
Resource Center**

java.oreilly.com is a complete catalog of O'Reilly's books on Java and related technologies, including sample chapters and code examples.

OnJava.com is a one-stop resource for enterprise Java developers, featuring news, code recipes, interviews, weblogs, and more.

Conferences

O'Reilly Media, Inc. brings diverse innovators together to nurture the ideas that spark revolutionary industries. We specialize in documenting the latest tools and systems, translating the innovator's knowledge into useful skills for those in the trenches. Visit *conferences.oreilly.com* for our upcoming events.

Safari Bookshelf (*safari.oreilly.com*) is the premier online reference library for programmers and IT professionals. Conduct searches across more than 1,000 books. Subscribers can zero in on answers to time-critical questions in a matter of seconds. Read the books on your Bookshelf from cover to cover or simply flip to the page you need. Try it today with a free trial.

Better, Faster, Lighter Java™

Bruce A. Tate and Justin Gehtland

O'REILLY®

Beijing · Cambridge · Farnham · Köln · Paris · Sebastopol · Taipei · Tokyo

Better, Faster, Lighter Java™
by Bruce A. Tate and Justin Gehtland

Published by O'Reilly Media, Inc., 1005 Gravenstein Highway North, Sebastopol, CA 95472.

O'Reilly books may be purchased for educational, business, or sales promotional use. Online editions are also available for most titles (*safari.oreilly.com*). For more information, contact our corporate/institutional sales department: (800) 998-9938 or *corporate@oreilly.com*.

Editor:	Mike Loukides
Production Editor:	Colleen Gorman
Cover Designer:	Ellie Volckhausen
Interior Designer:	Melanie Wang

Printing History:

June 2004:	First Edition.

 This book uses RepKover,™ a durable and flexible lay-flat binding.

ISBN: 0-596-00676-4

Table of Contents

Preface

In 2001, I was with Steve Daniel, a respected kayaker. We were at Bull Creek after torrential rains, staring at the rapid that we later named Bores. The left side of the rapid had water, but we wanted no part of it. We were here to run the V, a violent six-foot drop with undercut ledges on the right, a potential keeper hydraulic on the left, and a boiling tower of foam seven feet high in the middle. I didn't see a clean route. Steve favored staying right and cranking hard to the left after the drop to avoid the undercut ledge. I was leaning left, where I'd have a tricky setup, and where it would be tough to identify my line, but I felt that I could find it and jump over the hydraulic after making a dicey move at the top. We both dismissed the line in the middle. Neither of us thought we could keep our boats upright after running the drop and hitting the tower, which we called a haystack because of its shape. Neither of us was happy with our intended line, so we stood there and stared.

Then a funny thing happened. A little boy, maybe 11 years old, came over with a $10 inflatable raft. He shoved it into the main current, and without paddle, life jacket, helmet, or any skill whatsoever, he jumped right in. He showed absolutely no fear. The stream predictably took him where most of the water was going, right into the "tower of power." The horizontal force of the water shot him through before the tower could budge him an inch. We both laughed hysterically. He should have been dead, but he made it—using an approach that more experienced kayakers would never have considered. We had our line.

In 2004, I went with 60 kids to Mexico to build houses for the poor. I'd done light construction of this kind before, and we'd always used portable cement mixers to do the foundation work. This group preferred another method. They'd pour all of the ingredients on the ground—cement, gravel, and sand. We'd mix up the piles with shovels, shape it like a volcano, and then pour water in the middle. The water would soak in, and we'd stir it up some more, and then shovel the fresh cement where we wanted it. The work was utterly exhausting. I later told the project director that he needed cement mixers; they would have saved a lot of backbreaking effort.

He asked me how to maintain the mixers. I didn't know. He asked where he might store them. I couldn't tell him. He then asked how he might transport them to the sites, because most groups tended to bring vans and not pickup trucks. I finally got the picture. He didn't use cement mixers because they were not the right tool for the job for remote sites in Mexico. They might save a half a day of construction effort, but they added just as much *or more* work to spare us that effort. The tradeoff, once fully understood, not only failed on a pure cost basis, but wouldn't work at all given the available resources.

In 2003, I worked with an IT department to simplify their design. They used a multi-layered EJB architecture because they believed that it would give them better scalability and protect their database integrity through sophisticated transactions. After much deliberation, we went from five logical tiers to two, completely removed the EJB session and entity beans, and deployed on Tomcat rather than Web Logic or JBoss. The new architecture was simpler, faster, and much more reliable.

It never ceases to amaze me how often the simplest answer turns out to be the best one. If you're like the average J2EE developer, you probably think you could use a little dose of simplicity about now. Java complexity is growing far beyond our capability to comprehend. XML is becoming much more sophisticated, and being pressed into service where simple parsed text would easily suffice. The EJB architecture is everywhere, whether it's warranted or not. Web services have grown from a simple idea and three major APIs to a mass of complex, overdone standards. I fear that they may also be forced into the mainstream. I call this tendency "the bloat."

Further, so many of us are trained to look for solutions that match our predetermined complicated notions that we don't recognize simple solutions unless they hit us in the face. As we stare down into the creek at the simple database problem, it *becomes* a blob of EJB. The interfaces *become* web services. This transformation happens to different developers at different times, but most enterprise developers eventually succumb. The solutions you see match the techniques you've learned, even if they're inappropriate; you've been trained to look beyond the simple solutions that are staring you in the face.

Java is in a dangerous place right now, because the real drivers, big vendors like Sun, BEA, Oracle, and IBM, are all motivated to build layer upon layer of sophisticated abstractions, to keep raising the bar and stay one step ahead of the competition. It's not enough to sell a plain servlet container anymore. Tomcat is already filling that niche. Many fear that JBoss will fill a similar role as a J2EE application server killer. So, the big boys innovate and build more complex, feature-rich servers. That's good—if the servers also deliver value that we, the customers, can leverage.

More and more, though, customers can't keep up. The new stuff is too hard. It forces us to know too much. A typical J2EE developer has to understand relational databases, the Java programming languages, EJB abstractions, JNDI for services, JTA for transactions, JCA and data sources for connection management, XML for data representation, Struts for abstracting user interface MVC designs, and so on. Then, she's got to learn a whole set of design patterns to work around holes in the J2EE specification. To make things worse, she needs to keep an eye on the future and at least keep tabs on emerging technologies like Java Server Faces and web services that could explode at any moment.

To top it off, it appears that we are approaching an event horizon of sorts, where programmers are going to spend more time writing code to support their chosen frameworks than to solve their actual problems. It's just like with the cement mixers in Mexico: is it worth it to save yourself from spending time writing database transactions if you have to spend 50% of your time writing code supporting CMP?

Development processes as we know them are also growing out of control. No human with a traditional application budget can concentrate on delivering beautiful object interaction diagrams, class diagrams, and sophisticated use cases and still have enough time to create working code. We spend as much or more time on a project on artifacts that will never affect the program's performance, reliability, or stability. As requirements inevitably change due to increasing competitive pressures, these artifacts must also change, and we find that rather than aiding us, these artifacts turn into a ball, tied to a rope, with the other end forming an ever-tightening noose around our necks. There's a better way.

A few independent developers are trying to rethink enterprise development, and building tools that are more appropriate for the job. Gavin King, creator of Hibernate, is building a persistence framework that does its job with a minimal API and gets out of the way. Rod Johnson, creator of Spring, is building a container that's not invasive or heavy or complicated. They are not attempting to build on the increasingly precarious J2EE stack. They're digging through the muck to find a more solid foundation. In short, I'm not trying to start a revolution. It's already started.

That's the subject of this book. I recommend that we re-imagine what J2EE could and should be, and move back down to a base where we can apply real understanding and basic principles to build simpler applications. If you're staring at the rapids, looking at solutions you've been taught will work—but you still don't quite see how to get from point A to point B without real pain—it's time to rethink what you're doing. It's time to get beyond the orthodox approaches to software development and focus on making complex tasks simple. If you embrace the fundamental philosophies in this book, you'll spend more time on what's important. You'll build simpler solutions. When you're done, you'll find that your Java is better, faster, and lighter.

Who Should Read This Book?

This book isn't for uber-programmers who already have all the answers. If you think that J2EE does everything that you need it to do and you can make it sing, this book is not for you. Believe me, there are already enough books out there for you.

If you've already cracked the code for simplicity and flexibility, I'm probably not going to teach you too much that's new. The frameworks I hold up as examples have been around for years—although incredibly, people are only now starting to write about them. The techniques I show will probably seem like common sense to you. I'll take your money, but you'll probably be left wanting when you're done.

This book is for the frustrated masses. It's intended for those intermediate-to-advanced developers with some real experience with Java who are looking for answers to the spiraling complexity. I'll introduce you to some ideas with power and bite. I know that you won't read a phone book. You haven't got time, so I'll keep it short. I'll try to show you techniques with real examples that will help you do things better than you did before.

Organization of This Book

This book consists of 11 chapters and a Bibliography:

Chapter 1, *The Inevitable Bloat*

This chapter highlights the problems inherent in the large-scale enterprise Java frameworks that most programmers work with today. I will cover not only what's wrong with these bloated frameworks, but how they got that way. Finally, I will lay out the core principles we'll cover in the rest of the book.

Chapter 2, *Keep It Simple*

Many programmers fall into the same trap, believing that the more complicated their code, the better it must be. In fact, simplicity is the hallmark of a well-written application. This chapter defines the principle of simplicity, while drawing a distinction between simple and simplistic. I will also examine the tools and processes that help you achieve simplicity, like JUnit, Ant, and Agile development.

Chapter 3, *Do One Thing, and Do It Well*

Programmers need to resist the urge to solve huge problems all at once. Code that tries to do too much is often too entangled to be readable, much less maintainable. This chapter traces the path from being presented with a problem, to truly understanding the problem and its requirements, to finally solving the problem through multiple, simple, and targeted layers. It finally describes how to design your layers to avoid unnecessary coupling.

Chapter 4, *Strive for Transparency*

The programming community has tried for years to solve the problem of crosscutting concerns. Generic services, like logging or database persistence, are necessary for most applications but have little to do with the actual problem domain. This chapter examines the methods for providing these kinds of services without unnecessarily affecting the code that solves your business problem—that is, how to solve them transparently. The two main methods we examine are reflection and code generation.

Chapter 5, *You Are What You Eat*

Every choice of technology or vendor you make is an embodiment of risk. When you choose to use Java, or log4j, or JBoss, or Struts, you are hitching yourself to their wagon. This chapter examines some of the reasons we choose certain technologies for our projects, some traditional choices that the marketplace has made (and why they may have been poor choices), and some strategies for making the right decisions for your project.

Chapter 6, *Allow for Extension*

You simply can not know every use to which your application will be put when you write it. Any application that is worth the effort put into it will have a life outside the imagination of its authors. Your application needs to allow for extension after its release to the world. This chapter examines the techniques for providing extension points, from interfaces and inheritance to configuration and the plug-in model.

Chapter 7, *Hibernate*

Hibernate is an open source persistence framework that provides transparent object-to-relational mapping. It is a straightforward and simple implementation that focuses on the job of persisting your domain objects so that they can in turn focus on solving the business problems at hand.

Chapter 8, *Spring*

Spring is an open source application service provider framework on which to deploy enterprise applications. It has a simple, lightweight container for your objects, and provides access to a variety of core J2EE services. However, it does so without all the heavy requirements of standard J2EE frameworks, and with no intrusion into the design of your domain objects.

Chapter 9, *Simple Spider*

Building on the principles this book espouses, this chapter examines the construction of a sample application, the Simple Spider. This application provides indexing and search capabilities for a web site by crawling its pages, indexing them with Lucene, and providing multiple interfaces for searching the results.

Chapter 10, *Extending jPetStore*

Having built the Simple Spider, we now examine how easy it is to extend an application (the jPetstore sample from Chapter 8) if you follow the principles in this book. We replace the existing jPetstore search feature with the Simple Spider, then replace the persistence layer with Hibernate.

Chapter 11, *Where Do We Go from Here?*

Finally, this chapter looks ahead to what is coming on the horizon, new trends and technologies that are here or just around the corner, and how the ideas in this book are part of a changing landscape in enterprise Java development.

Bibliography

Contains a listing of resources and references.

Conventions Used in This Book

This book is by two authors, but with one voice. The stories come from the real-life experiences of Bruce and Justin. In everywhere but this paragraph, we've combined our voices, so that we don't confuse you. Don't worry. We both agree about everything that you see here.

The following typographical conventions are used in this book:

Italic
> Used for filenames, directories, emphasis, and first use of a technical term.

`Constant width`
> Used in code examples and for class names, method names, and objects.

`Constant width italic`
> Indicates an item that should be replaced with an actual value in your program.

`Constant width bold`
> Used for user input in text and in examples showing both input and output. Also used for emphasis in code, and in order to indicate a block of text included in an annotated call-out.

Comments and Questions

Please address comments and questions concerning this book to the publisher:

O'Reilly Media, Inc.
1005 Gravenstein Highway North
Sebastopol, CA 95472
(800) 998-9938 (in the United States or Canada)
(707) 829-0515 (international/local)
(707) 829-0104 (fax)

There is a web page for this book, which lists errata, examples, or any additional information. You can access this page at:

http://www.oreilly.com/catalog/bfljava/

To comment or ask technical questions about this book, send email to:

bookquestions@oreilly.com

For information about books, conferences, Resource Centers, and the O'Reilly Network, see the O'Reilly web site at:

http://www.oreilly.com

Acknowledgments

This book has been a real pleasure to write and I hope that translates to something that's a joy for you to read. The names on the cover are necessarily only a small part of the total team effort that it took to produce this book. It would be impossible to thank every person that contributed, but I feel the obligation to try.

Both Bruce and Justin would like to thank Michael Loukides for his gentle encouragement, expert touch, and steady hand. At times, it may have seemed like this book would write itself, but don't underestimate your impact on it. Thanks for giving us the freedom to do something unique, and the gentle guidance and leadership when the book required it. We also greatly appreciate our outstanding technical reviewers, including Stuart Holloway, Andy Hunt, Dave Thomas, and Glenn Vanderburg. We respect each of you deeply. It's truly an honor to have such a combined brain-trust review our book. Special thanks go to Rod Johnson for his quick response and thorough attention while editing the Spring chapter. I'm astounded by what he's accomplished.

Many heartfelt thanks also go to the production and marketing teams at O'Reilly, including David Chu for doing whatever it takes to speed the project along, Robert Romano for his work on the graphics, Daniel H. Steinberg for keeping us in front of his community, Colleen Gorman for her experienced, delicate editing, and Kyle Hart for her tireless promotion.

This book is about lighter, faster technologies and it relies heavily on the opinions and work of some pioneers. Thanks to the folks at IntelliJ, for use of a fantastic IDE. We used it to create many of the examples in this book. Thanks to Ted Neward, for his help in understanding JSR 175, and for his unique perspective. Ted, you scare me, only in a good way (sometimes). For his work on Spring, we thank again Rod Johnson. Thanks also to those who contributed to the open source JPetstore examples, including Clinton Began for his original JPetstore, which formed the foundation for Spring's version, and Juergen Hoeller's work to port that example to Spring. Gavin King and crew we thank for a fantastic persistence framework. Your remarkable accomplishments are rewriting Java history in the area of transparent persistence. We also would like to thank Doug Cutting and the entire Lucene maintenance team for their work on that excellent product. Dave Thomas and Mike Clark are Java leaders in the areas of test-driven development and decoupled designs. Thanks to both for providing credible examples for this book.

Bruce A. Tate

I would like to personally thank Jay Zimmerman for giving me a soap box for this critical message. As a mentor, you've taught me how to run a small business, you've trusted me with your customers, and you've been a jovial friend on the road. Thanks go to Maciej for helping to get the ball rolling and for help outlining this book. Thanks also go to Mike Clark for your ideas on unit testing, and your friendship. Most importantly, I thank my family. You are all the reason that I write. Thanks to Kayla and Julia for your smiles, kisses, and hugs when I am down; to my greatest love Maggie, for your inspiration and understanding; and most of all Connie, for 32 years of loving those who have been the closest to me. Connie, this book is for you.

Justin Gehtland

I would like to personally thank Stuart Halloway for being preternaturally busy all the time. I'd also like to say thanks to Ted Neward, Kevin Jones, and Erik Hatcher for forming a gravitational well pulling me towards Java. Mostly, I'd like to thank my wife Lisa and daughter Zoe, who prove to me constantly that work isn't everything. Someday, perhaps, I'll write a book you'd both like to read.

CHAPTER 1

The Inevitable Bloat

Java development is in crisis. Though Java's market share has been steadily growing, all is not well. I've seen enterprise Java development efforts fail with increasing regularity. Even more alarming is that fewer and fewer people are surprised when things do go wrong. Development is getting so cumbersome and complex that it's threatening to collapse under its own weight. Typical applications use too many design patterns, too much XML, and too many Enterprise JavaBeans. And too many beans leads to what I'll call *the bloat*.

Bloat Drivers

I'll illustrate the bloat by comparing it with the famous Lewis and Clark expedition. They started with a huge, heavily loaded 55-foot keel boat. Keel boats were well designed for traversing massive rivers like the Missouri and the Mississippi, but quickly bogged down when the expedition needed to navigate and portage the tighter, trickier rivers out West. Lewis and Clark adapted their strategy; they moved from the keel boats to canoes, and eventually to horseback. To thrive, we all must do the same. Java has not always been hard, and it doesn't have to be today. You must once again discover the lighter, nimbler vessels that can get you where you need to go. If the massive, unwieldy frameworks hinder you, then don't be afraid to beach them. To use the right boat, you've got to quit driving the bloat.

Over time, most successful frameworks, languages, and libraries eventually succumb to bloat. Expansion does not happen randomly—powerful forces compel evolution. You don't have to accept my premise blindly. I've got plenty of anecdotal evidence. In this chapter, I'll show you many examples of the bloat in applications, languages, libraries, frameworks, middleware, and even in the operating system itself.

Enterprise Mega-Frameworks

Java developers live with a painful reality: huge enterprise frameworks are en vogue. That might be good news to you if you're among the 10% of Java developers who are working on the hardest problems, and your applications happen to fit those enterprise frameworks perfectly. The rest of us are stuck with excruciating complexity for little or no benefit. Successful J2EE vendors listen to the market:

- Vendors can charge mega-dollars for mega-frameworks. Selling software means presenting the illusion of value. Big companies have deep pockets, so vendors build products that they can sell to the big boys.

- It's hard to compete with other mega-frameworks if you don't support the same features. Face it. Software buyers respond to marketing tally sheets like Pavlov's dogs responded to the dinner bell.

- Collaboration can increase bloat. Whenever you get multiple agendas driving a software vision, you get software that supports multiple agendas, often with unintended consequences. That's why we have two dramatically different types of EJB. The process satisfied two dramatically different agendas.

You can almost watch each new enterprise framework succumb to the bloat, like chickens being fattened for market. In its first incarnation, XML was slightly tedious, but it provided tremendous power. In truth, XML in its first iteration did almost everything that most developers needed it to. With the additions of XML Schema and the increased use of namespaces, XML is dramatically more cumbersome than ever before. True, Schema and namespaces make it easier to manage and merge massive types. Unfortunately, once-simple web services are taking a similar path.

But none of those frameworks approach the reputation that Enterprise JavaBeans (EJB) has achieved for bloat. EJB container-managed persistence (CMP) is the poster child for tight coupling, obscure development models, integrated concerns, and sheer weight that are all characteristic of the bloat (Figure 1-1).

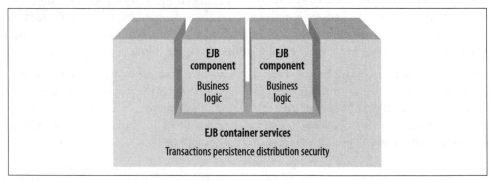

Figure 1-1. In theory, EJB's beans simplify enterprise programming

Figure 1-1 shows the EJB container-based architecture. Beans plug into a container that provides services. The premise is sound: you'd like to use a set of system services like persistence, distribution, security, and transactional integrity. The EJB is a bean that snaps into the container, which implements the set of services that the bean will use. Within the bean, the developer is free to focus on business concerns in the bean.

My favorite childhood story was *The Cat in the Hat* by Dr. Seuss, who should have been a programmer. I loved the game called "Up, up, with the fish," in which the Cat tries to keep too many things in the air at once. As an EJB programmer, it's not quite as funny, because you're the one doing the juggling. Consider this very simple example in Example 1-1. I want a simple counter, and I want it to be persistent. Now, I'll play the Cat, and climb up on the ball to lob the first toy into the air.

Example 1-1. Counter example: implementation

```
    package com.betterjava.ejbcounter;

    import javax.ejb.*;
    import java.rmi.*;

    /**
     * CMP bean that counts
     */

❶  public abstract class Counter implements EntityBean {

        private EntityContext context = null;

        public abstract Long getID( );
        public abstract void setID(Long id);

        public abstract int getCount( );
        public abstract void setCount(int count);

❷      public Object ejbCreate(Long id, int count)
          throws CreateException {

          setId(id);
          setCount(count);

          return null;
        }


        public void ejbPostCreate(Long id, int count)
          throws CreateException { }

        public void setEntityContext(EntityContext c) {
          context = c;
        }
```

Example 1-1. Counter example: implementation (continued)

```
      public void unsetEntityContext() {
        context = null;
      }

      public void ejbRemove() throws RemoveException { }
      public void ejbActivate() { }
      public void ejbPassivate() { }
      public void ejbStore() { }
      public void ejbLoad() { }

❸     public void increment() {
        int i=getCount();
        i++;
        setCount(i);
      }

      public void clear() {

        setCount(0);
      }

    }
```

The first file, called the bean, handles the implementation. Note that this class has the only business logic that you will find in the whole counter application. It accesses two member variables through getters and setters, the counter value and ID, which will both be persistent. It's also got two other methods, called clear and increment, that reset and increment the counter, respectively.

For such a simple class, we've got an amazing amount of clutter. You can see the invasive nature of EJB right from the start:

❶ This class implements the EJB interface, and you've got to use it in the context of an EJB container. The code must be used inside a container. In fact, you can use it only within an EJB container. You cannot run the code with other types of containers.

❷ You see several lifecycle methods that have nothing to do with our business function of counting: ejbActivate, ejbPassivate, ejbStore, ejbLoad, ejbRemove, setEntityContext, and unsetEntityContext.

❸ Unfortunately, I've had to tuck all of the application logic away into a corner. If a reader of this application did not know EJB, he'd be hard-pressed to understand exactly what this class was designed to do.

I'm not going to talk about the limitations of container-managed persistence. If you're still typing along, you've got four classes to go. As the Cat said, "But that is not all, no that is not all." Example 1-2 shows the next piece of our EJB counter: the local interface.

Example 1-2. Local interface

```
package com.betterjava.ejbcounter;

import javax.ejb.*;

/**
 * Local interface to the Counter EJB.
 */

public interface CounterLocal extends EJBLocalObject {

  public abstract Long getID( );
  public abstract void setID(Long);
  public abstract int getCount( );
  public abstract void setCount(int count);

}
```

This is the interface, and it is used as a template for code generation. Things started badly, and they're deteriorating. You're tightly coupling the interface to EJBLocalObject. You are also dealing with increasing repetition. Notice that I've had to repeat all of my implementation's accessors, verbatim, in the interface class. This example shows just one instance of the mind-boggling repetition that plagues EJB. To effectively use EJB, you simply must use a tool or framework that shields you from the repetition, like XDoclet, which generates code from documentation comments in the code. If you're a pure command-line programmer, that's invasive. But, "'Have no fear,' said the Cat." Let's push onward to Example 1-3.

Example 1-3. LocalHome interface

```
package com.betterjava.ejbcounter;

import javax.ejb.*;
import java.rmi.*;
import java.util.*;

/**
 * Home interface to the local Counter EJB.
 */
public interface CounterLocalHome extends EJBLocalHome {

  public Collection findAll( ) throws FinderException;

  public CounterLocal findByPrimaryKey(Long id) throws FinderException;

  public CounterLocal create(Long id, int count)
    throws CreateException;
}
```

In Example 1-3, you find the methods that support the container's management of our persistent object. Keep in mind that this class is a generic, standalone persistent class, with no special requirements for construction, destruction, or specialized queries. Though you aren't building any specialized behavior at all, you must still create a default local home interface that builds finder methods and templates for the lifecycle of the bean, like creation and destruction.

At this point, I'm going to trust that you've gotten the message. I'll omit the painful deployment descriptor that has configuration and mapping details and the primary key object. I'm also not going to include a data transfer object (DTO), though for well-documented reasons, you're not likely to get acceptable performance without one. Dr. Seuss sums it up nicely: "And this mess is so big and so deep and so tall, we cannot pick it up. There is no way at all."

You'd be hard-pressed to find a persistence framework with a more invasive footprint. Keep in mind that *every* persistent class requires the same handful of support interfaces, deployment descriptors, and classes. With all of this cumbersome, awkward goo, things get dicey. Some Cats have enough dexterity to keep all of those toys in the air. Most don't.

Progress

Developers do not want their programming languages to stay still. They want them to be enhanced and improved over time; so, we must continually add. Yet language vendors and standards boards can't simply remove older interfaces. In order to be successful, languages must maintain backwards compatibility. As a result, additions are not usually balanced with subtractions (Figure 1-2). That's a foolproof recipe for bloat.

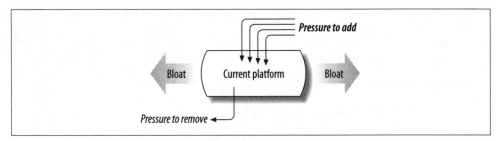

Figure 1-2. Backwards compatibility with progress leads to bloat

If you'd like to see an example of this principle in action, look no further than the deprecated classes and methods in Java. *Deprecated* literally means "to disapprove of strongly," or "to desire the removal of." In Java, Sun warns against the use of deprecated classes and methods, because they may be removed in some future release. I assume that they are defining either *remove* or *future* very loosely, because deprecated methods never disappear. In fact, if you look at the AWT presentation library for Java, you'll find many methods that have been deprecated since Version 1.1, over a half a decade ago. You can also look at the other side of the equation. The next few versions of Java are literally packed with new features.

If you're wondering about the impact of these changes on the overall size of the Java runtimes, then you're asking the right questions. Let's take a very basic metric: how big was the Zip file for the Windows version of the standard edition SDK? Table 1-1 shows the story. In Version 1.1, you would have to download just under 3.7 megabytes. That number has grown to 38 megabytes for JDK 1.4!

Table 1-1. Zip file size for standard edition Java developer kit in Version 1.1 and Version 1.4

JDK version, for Windows	Zip file size
JDK 1.1	3.7 MB
J2SE 1.2	20.3 MB
J2SE 1.3	33.2 MB
J2SE1.4	38.0 MB

You may ask, so what? Computers are getting faster, and Java is doing more for me than ever before. It may seem like you've got a free ride, but the ever-growing framework will cost you, and others:

- Some of the growth is occurring in the standard libraries. If the bloat were purely in add-on libraries, then you could perhaps avoid it by choosing not to install the additional libraries. But you can't dodge the standard libraries. That means that your resource requirements will increase.

- Java is harder to learn. Early versions of Java allowed most programmers to pick up a few books, or go to class for a week. Today, the learning curve is steeper for all but the most basic tasks. While the steep curve may not directly affect you, it does affect your project teams and the cost of developers.

- It's harder to find what you need. Since the libraries continue to grow, you need to wade through much more data to find the classes and methods that you need to do your job.

- You need to make more decisions. As alternatives appear in the basic Java toolkits (and often in open source projects), you've got to make more decisions between many tools that can do similar jobs. You must also learn alternatives to deprecated classes and methods.

- You can't fully ignore old features: people still use deprecated methods. How many Vectors have you seen in the past couple of years?

Platforms are not immune to the bloat. That's a fact of life that's beyond your control. My point is not to add needless anxiety to your life, but to point out the extent of the problems caused by the bloat.

Economic Forces

To be more specific, success drives bloat. The marketplace dictates behavior. Microsoft does not upgrade their operating systems to please us, or to solve our problems. They do so to make money. In the same way, commercial drivers will continue to exert pressure on Java to expand, so you'll buy Java products and align yourself with their vision. Beyond license fees, Sun does not make money directly from Java, but it's far from a purely altruistic venture. The Java brand improves Sun's credibility, so they sell more hardware, software, and services.

Market leaders in the software industry cannot stay still. They must prompt users to upgrade, and attract new customers. Most vendors respond to these challenges by adding to their feature set. For just one example, try installing Microsoft Office. Check out the size of the Word application. Though most users do little more than compose memos and email, Word has grown to near-Biblical proportions. Word has its own simple spreadsheet, a graphics program, and even web publishing built in. Most Word users have noticed few substantive changes over the years. To me, the last life-changing enhancements in Word were the real-time spelling checker and change tracking. Upgrade revenue and the needs of the few are definitely driving Word development today. Keep in mind that I'm an author, and spend way too much time in that application. Of course, we can't blame Microsoft. They're trying to milk a cash cow, just like everyone else. Yet, like many customers, I would be much happier with a cheaper word processor that started faster, responded faster, and crashed less.

Within the Java industry, BEA is an interesting illustration of this phenomenon. To this point, BEA has built a strong reputation by delivering an outstanding application server. From 2001 to the present, BEA and IBM have been fighting a fierce battle to be the market-leading J2EE application server. IBM increased their WebSphere brand to include everything from their traditional middleware (the layer of software between applications and the operating system) to extensions used to build turnkey e-commerce sites and portals. Two minor competing products, JBoss and Oracle9iAS, were starting to eat away at BEA's low-end market share. Both of these products were inexpensive. Oracle priced their product aggressively for users of their database, and JBoss was an open source project, so BEA was under tremendous pressure to build more value into their product and stay competitive. They responded by extending their server to enterprise solutions for building portal software, messaging middleware, and business integration. They also started a number of other initiatives in the areas of data (Liquid Data), user interface development (NetUI), and simplified application development (WorkBench). Building a great J2EE application server is simply not enough for BEA any more. They, too, must expand—and extend the inevitable bloat.

Misuse

Nothing drives bloat more than misuse. If you go to Daddy's toolkit and borrow his cool pipe wrench when you need to drive a nail, something's going to go awry. The book *Antipatterns*, by William J. Brown, et al. (Wiley & Sons), refers to this problem as the *golden hammer*. When you've got a golden hammer, everything starts to look like a nail. Misuse comes in many forms:

Framework overkill
> I've seen a departmental calendar built with Enterprise JavaBeans. I've also seen tiny programs use XML for a two-line configuration file.

Design patterns
> These days, it's almost too easy to use a design pattern. When you trade power for simplicity too many times, you get bloat.

Sloppy reuse
> If you try to stuff a round peg in a square hole, you'll have to adapt the hole or the peg. Too many adaptations will often lead to bloat. Cut-and-paste programming also leads to bloat.

Poor process
> Like fungus in a college refrigerator, bloat best grows in dark, isolated places. Isolated code with no reviews and one owner lets bloat thrive unchecked.

Many developers wear golden hammers as a badge of honor. Reaching for the wrong tool for the job is nearly a rite of passage in some of the places that I've worked. It's a practice that may save a few minutes in the short term, but it will cost you in the end.

Options

There are many possible solutions for dealing with the bloat in Java. Head-on is but one possibility. It takes courage and energy to take on the bloat, and you may not wish to fight this battle. You've got alternatives, each with a strong historical precedent:

Change nothing; hope that Java will change. This strategy means letting your productivity and code quality slide. Initially, this is the option that most developers inevitably choose, but they're just delaying the inevitable. At some point, things will get too hard, and current software development as we know it will not be sustainable. It's happened before, and it's happening now. The COBOL development model is no longer sufficient, but that doesn't keep people from slogging ahead with it. Here, I'm talking about the development model, not the development language. Java development is just now surpassing COBOL as the most-used language in the world, begging the question, "Do you want to be the COBOL developer of the 21st century?"

Buy a highly integrated family of tools, frameworks, or applications, and let a vendor shield you from the bloat. In this approach, you try to use bloat to your best advantage. You may put your trust in code generation tools or frameworks that rely on code generation, like EJB, Struts, or Model Driven Architecture (MDA). You're betting that it can reduce your pain to a tolerable threshold, and shield you from lower-level issues. The idea has some promise, but it's dangerous. You've got to have an incredible amount of foresight and luck to make this approach succeed. If you previously bet big on CORBA or DCE, then you know exactly what I mean.

Quit Java for another object-oriented language. Languages may have a long shelf-life, but they're still limited. For many, the decision to switch languages is too emotional. For others, like author Stuart Halloway, the decision is purely pragmatic. The long-time CTO of the respected training company DevelopMentor and tireless promoter of their Java practice recently decided to choose Objective C for an important project because Java was not efficient enough for his needs. Alternatives are out there. C# has some features that Java developers have long craved, like *delegation*, and C# hasn't been around long enough to suffer the bloat that Java has. Ruby is surprisingly simple and productive, and works very well for GUI prototyping and development.

Quit object-oriented languages for another paradigm. Every 15 to 20 years, the current programming model runs out of gas. The old paradigms simply cannot support the increasing sophistication of developers. We've seen programming languages with increasingly rich programming models: machine language, assembly languages, high-level languages, structured programming languages, object-oriented languages. In fact, today you're probably noticing increased activity around a new programming model called aspect-oriented programming (see Chapter 11). Early adopters were using object technology 15 years before it hit the mainstream. Unfortunately, new programming paradigms traditionally have been very difficult to time. Guess too early and you'll get burned.

Spend time and effort becoming a master craftsman. An inordinate amount of bloated code comes not from people who know too much about writing software, but from people who know too little. The temptation when faced with a problem that you don't fully understand is to put everything and the kitchen sink into the solution, thus guarding against every unknown. The problem is that you can't guard against unknowns very effectively; frankly, all the extra complexity is likely to generate side effects that will kill the application. Thoroughly understanding not just your problem domain but the craft of software development as well leads to better, smaller, more focused designs that are easier to implement and maintain.

Each of these techniques has a time and a place. Research teams and academics need to explore new programming models, so they will naturally be interested in other programming paradigms. Many serious, complex problems require sophisticated enterprise software, and the developers working on these problems will look to complex frameworks that can hopefully shield them from the bloat. Small, isolated development projects often have fewer integration requirements, so they make effective use of other programming languages, or paradigms. But for most day-to-day Java applications, the alternatives are too risky. My choice is to actively fight the bloat.

Five Principles for Fighting the Bloat

You can't fight the bloat by being simple-minded. You can't simply fill your programs with simple cut-and-paste code, full of bubble sorts and hardwiring. You cannot forget everything you've learned to date. It's an interesting paradox, but you're going to need your creativity and guile to create simple but flexible systems. You've got to attack the bloat in intelligent ways.

The bloat happened because the extended Java community compromised on core principles. Many of these compromises were for good reasons, but when core principles slide often enough, bad things happen. To truly fight the bloat, you've got to drive a new stake in the ground, and build a new foundation based on basic principles. You've got to be intentional and aggressive. In this book, I'll introduce five basic principles. Together, they form a foundation for better, faster, lighter Java.

1. Keep It Simple

Good programmers value *simplicity*. You've probably noticed a resurgence of interest in this core value, driven by newer, Agile development methods like eXtreme Programming (XP). Simple code is easier to write, read, and maintain. When you free yourself with this principle, you can get most of your code out of the way in a hurry, and save time for those nasty, interesting bits that require more energy and more attention. And simple code has some more subtle benefits as well. It can:

- Give you freedom to fail. If your simple solution doesn't work, you can throw it away with a clear conscience: you don't have much invested in the solution anyway.
- Make testing easier. Testability makes your applications easier to build and more reliable for your users.
- Protect you from the effects of time and uncertainty. As time passes and people on a project change, complex code is nearly impossible to enhance or maintain.
- Increase the flexibility of your team. If code is simple, it's easier to hand it from one developer to the next.
- Self-document your code, and lessen the burden of technical writing that accompanies any complex application.

More than any core principle, simplicity is the cornerstone of good applications, and the hallmark of good programmers. Conversely, complexity is often a warning sign of an incomplete grasp of the problem. This doesn't mean that you need to build applications with simple behavior. You can easily use simple constructs, like recursion, and simple classes, like nodes, to get some complex structures and behaviors. Figure 1-3 shows one simple node class consisting of a collection and a string. That's a simple structure, but I use it to represent a family tree, with many complex relationships. I've captured the complex relationships in concept, including children, spouses, parents, grandparents, uncles, and nieces.

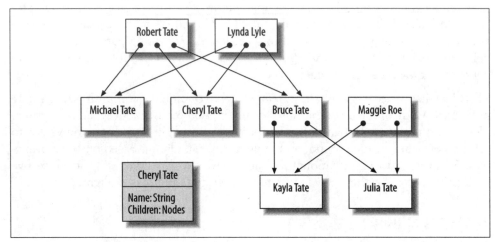

Figure 1-3. A simple node class, a string, and a collection form the foundation of a family tree

I'm not advocating simplicity across the board, above all else. I'm merely suggesting that you value simplicity as a fundamental foundation of good code. You don't have to over-simplify everything, but you'll be much better off if you pick the simplest approach that will work.

2. Do One Thing, and Do It Well

Focus is the second principle, and it builds upon simplicity. This basic premise has two underlying concepts: concentrate on one idea per piece, and decouple your building blocks. Object-oriented programming languages give you the power to encapsulate single ideas. If you don't take advantage of this capability, you're not getting the full benefits of object-orientation.

Focus is the premise behind perhaps the most popular design pattern ever, model-view-controller (MVC), shown in Figure 1-4. Each component of this design pattern elegantly separates the concerns of one particular aspect of the problem. The view encapsulates the user interface, the model encapsulates the underlying business logic, and the controller marshals data between them.

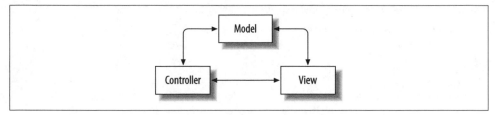

Figure 1-4. Each rectangle encapsulates a single aspect of an application

These ideas seem simple, but they carry incredible power:

- Building blocks, designed with a single purpose, are simple. By maintaining focus, it's easier to maintain simplicity. The converse is also true. If you muddy the waters by dividing your focus, you'll be amazed at how quickly you get bogged down in complex, tedious detail.

- Encapsulated functionality is easier to replace, modify, and extend. When you insulate your building blocks, you protect yourself from future changes. Don't underestimate the power of decoupled building blocks. I'm not just talking about saving a few hours over a weekend—I'm talking about a principle that can change your process. When you decouple, you have freedom to fail that comes from your freedom to refactor.

- You can easily test a single-purpose building block. Most developers find that testing drives better designs, so it should not come as a surprise that decoupled designs are easier to test.

3. Strive for Transparency

The third principle is *transparency*. When you can separate the primary purpose of a block of code from other issues, you're building transparent code. A transparent persistence framework lets you save most any Java object without worrying about persistence details. A transparent container will accept any Java object without requiring invasive code changes.

The EJB counter in Example 1-1 is a framework that is not transparent. Look at the alternative counter, in Hibernate or JDO, shown in Example 1-4.

Example 1-4. Transparent counter

```
package com.betterjava.ejbcounter;

import java.util.*;

public class Counter {

  private string name;
  private int count;
```

Example 1-4. Transparent counter (continued)

```
  public void setName(long newName) {
    name = newName;
  }

  public string getName( ) {
    return name;
  }

  public int getCount( ) {
    return count;
  }

  public void clear( ) {
    count = 0;
  }

  public void increment( ) {
    count += 1;
  }
}
```

That's it. The code is transparent, it's simple, and it encapsulates one concept—counting. Transparency, simplicity, and focus are all related concepts. In fact, in this example, we used transparency to achieve focus, leading to simplicity.

4. Allow for Extension

Simple applications usually come in two forms: *extensible* and *dead-end*. If you want your code to last, you've got to allow for extension. It's not an easy problem to solve. You probably want your frameworks to be easy to use, even when you're solving hard problems. OO design principles use layered software (which we call *abstractions*) to solve this problem. Instead of trying to organize millions of records of data on a filesystem, you'd probably rather use a relational database. Rather than use native networking protocols like TCP/IP, you'd probably rather use some kind of remote procedure call, like Java's remote method invocation (RMI). Layered software can make complex problems much easier to solve. They can also dramatically improve reuse and even testability.

When you build a new abstraction, you've got to engage in a delicate balancing act between power and simplicity. If you oversimplify, your users won't be able to do enough to get the job done. If you undersimplify, your users will gain little from your new abstraction level. Fortunately, you've got a third choice. You can build a very simple abstraction layer and allow the user to access the layer below yours. Think of them as convenient trap doors that let your users have access to the floors below.

For example, you might want to build a utility to write a message. You might decide to provide facilities to write named serialized messages. Most users may be satisfied with this paradigm. You might also let your users have full access to the JMS connection, so they can write directly to the queue if the need arises.

5. You Are What You Eat

My mother always told me that I am what I eat. For once, she was right. Applications build upon a foundation. Too many developers let external forces easily dictate that foundation. Vendors, religion, and hype can lead you to ruin. You've got to learn to listen to your own instincts and build consensus within your team. Be careful of the concepts you internalize.

Look at it this way: a little heresy goes a long way. You can find a whole lot of advice in the Java community, and not all of it is good. Even commonly accepted practices come up short. If you've been around for 10 years or more, you've probably been told that inheritance is the secret to reuse (it's not) or that client-server systems are cheaper (they're not) or that you want to pool objects for efficiency (you don't). The most powerful ideas around the whole high-tech industry bucked some kind of a trend:

- Java lured C++ developers away with an interpreted, garbage-collected language. C++ developers typically demand very high performance. Most conventional wisdom suggested that customers would be much more interested in client-side Java than server-side Java due to performance limitations. So far, the opposite has been true.

- Many Java experts said that reflection was far too slow to be practical. Bucking the trend, many new innovative frameworks like Hibernate and Spring use reflection as a cornerstone.

- Whole consulting practices were built around EJB. We're only now beginning to understand how ugly and invasive that technology is, from top to bottom.

Java development without a little heresy would be a dull place, and a dangerous one. You've got to challenge conventional thinking. When you don't, bloat happens.

Summary

In this book, I'm going to take my own medicine. I'll keep it simple and short. At this point, you're probably wondering how five simple principles can change anything at all. Please indulge me. In the pages to come, I'll lay out the five simple principles. I'll then show you the ideas in practice. You'll see how two successful and influential frameworks used these principles, and how to build applications with these frameworks. You'll see an example of a persistent domain model, an enterprise web application, a sophisticated service, and extension using these core concepts. My plan is simple. I'll show you a handful of basic principles. I'll show you how to succeed with the same ideas to build better, faster, lighter Java.

If you tend to value a book by the weight of its pages, go find another one. If you'd rather weigh the ideas, then welcome aboard. It all begins and ends with simplicity. And that's the subject of Chapter 2.

CHAPTER 2

Keep It Simple

Simplicity should be a core value for all Java programmers, but it's not. Most developers have yet to establish simplicity as a core value. I'll never forget when one of my friends asked for a code review and handed me a nine-page, hideously complex blob with seemingly random Java tokens. All kinds of thoughts swarmed through my mind in a period of seconds. At first, I thought it was a joke, but he kept staring expectantly. My next thought was that he hated me; I couldn't think of anything I'd done to deserve it. Finally, I began to read. After three pages of pure torture, I glanced up. He was grinning from ear to ear. My slackened jaw fell open, and I finally realized that *he was proud of this code*.

It's a cult. If you've coded for any length of time, you've run across someone from this warped brotherhood. Their creed: if you can write complicated code, you must be *good*.

The Value of Simplicity

Simplicity may be *the* core value. You can write simple code faster, test it more thoroughly with less effort, and depend on it once it's done. If you make mistakes, you can throw it away without reservation. When requirements change, you can refactor with impunity. If you've never thought about simplicity in software development before, let's first talk about what simplicity is not:

- Simple does not mean simple-minded. You'll still think just as hard, but you'll spend your energy on simplicity, elegance, and the interactions between simple components. e=mc^2 is a remarkably simple formula that forms the theory of relativity, one of the most revolutionary ideas ever.

- Simple code does not necessarily indicate simple behavior. Recursion, multithreading, and composition can let you build applications out of simple building blocks with amazingly complex behavior.

- Writing simple code does not mean taking the easy way out. Cutting and pasting is often the fastest way to write a new method, but it's not always the simplest solution, and rarely the best solution. Simple code is clean, with little replication.

- A simple process is not an undisciplined process. Extreme programming is a process that embraces simplicity, and it's quite rigorous in many ways. You must code all of your test cases before writing your code; you must integrate every day; and you must make hard decisions on project scope in order to keep to your schedule.

Simple code is clean and beautiful. Learn to seek simplicity, and you'll step over the line from engineer to artist. Consider the evolution of a typical guitar player. Beginners aspire to play just about anything that they can master. Intermediate players learn to cram more notes and complex rhythms into ever-decreasing spaces. If you've ever heard one of the great blues players, you know that those players have mastered one more skill—they learn what *not* to play. Bo Diddley embraces silence and simplicity with every fiber of his being. He strips his music to the bare essence of what's required. Then, when he does add the extra, unexpected notes, they have much more power and soul.

Coding simply accrues benefits throughout the development process. Take a look at the typical object-oriented development iteration in Figure 2-1. Here, I'm trying to show the typical steps of an object-oriented cycle. Notice that you can see the tangible impact of simplicity in every phase of each iteration. I should also point out that you can have a dramatic impact outside of the typical development iterations, and into the production part of an application's lifecycle, because your code will be easier to fix and maintain.

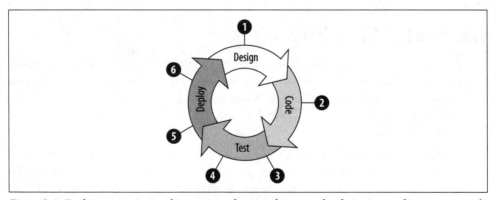

Figure 2-1. Each iteration in an object-oriented project has steps for designing, coding, testing, and reacting to the results of those tests

Here are some reasons to write simple code. They correspond to the numbers in Figure 2-1:

1. Given simple tools, takes less time, and is less prone to error.
2. Easier to write.

3. Usually easier to test.

4. Usually more reliable in production.

5. Easier to refactor before deployment.

6. Easier to refactor to fix production problems.

7. Easier to maintain.

You're probably wishing I would get right to the point and talk about new design patterns that help create simpler code. Here's the bad news: you can't address simplicity that way. You've got to pay attention to the process you're using to build code, the foundation you're building on, and the basic building blocks you're using in your everyday programming life before you can truly embrace simplicity.

Choosing the Foundations

If you want to build simple applications, you're going to have to build on simple frameworks. You need processes, tools, frameworks, and patterns that support the concepts in this book. Face it: if you build on top of an unintelligible, amorphous blob, you're probably going to be writing code that looks like sticky, tangled masses of goo. That goes for foundations you code, technologies you buy, and design patterns you reuse.

Technology you buy

Two values should govern every layer that you add to your system: value and simplicity. When it comes to value, remember that there are no free rides. Each layer must pay its own way. When I say *pay*, I'm generally not talking about the software sales price. Over your development cycle, most of your costs—like time and effort to develop, deploy, and maintain your code—will dwarf the sales price of any given component. You'll want to answer some pointed questions for each and every new piece of software:

How does it improve your life?
> Many a project has used XML for every message, configuration file, or even document. If two elements of a system are necessarily tightly coupled, XML only adds cost and complexity. Often, pure text with hash tables works fine. Likewise, even if the two elements are loosely coupled but the data is simple enough (key/value pairs, or a simple rectangular table), then XML is probably still overkill.

What is the cost?
> If a technology marginally improves your life, you should be willing to pay only a marginal cost. Too often, developers compromise on major values for minimal gain. Adopting EJB CMP for a project because it comes free with an application server often seems wise, until the true, invasive complexity of the beast shows itself.

Is it easy to integrate and extend?

Many technologies work well within their own domain, but make assumptions that make even basic extensions difficult. Be especially careful with frameworks for distributed communication, persistence, and user interfaces.

Will it cause you to compromise your core principles?

If you're striving for simplicity and independence, you should not consider ultra-invasive technologies. If you need portability at any cost, then you shouldn't use a tool that forces you to adopt nonstandard SQL.

Can you maintain it and manage it in production?

Client-server technologies often broke down because they were too expensive to deploy. Web developers live with the limitations of the user interface because the deployment advantages on the client are so significant.

Is it a fad technology that will leave you hanging when it falls from fashion?

Look across the pond at developers moving from Micrsoft's ASP to ASP.NET. While ASP was the platform, VBScript was the language of choice for many developers. Sure, it was nonstandard (the standard is JavaScript, or Ecmascript, depending on who you ask), but it looked just like VB and was comfortable. With the advent of ASP.NET, guess which language is still supported? Hint: it isn't VBScript. Now there is a *lot* of rewriting going on that need never have happened.

"Buy over build" is a great motto, but you've got to watch what you buy. It's really just a cost comparison. How much would it cost you and your team to develop the equivalent functionality with the equivalent stability but more targeted to your specific needs? When you look at it this way, everything is a "buy." Your own development shop is just one more vendor.

Design patterns

Treat design patterns like a framework that you purchase. Each one has a cost and a benefit. Like a purchases framework, each design pattern must pay its own way. If you want to embrace simplicity, you can't build in each and every design pattern from the famous Gang of Four book, *Design Patterns*, by Erich Gamma, Richard Helm, et al. (Addison-Wesley).

True, many design patterns allow for contingencies. That's good. Many Java gurus get in trouble when they try to predict what the future might hold. That's bad. The best rule of thumb is to use design patterns when you've physically established a need, today. You need expertise on your team that can recognize when a given situation is crying out for a particular pattern. Too often, developers buy the Gang of Four book, or one like it, crack it open to a random page, and apply a pattern that has no problem. Instead, it's better to find a difficult problem, and then apply the right pattern in response. You need experts on a team to apply any technology. Design patterns are no exception. In other words, don't impose design patterns. Let them emerge.

Your own code

Of course, much of your foundation will be code that you or your peers write. It goes without saying that the simplicity of each layer affects the simplicity of the layers above.

You may find that you're forced to use a particularly ugly foundation that looks only slightly better than a random string of characters. Further, you may find that it's impossible to junk it and start from scratch with a simpler foundation. When this happens, you can do what moms and pet owners do when they need to feed their charge a bitter pill: they hide it in peanut butter or cheese. I call this technique *rebasing*. When you rebase, your overriding concern is the interface. Your goal is to give your clients a better interface and usage model than the code below you. An example of rebasing is providing a *data access object* layer, which hides the details of a data store, over the EJB entities. You can then keep that skeleton deep in the closet, or clean it out at your leisure. Your clients will be protected, and be able to provide a much cleaner interface.

Process and Simplicity

Kent Beck, the father of XP, says "Pick the simplest thing that will work." Building the simplest house or making the simplest of car repairs is difficult without the right tools and process. Building great software is no different. If you want to build simple software, you've got to strip all the extraneous junk out of your process that clutters your mind, your motivations, and your code. As you've seen in Chapter 1, I don't think that most development shops are moving in the right direction. The same forces that bloat frameworks, languages, and tools can also convolute the everyday development process:

Overkill
> Heavy-duty processes used in the mainstream are designed for the most difficult problems. For the most part, UML diagrams such as sequence diagrams, class diagrams, and the like provide more harm than value. To me, UML belongs in books, on white boards, and possibly in the classroom, but rarely in design documents.

Complexity
> When you do need to add tools like UML, keep it simple. A box with the class name and the two most important methods is often more useful than a multi-symbol mish-mash with every UML bell and whistle embedded.

Indirection
> It's hard to keep those phone book–sized requirements documents in sync with the code. It's even harder to keep that 350-class set of UML diagrams up to date. I've got another, more effective rule for synchronizing documents: code always wins. Code is the primary artifact that you'll deliver.

Rigidity

> Those that sell methodology also often sell dogma. It doesn't matter whether you're going with a high-end process like Rational Unified Process (RUP) or a lower-intervention process like XP.

Over-specialization

> Too many complex development frameworks segregate team members into roles that are too specialized, and code becomes isolated from documents, programmers from testers, and code from the warning, healing light of day.

Effective development processes do none of these things. The best development processes add just enough rigor to get the job done. They let you work primarily on the artifacts that you will deliver directly to your customer, and minimize the work spent on other documents that live to support the process.

But few methods work out of the box. To make a development method effective, tailor it to your needs. Teams vary in size, skill, preference, and prejudice. If you don't like class diagrams or object interaction diagrams, don't use them. If pair programming feels like overkill, don't do it. If you can't deal with an on-site customer, use some other way to introduce an effective surrogate. If a particular diagram is not clear or useful, don't create it. As James Duncan Davidson, the author of Tomcat and Ant, once told me, "If it feels good, do it. If it doesn't, quit."

The Best of Agile

Programming methods like XP and SCRUM advocate simplicity, and make it easier to achieve. Many of the authors of these methods are part of the Agile Alliance, which defines Agile software development principles. These ideas are rapidly shaping the way modern teams build software. The methods run contrary to many of the other methods that you may use. These rules in particular cut against the grain:

Code rules

> While other methods like RUP require you to build many different types of diagrams as artifacts, Agile methods encourage you to focus on working code as the primary artifact. Everything else is secondary.

Embrace change

> Other methods try to limit change; Agile methods encourage it. Developers refactor whenever they think it's necessary or helpful. Safety measures like continuous integration and automated tests protect the code base. Customers understand that as new features are added, others are removed.

Agile methods make it much easier to develop simple code. They can help you to minimize your development process to the bare essentials that you'll need to get the job done. Even if you don't fully embrace all Agile ideas, you can make tremendous gains by embracing some of the Agile principles:

Strive for simplicity
> This is a cornerstone of all Agile methods, and among the most important.

Get and make use of feedback as early as possible
> The rest of the principles are based on this one: shortening the feedback loop and applying what you learn as soon as possible is vital to being agile.

Automate testing
> Some of the methods are stronger, requiring test cases before code. While such a principle may seem cumbersome and time-consuming, most developers find that in the long run, testing actually saves you time by catching problems early, while they are still easy to solve.

Integrate continuously
> Paradoxically, integrating more frequently actually takes less time. When you do, you catch errors quickly and find potential stumbling blocks before they get out of control.

Refactor
> To be agile, you must respond to change. That means you need to refactor early and often. It also means you need to build in the safety precautions that protect you from potential damage caused by refactoring.

These principles stand alone, and work well with just about any development process. When you use them together, you multiply their benefit. All of the principles build upon simplicity, a core value, but simplicity is difficult to maintain through successive iterations without refactoring. Automated unit tests and continuous integration build in a safety net to protect the code base from errors injected through refactoring. JUnit is rapidly becoming one of the most critical Java tools in my toolbox and the toolboxes of the best developers that I know.

Other ideas can help you to tailor your process, too. You can remove some requirement documents such as rigid functional specifications and heavy-duty use cases, and replace them with better customer contact and simple stories. You can work from source code, and relegate heavy-duty diagrams to the whiteboard. Seek regular informal communication, whenever and wherever you need it. Eschew all wasteful meetings. Abhor complexity, in any form. These ideas are independent of any methodology. They represent a philosophy, from the inside out, based on simplicity.

Pick Your Battles

A couple of years ago, I had a mental breakthrough: I was coding scared. I was afraid of trying simple solutions because I feared that they would not be rich enough. I didn't want to ever discard code; often, I'd invested too much of myself in it. I was afraid to change anything because I might break something else. I wasn't always that way. As the frameworks that I used and the algorithms that I used became more complex, I became more fearful. Fearful programming is an easy habit to make, and also an easy one to break. All you've got to do is embrace the simple solution instead of cracking open that jar of scorpions that you've been dreading. If you feel trapped, you'll code scared. The secret is leaving yourself an escape hatch.

The bottom line is this: you can't embrace simplicity without also embracing refactoring. Don't be afraid of serious changes, or even throwing away code. You'll likely find that you fear the wrong things. Because you've saved time with simple solutions along the way, you'll have more time to deal with your toughest problems when you need it most.

Think of your programming as the simple decision chart in Figure 2-2. Your goal is to keep as much code as simple as possible for as long as possible. The left-hand side of the chart represents simplicity. The right side is your escape hatch. You can use the escape hatch to inject as much complexity as you require. You'll find that you won't need your escape hatch nearly as much as you thought.

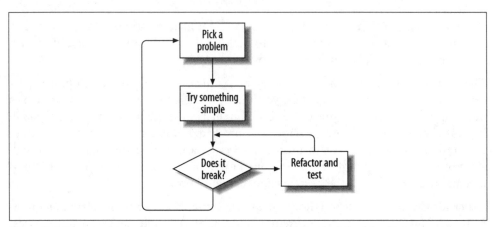

Figure 2-2. Your goal is to keep as many decisions as possible to the left of the diagram

The chart says to try something simple. How simple? Use your judgment. You don't want to waste time with solutions that you *know* will break; neither do you want to *guess* which things will break, or are likely to break. It's an important distinction that most programmers do not observe, especially as they become more experienced.

The bottom line is this: when you guess wrong, and you guess simple, it's cheap. When you guess wrong, and you guess complex, it's very expensive. You can apply this type of thinking in many places.

Algorithms

When you hear about simplicity, it's usually in the context of algorithms. I'm not saying that you should always reach for that bubble sort, but I am saying that you should leave all of the tiny, ugly optimizations out until you measure the need for change. Take the example of object allocation. Which code is easier to read, this one:

```
String middle = "very, ";
String prefix "This code is ";
String suffix = "ugly.";
String result = "";
StringBuffer buffer = new StringBuffer( );

buffer.append(prefix);
for (int i= 0; i<5; i++) {
  buffer.append(middle);
}
buffer.append(suffix);
result = buffer.toString( );
```

or this one:

```
String result = "This code is ";

for (int i= 0; i<5; i++) {
  result = result + "much, ";
}
result = result + "simpler, and neater.";
```

If you've ever read an earlier Java book with performance tips, you were probably warned that the first example is better code. In fact, some applications had real problems with object allocation. As a result, you can still see huge blobs of code like the first one all over the place.

But remember what I said about developer intuition? It stinks, and things change. Now, compilers can heavily optimize object allocation. But let's give it the benefit of the doubt, and say that you are working on an older compiler. And let's further assume that the loop is a little longer. Would you really notice the difference? Unless you were doing nothing but processing huge numbers of strings, you would never see the difference. And you'd be forced to maintain a bigger blob of uglier code until the end of time. Trade a little less performance for better readability every time. Your correct guesses will save you more than enough time to refactor the wrong ones.

Architecture

Most of the applications that you build with Java are distributed, and it's easy to distribute more broadly than you need. Distribution can add flexibility, scalability, and availability. Distribution also forces some decisions and architectures that make your code much more difficult to write and understand. When in doubt, guess simple. I'm not suggesting that you hardwire your application so that distribution is impossible. I'm merely making the point that distance will cost you. Keep in mind that the vendors that build generic J2EE architectures sell either hardware, software, or both. The network may be the computer, but it's an expensive, unreliable computer. Use it when you must, but lean on it only when it's necessary.

Performance

Most of the developers that I know try to optimize as they go. The best of them are wrong more than half of the time. You probably can't predict exactly which piece of code will cause bottlenecks in your system. Don't try. When you do, you introduce (probably useless) complexity into your application, reducing your ability to maintain and adapt your code over time. Instead, code simple solutions and save your time for measuring and repairing the bottlenecks as they occur. Let your tools, like a good profiler, do the heavy lifting.

Design patterns

There's an inside joke among many Java consultants. You can often tell which books inexperienced developers are reading by reading their code. Sometimes, it's the reader's fault. When you read about a technique, you're anxious to try it out. But don't just start coloring on the walls. Use a coloring book first—like a sample application.

Sometimes, the problem lies with authors, who often oversell ideas or solutions. Other times, the problem lies with frameworks. If you want to know what I mean, pick up a book that deals with EJB design patterns. Now, count the number of design patterns that do nothing more than work around EJB features that stink. Or look to the seminal Gang of Four patterns; they are workarounds for problems with C++.

For this reason alone, many influential consultants abhor design patterns. I'm not in that camp. But let the need for a design pattern emerge before you work it into an application. In other words, wait until you have a problem before you look for a solution.

Your Safety Net

Agile methods like XP have introduced new practices and philosophies into mainstream development that will change the way that you code forever. One of the practices that is gaining rapidly in popularity is *unit test automation*. Remember that refactoring is a foundation. In order to refactor, you've got to test all of the classes related to your refactored class. That's a pain. That's why unit testing is a fundamental building block for simplicity, because it provides the confidence to refactor, which enables simplicity, like the pyramid in Figure 2-3.

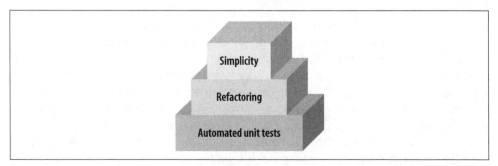

Figure 2-3. Automated unit tests provide the foundation for simplicity

You can see how these concepts build on one another. You're free to choose simple concepts because you can refactor if the simple solution is insufficient. You're free to refactor because you'll have a safety net. Automated tests provide that net.

Chances are good that you're already using JUnit. If so, you can skip ahead to the next section. If you're not using JUnit, you need to be. JUnit is an automated testing framework that lets you build simple tests. You can then execute each test as part of the build process, so you know immediately when something breaks. At first, most developers resist unit testing because it seems like lots of extra work for very little benefit. They dig in their heels (like another Dr. Seuss character, saying "I do not like green eggs and ham"). I'm going to play the part of Sam I Am, the green-eggs-and-ham pusher, and insist that you give it a try. Automated unit testing is foundational:

JUnit testing lets you run every test, with every build. Further, you can create automated tests with no more effort than it takes to build a single test (after you've done a little set up). When something breaks, you know immediately. You run tests more often and have built-in regression tests to catch errors.

JUnit testing gives you the courage to try new things. When you've got a unit test as a safety net, you can reorganize or rewrite ugly code.

JUnit lets you save and use debugging code that you're going to write anyway. If you're like most programmers, you already write a whole lot of print or log statements to debug. JUnit can give you the same type of information in a more useful form: you can check it with your computer instead of your eyeballs.

JUnit forces you to build better code. The JUnit framework will be a client of your code. If you want to be able to test, you'll have to build code that's easy to use and reuse. That means you'll need to reduce coupling and improve encapsulation.

In *Green Eggs and Ham*, Sam I Am asks the same question over and over because he knows that he's got something that may look repulsive, but is worthwhile. I know traditional software testing has beaten many of us down. It's usually difficult, and provides few tangible rewards. Don't equate JUnit with traditional testing. It has made believers out of thousands of Java developers. It'll rock your world.

Getting Started with JUnit

I'm going to introduce JUnit and Ant. If you're already well-versed in the value of both together, you'll want to skip ahead to the section "Refactoring for Testability." In case you haven't seen JUnit before, I'm going to tell you just enough to get you started, so you'll be able to understand the other concepts in this chapter. If you want to learn more, check out the books and other sources in the bibliography.

JUnit is a framework that lets you build simple test cases that test your code. JUnit test cases actually use your code and then make assertions about what should be true if the code is working properly. If the test fails, JUnit notifies you. I'll show you how to use JUnit in two ways:

Development tool

You make a simple test, and write just enough code to make it pass. This process, called *Test-Driven Development*, helps you focus efficiently, and deliver better quality. You'll run JUnit from the command line, or a GUI, or from within a supported development environment like Eclipse or IDEA.

Automated watchdog

In this model, after you've already created some test cases with your code, you run them with each build. You plug JUnit tasks into Ant.

You can learn JUnit best by example. We'll start with the development tool approach. Let's say that you have this simple Adder class, with one method called add that adds integers (Example 2-1).

Example 2-1. Add two numbers together (Adder.java)

```
public class Adder {

  public static int add(int x, int y) {
    return (x+y);
  }

}
```

If you weren't a JUnit programmer, you'd probably want to make sure that this class worked. You'd probably build a simple application, shoot out a couple of logging or print statements, or embed your tests into main. Most of that stuff gets used rarely at best, and discarded at worst.

Turn it around and start saving that work. Install JUnit, and get busy. You can get the free download and installation instructions from *http://junit.org*. Once you've installed it, try a simple test case, like Example 2-2.

Example 2-2. Build a JUnit test for Adder (TestAdder)

```
import junit.framework.*;

public class TestAdder extends TestCase {

  public TestAdder(String name) {
    super(name);
  }

  public void testBasics() {
    assertEquals(10, Adder.add(5,5));
    assertEquals(0, Adder.add(-5, 5))
  }

}
```

Take a look at Example 2-2. You'll see the class name for the test, which subclasses from a JUnit TestCase. Next, you'll see a constructor and a simple test method called testBasics. The test makes two basic assertions about Adder. If Adder.add(5, 5) returns 10, and Adder.add(-5,5) returns 0, the test passes.

To run the test, type `java junit.swingui.TestRunner`. You'll see the JUnit graphical user interface, like the one in Figure 2-4. You can then type the name of your test.

Figure 2-4. This JUnit test runner shows the status of the tests

Alternatively, you can run the test on the command line, like this:

```
C:\home\project\src>java junit.textui.TestRunner TestAdder
```

You can replace *TestAdder* with the name of your test. You'll see the results quickly:

```
.Time: 0
OK (1 test)
```

You'll see a "." character for each test that JUnit runs and a report of all of the tests that you ran.

Organizing tests

After you've created a number of individual test cases, you may want to organize them in groups called test *suites*. A suite is a collection of tests, and they can be nested, as in Figure 2-5. These organizational techniques let you organize similar tests for strategy, behavior, or convenience. For example, you may not want to run all of your long-running performance tests with each build, so break them into separate suites.

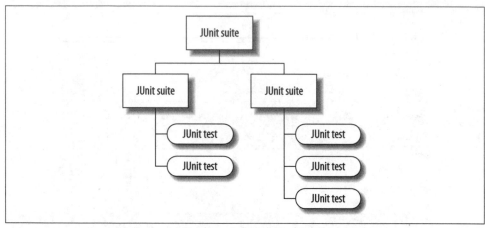

Figure 2-5. JUnit organizes test cases into suites

You have a couple of options for building your suites. You may want to explicitly add each test to a suite in order to manually control what goes into each one. Most developers prefer an easier alternative: let JUnit collect all of the tests within a class automatically, through reflection. JUnit puts all of the methods that start with the word "test" into a suite. Add the following method to your test class:

```
public static Test suite() {
    return new TestSuite(TestAdder.class);
}
```

After you've organized your tests into suites, you may want an easier way to invoke the tests. Many people prefer to have tests grouped into a main( ) method. You can do so easily, like this:

```
public static void main(String args[]) {
    junit.textui.TestRunner.run(suite());
}
```

Initialization and clean up

Often, within a test, you may want to do some set up work that's common to several tests, like initializing a database or a collection. Additionally, you may want to do some special clean-up work in code that's common to several tests. JUnit provides the setup and `tearDown` methods for these purposes. You can add these methods to your test class, substituting your initialization and clean-up code in the commented areas:

```
protected void setUp( ) {
   // Initialization
}

protected void tearDown( ) {
   // Clean up
}
```

Assertions

JUnit allows several kinds of assertions. Each of the following methods allows an optional descriptive comment:

assertEquals
> Passes if the two parameters are equal. You can specify a tolerance (e.g., for floating point arithmetic), and the assertion will pass if the difference between the parameters is less than your specified tolerance.

assertNull
> Passes if the single parameter is null.

assertSame
> Passes if the parameters refer to the same object.

assertTrue
> Passes if the parameter, containing a Boolean expression, is True.

Whenever you are asked to pass in two values to compare (the expected and the actual), pass the *expected* value first.

Exceptions and intentional failure

Under some circumstances, you may want to fail a test. You may have logic within your test that is unreachable under normal circumstances. For example, you might have an exception that you wish to test. Use a Java catch block, with other JUnit techniques:

```
public void testNull( ) {
   try {
      doSomething(null);
      fail("null didn't throw expected exception.");
   } catch (RuntimeException e) {
      assertTrue(true);                         // pass the test
   }
}
```

Those are the JUnit basics. You can see that the framework packs quite a punch in a very simple package. In the next couple of sections, I'll show how JUnit can change the way that you code in ways that you may not expect. For a complete and excellent treatise on JUnit, see "Pragmatic Unit Testing in Java with Junit" by Andrew Hunt and David Thomas, the Pragmatic Programmers (*http://www.pragmaticprogrammer.com*).

Automating Test Cases with Ant

I cut my programming teeth in an era when a build guru was a full-time job. The build was a dark, foul-smelling place where working code went to die. Integration was another circle of Hell. For me, it's not like that anymore, but many of my clients fear builds, so they avoid integration until it's too late.

If you want to shine a little light into those dim recesses, you need information. That means that you've got to bite the bullet and integrate regularly. Ant makes it much easier for developers and teams to build at any moment. You are probably already using Ant, and I won't bore you with another primer here. I will, however, show you how to plug JUnit into Ant.

To extend Ant for JUnit, most developers use a separate target called test. Here, you'll build the target test cases and copy them to a common directory. Next, you'll run the test cases with a special task, called JUnit. Here's the JUnit test underneath the test class that I used for our examples:

```
<junit showoutput="on" printsummary="on"
       haltonfailure="false" fork="true">
    <formatter type="brief" usefile="false"/>
    <formatter type="xml"/>
    <batchtest todir="${test.data.dir}">
        <fileset dir="${test.classes.dir}">
            <include name="**/*Test.class"/>
        </fileset>
    </batchtest>
    <classpath>
        <fileset dir="${lib.dir}">
            <include name="**/*.jar"/>
            <include name="**/*.zip"/>
        </fileset>
        <pathelement location="${build.classes}"/>
        <pathelement location="${test.classes.dir}"/>
    </classpath>
</junit>
```

This example tells Ant that you're using JUnit. You can have JUnit halt the build upon failure, but sometimes it's useful to get a test report with more than one failure (in order to gather more information), so we opt not to halt on failure. The batchtest parameter means that you want JUnit to run all tests in a given directory.

Next, tell JUnit to create a report with another custom task called JUnitReport. This Ant task is optional, but quite useful for teams or larger projects. Here's the Ant task that we use for examples in this book:

```
<junitreport todir="${dist.test.dir}">
    <fileset dir="${test.data.dir}">
        <include name="TEST-*.xml"/>
```

```
        </fileset>
        <report format="frames" todir="${dist.test.dir}"/>
    </junitreport>
```

Now, you can see more of the power of JUnit. Your build is suddenly giving you a striking amount of information. Sure, you'll know if your code compiles. But now you'll also be able to get a thorough sniff test of *runtime behavior*! You'll be able to point to the test cases that break, right when you break them.

You're changing your worldview ever so slightly. A successful build becomes one that compiles *and runs* successfully. If you've never tried it, you have no idea how powerful this paradigm shift can be. These two tools, Ant and JUnit, form the secret recipe to avoiding integration Hell. All you need to do is keep the build working and make sure the test cases pass every day. Don't let them get too far out of sync. You'll find that integration becomes a tiny part of your everyday rhythm. My guess is that you'll like these green eggs and ham much better than you ever thought you would.

Refactoring for Testability

After using JUnit for a while, most people begin to write their test cases *before* the code. This process, known as test-driven development, changes the way that you look at programming in unexpected ways. The reason is that each new class that you create has more than one client: your test case, and your application, as in Figure 2-6.

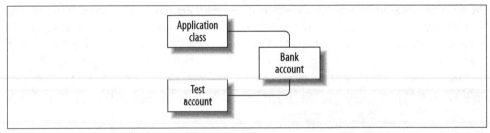

Figure 2-6. Testing improves the design of your application by reducing coupling

Since you'll reuse classes that you want to test, you'll have to design in all of the things that improve reuse from the beginning. You'll naturally spend more time up-front separating the concerns of your classes, but you'll need to do less rework moving forward.

Reuse and testability

To find out how to accomplish test-driven development, let's listen to the experts. In Hunt and Thomas's book *Pragmatic Unit Testing* they present the following example of a method that sleeps until the top of an hour:

```
public void sleepUntilNextHour( )
    throws InterruptedException {

    int howLong;
```

```
// calculate how long to wait here...

    thread.sleep(howlong);
    return;
}
```

This code is probably not going to be very testable. The code doesn't return anything, and does nothing but sleep. If you think about it, the operating system call to sleep is probably not going to break. If anything, it's the calculation of how long to sleep that's going to give you trouble. The refactored code looks like this:

```
public void sleepUntilNextHour()
    throws InterruptedException {

    int howlong = milliSecondsToNextHour(new Date());

    thread.sleep(howlong);
    return;
}
```

We've taken a method with poor testability and built a likely target for tests: milliSecondsToNextHour. In the process, we have also increased the likelihood that the code can be reused. The method milliSecondsToNextHour will work with any date and time, not just the current one.

Coupling

Mike Clark is a noted author, the creator of *JUnitPerf* (an open source JUnit testing framework for building performance tests), and a JUnit expert and contributor. He strongly believes that unit tests will reduce the coupling in your code. For instance, if you want to be able to test the persistent classes of your application without actually wiring into a database, you'll probably want to cleanly separate the persistence layer and data source, so that it's not intrusive. Then you can test your class with a simpler data source, like a collection.

If you write your test cases first, you'll get pretty immediate feedback when you try to couple things too tightly. You won't be able to build the right set of tests. For the most part, that means separating concerns as clearly as possible. For example, testing could drive the following design decisions:

- In order to effectively test your order processing in a messaging architecture without using your full messaging infrastructure, your test cases would motivate you to separate your message processing from the message parsing and delivery. You would probably wish to code a separate Order value object, an OrderHandler to process the order, an OrderProducer to package an order, and the OrderConsumer to parse the message.[*] The end result is a cleaner design with looser coupling (Figure 2-7).

---

[*] Bitter EJB.

- To test a domain model without worrying about EJB, you'd probably want to separate your domain model from your session bean façade. You'd then have a domain model with clean separation from the façade, and the services that the façade provides. You could then build lightweight, independent tests for the session beans. Once again, test-driven development drives us to the best design.

- If you want to be able to test the persistent classes of your application without actually wiring into a database, you'll probably want to cleanly separate the persistence layer and data source. Then you can test your class with a simpler data source, like a collection.

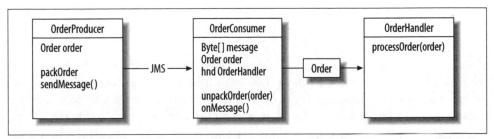

Figure 2-7. Testability improves a design with only a single producer and consumer to a design that breaks out an order and handler

In each of these cases, a need for better testability drives a better design. With practice, you'll find that each individual component of a system is ever-so-slightly more complex, but the overall system will fit together much more smoothly, improving your overall simplicity tremendously.

Summary

Simplicity is perhaps *the* core value of Java development. It makes you more productive, improves the readability of your code, reduces bugs, and makes it easier to layer core concepts. It's a concept that does not stand alone. You must consider the foundation that you're using—whether it's a framework, design pattern, or your own code. You've also got to worry about your development process, because complex development processes frequently lead to complex code.

Finally, you've got to embrace the practices of refactoring and testing to have the freedom that leads to simplicity. One XP principle is to try the simplest thing that will work. This adage works well within XP because if you're wrong, you can refactor. Since you started with a simple solution, you're not going to lose much. Refactoring, through, can be dangerous, so you need a safety net. Automated unit tests provide that safety net.

In the next chapter, I'll introduce the principle "Do one thing, and do it well." You'll learn how to focus the goals of each part of your system. As you'd probably expect, I'll also spend some time talking about reducing coupling.

CHAPTER 3
Do One Thing, and Do It Well

There's only one way to eat an elephant: a bite at a time. That's also the best way to code. Each bite of clear, simple Java code must have a single purpose. The best Java programmers keep a maniacal focus on a single problem at a time and go to extraordinary lengths to maintain that focus. If you want to improve, emulate them.

I'm a whitewater kayaker. For a long time, I walked around every serious rapid that I faced. I could see how to run a one-shot waterfall or drop, but I couldn't get my head around the linked moves that would take me safely through Humpty-Dumpty on the Little River, or .25-mile Pine Creek on the Arkansas. A light clicked on for me on the Watauga River in Tennessee. I learned that I just couldn't bomb down continuous Class IV rapids with a preconceived set of moves in my head. Instead, I needed to find the natural break points *within* the rapids, and run many little ones. I learned to read the river and find the natural resting places within the whole. Then I could conquer one section, set up, and attack the next section. When I approached the problems this way, I received unexpected benefits. Coding, to me, is similar:

- It's usually easier to clearly define a piece of a big problem than the whole. We all tend to get overwhelmed by large problems, but not as much by many smaller ones. Our brains just work that way, whether we're on a river or behind a keyboard.

- When things go wrong, it's easier to adjust or adapt if your plan is segmented. Plans change; it's harder to change a grand, sweeping plan than several smaller ones.

- You can protect yourself from disaster. On the river, I now plan for safety one small section at a time. While coding, we must build test cases that identify problems quickly in each logical section.

- You can better reuse techniques and code. On the river, I learn new moves that I can use elsewhere. Instead of frantically paddling through a section, I use a draw stroke to avoid one rock, an aggressive brace and sweep to punch a hydraulic, and so on. In code, I build collateral and learn techniques to solve smaller, more general problems. Each design pattern that you learn in context is worth any 20 that you read about.

Whether you're a kayaker running a Class V rapid, a physicist working on a space station, or a programmer dealing on a massive problem, your approach should be the same.

Understand the problem

> You must understand a problem to solve it well. Effective programming goes beyond your code editor and debugger. You need to be able to accurately gather requirements, and control the scope and expectations of your customers. There is nothing worse than a solution without a problem; it just generates more problems.

Distill the problem to its essence

> It's often said that programming is more of an art than a science. Nowhere is this axiom more obvious than in the ability to cut through clutter and find the core problem. You've got to recognize what belongs in the center of your problem space and what you can push out to other classes around the perimeter, or out of the project altogether. Most of the time, less is more.

Layer the architecture

> If you're solving a difficult problem and you can only focus on one thing at a time, you must layer your architecture, with each layer handling one task. The broadest, most successful design patterns help you build effective, decoupled layers. Model-view-controller lets you design user interfaces with three layered components. Façades allow you to build clean interfaces between major layers in your application. If you like to study design patterns, pay attention to how often this theme arises.

Periodically refine your approach

> Left to its own devices, software loses focus over time. You've got to make a concentrated effort to refactor, decoupling your software into autonomous layers. Automated tests will help you refactor with confidence and design decoupled code in the first place. Getting feedback from teammates and clients often helps make sure the approach still solves the right problems.

In this chapter, we explore each of these concepts in detail. You don't need to go through them all to see a difference in your programming—you can benefit from each technique individually. But combining them multiplies their impact.

Understanding the Problem

Communication is a huge part of programming. Writing better Java won't do you any good if you're building the wrong thing: you must understand before you can code. As you advance in your programming career, you'll find that more and more of your job demands effective communication. It doesn't really matter where your requirements come from—your team lead, an analyst, or the customer. In each case, your first job is to accurately gather each requirement and focus your customer on what you can reasonably achieve with your resources at hand. Don't plow your customer under with enormous requirements and arcane design documents. If the customers can't understand your documents, they can't focus on the real issues. Like your code, keep your requirements simple and clear.

If you don't like communication, I've got news for you: things are going to get worse before they get better. In a global economy, you've got to be efficient. Increasingly, that means developers must handle more and more of the software development process. Out of college, I worked for the largest software company in the world. We had more testers than coders on a project (often, by a factor of 3 to 1), and teams of 10 planners supporting 40 developers. The overall effort was 200 developers strong. Now, that project might use 10 developers and half the original timeframe to develop the same piece of software. Since the development of better automation and unit testing, each modern developer must shoulder more of the testing load. Coders also do more design work and planning than ever before. However, experience shows that many of those developers are not equipped to handle many of the increased planning and analysis roles that they face.

Gathering Requirements

This book would not do its readers justice if we didn't talk about dealing with change from a process perspective. If you're one of those shops that tries to do more with less, you need to do two things in the planning process: first, weed out software requirements that don't contribute much to the final project, and second, weed out unnecessary work that supplements traditional development but does not contribute much to the overall content or quality of your code.

Many programmers believe that they need to build object-oriented design documents like class diagrams or object interaction diagrams in order to support development. The danger with this approach is that you can spend too much time maintaining your design documentation, and not enough time building working code. The best design resources are a lightweight requirements list, working code, and an on-site customer. A requirements document often consists of little more than single line items, each taking less than half a day to several days to complete. Often, you don't need formal project management software. I've managed requirements with expensive project management tools, word processor documents, and spreadsheets. Low tech usually works better than high tech.

Controlling Scope Creep

Once you've got requirements together, you'll want to keep a manageable scope. I often spend a good deal of my time improving communication and understanding at client sites. By far, the biggest problems I encounter come from controlling the scope and expectations of the project. Often, the power comes from a pocketbook, so it's tempting for those in charge to try to add whatever features they want, whenever they want them. There's a necessary tension between productivity and change. Many teams succeed because they adapt to rapidly changing requirements, but just as many projects falter because teams fail to adequately control scope. This is the central problem in software development. The only way to effectively develop software is to succeed at solving this problem.

Managing good change

Iterative development is effective partially because it allows you to adapt. But regardless of the process that you use, your customers must understand the overall cost of change. Whenever someone requests significant changes, you can't threaten to beat them with a plastic whiffleball bat. You've got to be receptive but firm. Your first response should be something like, "We'll try to work it in. Let me tell you what it will cost." This type of answer immediately gives your customer positive feedback, and also lets them know that change affects the overall cost of the project. It doesn't matter who the customer is. Whether your project is internal or external, some facts never vary: development takes money, time, and manpower. You can only do so much with a given pool of resources.

Figure 3-1 illustrates the three ways you can react to expanded requirements:

1. Reduce the remaining scope by removing an unimplemented item of the same cost from this release.

2. Increase the time allotted: request more time, and ask for more money.

3. Increase your manpower: ask for more money, and increase your team size.

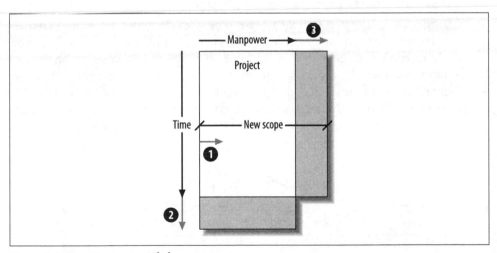

Figure 3-1. Reacting to expanded requirements

You can also combine two or more of these options. The first method is by far the best.

Notice that increasing hours is not a viable option. Heavy overtime means that the project managers are not doing their job. (Increasingly, the developer is the project manager!) Heavy overtime usually leads to defections, mistakes, and sloppiness that cost more in the long run. Nor should you increase your manpower in other ways. Unless you're grossly understaffed, increasing the size of an optimal team is going to sacrifice efficiency, and may even delay the project further. Scheduling conflicts also cause problems. If you frequently slip your schedules, you're delaying the value to your customers, and that's rarely a good idea.

By far, the preferred way to pay for a change in a release is to push other functions out of the release. If you get into the habit of negotiating a healthy give-and-take with your customers, they'll get better at understanding of what's most important to them, and you'll get accustomed to delivering on your commitments.

Curtailing disruptive change

The ability to react to your customers is important, but not all change is good. Disruptive change keeps your code out of the hands of your customers, and code that's in the lab doesn't do your customers any good. Disruptive change takes several forms:

- Unchecked scope creep can quickly derail any project. You must consciously mitigate each change in scope, and do so with minimal disruption to your team and schedule. That usually means pulling features out for each one that you add.

- Changes that are outside the central purpose of a project reduce focus. This kind of disruptive change often deals more with infrastructure and middleware than with end applications. For example, I have seen customers build messaging into their persistence frameworks, or business logic into their user interfaces. These types of short-term compromises usually backfire.

- Changes outside of the normal release schedules disrupt a team, and changes that happen very late in an iteration (for example, after a code freeze) are especially disruptive. In general, you improve your ability to change by shortening iterations rather than forcing unnatural change into an ongoing iteration. Figure 3-2 shows the cost of change at each step in the development cycle. The sawtooth pattern is characteristic of the cost of change in an iterative development process. It's better to have the customer wait for the next iteration.

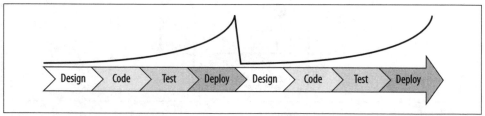

Figure 3-2. At the end of each cycle, especially after a code freeze, change gets more expensive

In general, certain types of changes cause more chaos than others: late changes, large changes, and shifts in focus. The reality, though, is that you're going to have change, and unless you're both disciplined and lucky, you're going to have to deal with some late change. The rest of this chapter, and this book, deals with adapting to change.

Distilling the Problem

Virtuosos in any profession have a common gift: they can distill a problem to its basic components. In physics, Einstein identified and captured many complex relationships in a simple equation, $e=mc^2$. Beethoven captured and repeated a motif consisting of four notes in his fifth symphony that's endured for centuries. Programming demands the same focus. You've got to take a set of requirements, identify the essential elements, strip away everything that doesn't belong, and finally break down and solve the problem.

To improve your programming, you don't have to live in a cave, reading about a design pattern that covers every possibility. You don't need to know the latest, hottest framework. You've just got to focus on the right problem, distill it to the basics, and hammer out the simplest solution that will work. In this section, I'm going to take a set of requirements, distill them, and turn them into code.

Collecting Requirements

Let's take a simple example. Say that you're building an ATM. Your job is to build the support for an account. In keeping with Agile programming practices, you've decided to keep a simple set of requirements in a table. You'll record the requirement number, a brief description, a size (timeline), and choose a programmer. Your team is small and your cycles are short, so that's all that you think you'll need. Table 3-1 shows the basic requirements.

Table 3-1. Requirements for account project

Number	Description	Size (hours)	Assigned
1	Keep a balance and account number		
2	Report a negative balance		
3	Have a six-digit account number		
4	Don't let users change the account number		
5	Remember the balance when the user comes back		
6	Let users make deposits		
7	Let users make withdrawals		
8	Display the balance		
9	Display debit/credit buttons		
10	Print a new balance when the user is done		

Table 3-1. Requirements for account project (continued)

Number	Description	Size (hours)	Assigned
11	Make the account secure		
12	Display the bank's logo		
13	Use lighter colors		
14	Let the users print out their balance		
15	Make the user type a four digit password		
16	Make the user insert a card		
17	It should be transactional (it all works, or it all fails)		

These requirements are typical of the types of things you'll get from your customers. They are far from complete, but that, too, is normal. The job of the requirements document is to accumulate requirements as you understand more about your application. At the moment, you're the one assigned to this task. You'll size tasks later. At this point, you should focus on the problem at hand. Your job is to build support for an account.

Whittling Away the Noise

Your first job is to whittle away some of the noise. Take any of the issues that may fit neatly elsewhere and push them out to the perimeter. Immediately, you recognize that you should separate the user interface from the base account. You also see that keeping a balance means that the account will need to be persistent. You'll use your relational database. Security probably doesn't belong in the account itself; it would probably be better left to another layer of the architecture, like perhaps a façade, but security is also a special case. Too many developers treat security as an afterthought, something they can sprinkle on top of an application to make it "safe." No such pixie dust exists, though; security layers should be treated with the same respect you show to everything else in your code.

Essentially, you need to build a persistent account. Rather than trying to build a design document, you'll start to code. It's a small enough problem to get your head around, and you can always refactor. In fact, you'll probably refactor several times as you think of ways to simplify and improve your design. The new set of requirements is shown in Table 3-2.

Table 3-2. Updated, whittled-down requirements

Number	Description	Size (hours)	Assigned
1	Keep a balance and account number	2	BT
2	Report a negative balance	1	BT
3	Have a six-digit account number	1	BT
4	Don't let users change the account number	1	BT

Table 3-2. Updated, whittled-down requirements (continued)

Number	Description	Size (hours)	Assigned
5	Remember the balance when the user comes back	4	BT
6	Let users make deposits	1	BT
7	Let users make withdrawals	1	BT
17	It should be transactional (it all works, or it all fails)	?	BT

Keep in mind what you're trying to accomplish. You're not discarding the rest of the tasks. You'll still need security and a user interface. Instead, you first want to carve out a manageable size of development. When that's completed and tested, you can go ahead and layer on the other aspects of the application, like the user interface and the persistence. Also, keep in mind that as an example, these requirements may have a finer grain than they would in a production project. When you've got a rough unit, you can start to code.

I'm going to omit the JUnit test cases to keep this example (and this book) brief, but I recommend that you code test cases first, as we did in Chapter 2. The next task is to rough out an interface. You don't yet need a full implementation. I recommend that you oversimplify, attaching everything to a single class until the ultimate design becomes clear. For this example, start with the implementation for requirements 1, 6, and 7, in a simple class called Account. Scoping and a simple constructor can take care of requirement 4. Stub out the rest with empty methods, so that you've got a simple interface.

Start by organizing in a package, and add a simple constructor:

```
package bank;

public class Account {

    float balance = 0;
    private String accountNumber = null;


    Account (String acct, float bal) {
        accountNumber = acct;
        balance = bal;
    }
```

Next, add the accessors for the members. Remembering your requirements, you want to keep the account number private, so you scope it accordingly, and omit the setter.

```
    public float getBalance () {
        return balance;
    }

    public void setBalance(float bal) {
        balance = bal;
    }
```

```
    private String getAccountNumber () {
      return accountNumber;
    }

    public float debit(float amount) {
      balance = balance - amount;
      return balance;
    }

    public float credit(float amount) {
      balance = balance + amount;
      return balance;
    }
```

Finally, add some stubs for methods that you'll need later. You may not decide to do things in this way, but it helps the ultimate design to emerge if you can capture some placeholders.

```
    public void save() {}
    public void load() {}
    public void beginTransaction() {}
    public void endTransaction() {}
    public void isValid(String accountNumber) {}


}
```

This is a reasonable start. You've covered requirements 1, 3, 4, 5 and 6, and you've got a head start on the rest. You're probably not completely happy with the design. It's already time to refactor. Since you've been writing unit tests all along, you can do so with confidence, knowing that your tests will let you know if you break anything along the way.

Refining Your Design

Sometimes, a metaphor can help you analyze your design. In this case, think of the job that we want the account to do. At least four things surface:

1. The getters and setters should tell you that this class holds data. That's a classic data access object, or value object, depending on the terminology you're used to.

2. The validation, debit, and credit methods should tell you that you're doing business logic.

3. The class saves and retrieves data from the database.

4. The beginTransaction and endTransation suggest that you're also doing transactional processing.

Some of my past clients would have stopped designing at this point. If you're an EJB programmer, you're thinking that you've got a match: the class is transactional, persistent, and possibly distributed. Step away from that sledge-o-matic, and pick up a plain old ordinary hammer. It's time to break this puppy down.

Not many would complain if you suggested that it's a good idea to separate the business logic from the value object. Today, many modelers like to always separate value objects from the business domain. Persistence frameworks and other middleware made it easier to build systems that way. But designs are simpler and much easier to understand when you can leave them together.

Now, think about the save and load methods, as well as the transactional methods. Another metaphor is useful in this situation: think of a folder that holds paper. The paper represents your data and the folder represents a value object. Think of the save and load methods as filing the folder for later access. You would not expect the folder to be able to file itself. In principle, it makes sense to break the persistence methods away from the accessor methods and the business logic. For now, let's move the transactional methods with the persistence.

The result is clean, well-defined business logic, and a data access object (DAO) built explicitly to access the database. The DAO should be able to save and retrieve accounts. Here's the code to load an account using JDBC:

```
public static Account load(String acct) throws NotFoundException, SQLException {

    Account valueObject;
    ResultSet result = null;
    String sql = "SELECT * FROM ACCOUNT WHERE (accountNumber = ? ) ";
    PreparedStatement stmt = null;
    stmt = conn.prepareStatement(sql);

    try {

      stmt.setString(1, acct);
      result = stmt.executeQuery( );

      if (result.next( )) {

        account.setAccountNumber(result.getString("accountNumber"));
        account.setBalance((float)result.getDouble("balance"));
        return account;

      } else {
        throw new NotFoundException("Account Object Not Found!");
      }
    } finally {
      if (stmt != null) {
        stmt.close( );
      }
    }
  }
```

The save code is similar. It's a little ugly, but that's okay. You'll only be reading this code when you're interested in the database details. You'll be able to test the business logic of the account without wiring it to the data access object. You'll also be able to add sophistication to the business logic without thinking about persistence, and you can change the persistence layer without impacting the business logic.

Consider transactions for a moment. Rather than bringing in the heavyweight artillery like JTA or EJB, start with the simplest solution. You can lean on the transaction support of your database engine and access it through your JDBC connection. That means the JDBC connection should probably be attached elsewhere, because you'll want all of your different data access objects to potentially participate in the same transaction. For example, if a user opened an account, you'd probably want to update the user and the first account deposit at the same time.

You know you need to refactor. Where's the correct place for the JDBC connection, and the associated transaction support? It's not in the account itself or the Account data access object. You'll need to create something, and you'll need some type of connection manager. If that strategy doesn't work out, you can always refactor again. Lean on these types of iterative refinements to improve your design as you progress.

Although this is a trivial example, it demonstrates how the process works. You write tests, code a little, refactor a little, and repeat the cycle until your eventual design emerges. After wading through these details, it's time to look at issues at a higher level.

Layering Your Architecture

This book is about building complex code in a simple way. The principle in this chapter, "Do one thing, and do it well," may seem like it argues against building complex software. But it simply means each major piece focuses on a single aspect of the overall solution.

You can organize an application in layers, so that you'll only have to deal with small, focused chunks of the application at any given point of time. In this section, I'll talk about the anatomy of a layer, the interfaces between layers, and the typical layers that you're likely to find in better Java applications. Before I start piling on generic information about how you should build layers, here's what you should not do:

- Don't bite off too much in any given layer. Your layers should have a simple purpose, and they should be easy to digest at one sitting. If your layers are too fat, they'll be too hard to test, maintain, and understand.

- Don't add a layer because you read about it in a book. In most cases, you should add new layers and design patterns based on real, experienced need, not assumed need.

- If you're testing as you go, your tests will dictate some level of layering. Don't resist. Your tests mirror usage patterns in many ways, and they'll make your code easier to reuse and decouple as the need arises.

- Pay attention to names. Think of each independent layer as a library of services, even if there's just one client at the moment. If you misname your services, your layer will be misused. If a name becomes a problem, change it. If it's too hard to change names, get a tool that lets you do so. Intellij's IDEA was used to build some of the software in this book, and its refactoring tools are extremely useful.

All developers layer; some just do so more effectively and intentionally. In the last section, you probably noticed that I threw some requirements out to handle later. I did so because the postponed requirements were natural layers for the emerging architecture. I explicitly defined layers for the business domain model and the data access object. I implicitly defined a layer for the user interface, a potential façade, and security. Let's look at the anatomy of a layer.

The Basics of Layering

OOP makes effective layering much easier. Each layer should do one fundamental thing. There are many different layers, but they only do a few different types of things:

Abstraction
> Often, a software layer does what you need it to, but it may have an interface that's complex or awkward for your application. An abstraction layer presents a simpler interface for its clients. Façade layers are abstraction layers.

Application
> These layers do the specific work of an application. The Account object is a functional application layer.

Service
> These layers are similar to application layers, but they provide common services potentially needed by many applications. The line between a service layer and an application layer can be blurry.

Interfaces Between Layers

Figure 3-3 shows how the layers fit together. Ideally, you want a strict hierarchy. Typical layers are clients of layers below, and provide services for layers above. The lower-level layer usually exposes and maintains the interface, but that's not always the case. When you expose an interface (like the darker areas of Figure 3-3), you need to harden it more. Peer layers are at the same level of abstraction and do roughly the same type of work. Peer interfaces might have a tighter level of coupling than other layers, because peers often share bi-directional interfaces. Often, you might not want that tighter coupling.

Think about the business model that we defined in our example above. The lower-level services that you use, those defined by the Java JDK, know nothing about our

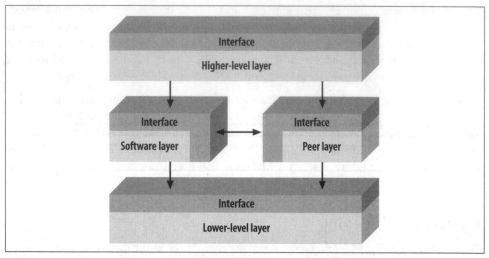

Figure 3-3. A typical intermediate software layer has layers above and below

account. The account uses JDK library classes like String. If the interface of the JDK changes, then you've got to move Account to change with it. The Account, on the other hand, knows nothing about the DAO layer. The Account DAO layer that saves and loads an account is a client of the Account.

Most people think about interfaces as two equal operators, like two people shaking hands with presumably the same equipment. Usually, that's not the case. Most interfaces impose a direction. One layer presents an interface, and the others use it. Your interface should simultaneously provide complete services to the consuming layer while protecting the inner workings of the presenting layer.

In general, you'd like your layers to observe a strict hierarchy. Lower-level layers should not have direct knowledge of higher-level layers. Peer relationships can be especially troublesome, and deserve strict attention.

A word about good interfaces

You can make your layers much more effective if you concentrate on building a good interface around them. An interface bears some resemblance to food: everyone knows when it's good and when it's not, although not everyone will agree; it also takes whole lot more skill to make it right than to consume it. You could write a whole book on interfaces and still not say everything that needs to be said, but here are some guidelines for good interfaces. They should be:

Complete
> You should be able to use your layer to do everything that you need to do through your interface. Everything doesn't need to be easy, but everything does need to be available.

Compact

Don't allow unnecessary duplication in your interface. When you duplicate, you're more prone to error, and you create additional maintenance burdens. Don't build in future requirements until you need them; don't add too many convenience methods; don't expose private methods.

Convenient

It should make it easy to do the things that you do the most. Convenience and compactness are often at odds. You'll want to assure compactness first, then convenience. That doesn't mean that you can completely blow off convenience.

Hardened

An interface should protect you from incorrect usage. If a null value breaks your code, throw the appropriate exception.

Consistent and predictable

An interface should observe standards, and should do similar tasks in similar ways.

Well-factored

Often, a few smaller, more focused interfaces are better than one all-encompassing interface.

Interfaces can take many forms, but all should observe these basic principles. They apply to messaging models, distributed remote procedure calls, and basic method invocations, too. The need for good programming hygiene is magnified between major levels of your architecture. Two excellent books for good interface design are *The Pragmatic Programmer* by Andrew Hunt and David Thomas and *Effective Java* by Joshua Bloch, both published by Addison-Wesley.

Common Layers

In my classes, many of my students ask me what layers a Java application should have. I tell them that it depends on what you want to do. Java application architectures are converging around a common architecture in several critical places. In truth, many of those layers are unnecessary, or mandated by ineffective architectures like EJB CMP. In other places, certain effective layers, in the right circumstances, are beginning to emerge.

Business domain models

Some development shops are moving away from a classic business domain model. Frankly, for some applications (like those built to baby-sit big relational databases), I'd have to agree with their direction. When you're doing nothing but viewing and entering relational data, a full object-oriented model is overkill.

When you do have a legitimate need for an effective business model, it should usually be the center of your application. Build services and interfaces around that layer to persist, display, notify, and manipulate that model. The model is too important, and often too complex, to clutter with other details—so transparency becomes extremely important.

Data access

Many strategies and frameworks exist to persist business objects. At the low end is a simple data access object implemented with JDBC. At higher levels, full persistence frameworks build in value-add services like lazy loading and caching across clusters. Since EJB CMP left such a bad taste in people's mouths for so long, Java developers are moving back toward simpler JDBC-based architectures, and also toward transparent persistence solutions such as JDO and Hibernate.

Communication

The era of CORBA, where a single business domain model was distributed across many different nodes, is dying rapidly. Instead, you're more likely to see strategic communication between hierarchical layers of an application (like session beans between an application server and a presentation server), and between major applications. As such, packaging a service with a technology like web services or JMS with XML is much more prevalent. Older systems come into play here; also, disparate technologies like Microsoft's .NET platforms are increasing in popularity.

Façades

A façade is often the primary client of your business model. Your goal is to provide a higher-level interface for the rest of the world. Before you add a façade layer, you must understand the value that it's providing. I've seen clients mirror the interface of their DAO layer, verbatim, within their façade. Façades are much more interesting when you're doing some consolidation, such as returning all members of a department across a distributed interface instead of making a separate round trip for each one.

For distributed architectures, you often want to present a simple, coarse-grained interface to clients, instead of a complex, complicated business domain model. The façade layer rolls many fine-grained methods up to a simpler interface.

If you're one of those developers who tend to believe everything written by a major software vendor, now would be a good time to pick up some rotten tomatoes and eggs. I'm going to get a little heretical. Your façade layer need not be distributed at all. You can simply deploy your presentation layer and your business layers on the same box. If your façade is not distributed, you probably don't need those session beans. And if you're not getting transactional integrity or security from your façade, you may not need a façade layer at all. You'll see more about the role of an effective façade in Chapter 4.

User interfaces

One of the most famous patterns for layering software is the model-view-controller architecture made popular by the Smalltalk community. Java model-view-controller architectures break user interfaces into three separate sections: a browser-based user interface, a controller, and a wrapper around the domain model.

Java developers fully embrace this concept and generally support an open source implementation called Struts to separate the user interface layers for a web-based application. Figure 3-4 shows the typical arrangement. A browser-based HTML interface calls a controller servlet, via HTTP. This servlet invokes an action, which wraps the domain model. Then, the controller calls a JSP, which compiles to a servlet, and returns a page to the client, possibly with results from the domain model.

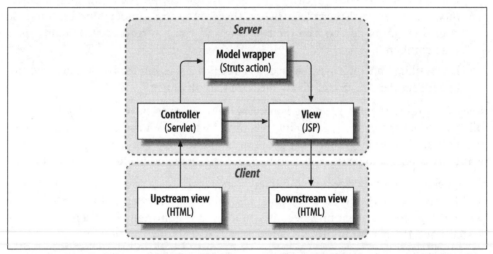

Figure 3-4. The model-view-controller architecture provides an approach to layering user interface code (this figure is a slight variation of the original, and supports web user interfaces via Struts)

In the near future, JavaServer Faces may present a more attractive option than Struts, because it supports more sophisticated user interfaces. Still, I'm skeptical about JSF for a few reasons:

- As with all event-based client-server models, JSF potentially increases communication costs between the client and server.

- JSF has been designed in a closed committee. That's often been a recipe for disaster.

- JSF is complex and will require specialized tools to be effective. The tools from some vendors tend to be proprietary, so it's important to watch the requirements evolve.

Starting with clean layers is only the first step. In the best of cases, you're going to want to refine your designs, and adjust your approaches. That's the subject of the next section.

Refactoring to Reduce Coupling

You may start with a cleanly defined design and you may layer your design, as we've discussed, so that each layer does one autonomous job. You may have coupling only at the appropriate places. But if you don't try to maintain that design, it won't last. Your code will naturally move toward tighter coupling unless you fight that tendency. In the last part of this chapter, we review some of the types of coupling, and how to avoid them. The benefits of looser coupling include:

- Decoupling protects major subsystems of your architecture from each other. If the coupling between your model and view are low, then changes in one will not severely affect the other.

- Loosely coupled code is easier to read. If you couple your business domain model to your persistence framework, then you need to understand both to read your domain model. Loosen the coupling and you can read your domain model unencumbered.

- Decoupling can improve reuse. It's harder to reuse big blobs of software, just like it's harder to reuse a full engine than a spark plug.

Keep in mind that some coupling is natural. You've got to have some degree of coupling to do anything at all. Coupling gets out of hand when things that don't belong together are bound together. Your goal should be to avoid accidental coupling—you want any coupling in your application to be intentional and useful.

Also, keep in mind that decoupling often comes at a price. You can add JMS queues and XML messages between every class, but you'll work harder and your application will be dog slow. Decoupling becomes much more important between major subsystems and layers of your architecture.

Microcoupling

Most of the code written today has many relationships, and most of those relationships are tightly coupled. Anything from a method call to the use of a common variable increases your coupling. Like I said earlier, that's not inherently bad. You just want to keep it intentional, and keep your coupling confined to an area of the architecture.

Your software design strongly suggests where your coupling should be. Excessive coupling across packages, and across layers—in general, excessive coupling across a focused idea—breaks down your ability to do one thing and do it well. When you find it, refactor it.

Direct access

The easiest type of coupling to find is direct access. When you directly call a method on another class or access its member functions, you're coupled to it. You can break coupling in a number of ways. When you're trying to loosen the coupling from two classes, often the easiest way to is to insert some kind of intermediary. The Java programming language includes interfaces for this purpose. Bear in mind that interfaces are useless for decoupling unless they are paired with a factory. This line of code:

```
MyInterface myinterface = new MyObject();
```

is no less tightly coupled than this one:

```
MyObject myobject = new MyObject();
```

Whereas this one accomplishes the task and is completely decoupled:

```
MyInterface myinterface = MyFactory.getObject();
```

Think about cars. They work because they have combustion engines that drive axles, which spin wheels. In order to drive a car, you don't manipulate the engine and axles directly; you turn a steering wheel, press gas and brake pedals, and maneuver a shift. The steering wheel, pedals, and shift make up the interface to a car. There is a big difference between a '72 Beetle and a '04 Ferrari under the hood, but anybody can drive either because they share an interface.

An interface lets you couple to a capability rather than an implementation. Let's say that you're building classes that you'd like to fire when an event occurs. You could have your code explicitly call the fire method on all of the classes that you want to notify. This approach is limited to behavior that you can anticipate at compile time.

A slightly better approach is to build a class that supports the method fire. Then, everything that needs to be triggered can inherit from that class. That's the solution many novice Java developers use. It's limiting, because you may want to trigger other types of classes too. Instead, use an interface called Firable:

```
interface Firable {

    public void fire();

}
```

Notice that you don't see an implementation. Now, whenever you want a Firable class, you simply implement the interface:

```
public class AlarmClock implements Firable {

  public void fire() {
    System.out.println("Ring!");
  }
}
```

Now, other classes can use your "fire" method without coupling directly to yours:

```
public void wakeUp(Firable clock) {
  clock.fire();
}
```

The idea is to couple to an idea rather than an implementation. You don't want to build an interface that repeats every method of a class. Instead, break out the concepts that you want to expose in the interface. If you find yourself addicted to JUnit as I have, you'll use this trick with some frequency. The nice thing about this approach is that you don't have to have any special behavior to test the alarm clock. You can also quickly mock a Firable class to help test code that fires your interface.

Interfaces serve as intermediaries, and you can decouple with other kinds of intermediaries as well. A façade is an intermediary that is nothing more than a thin wrapper. At first glance, you might think that you're trading coupling from one area of the application to the other, so you gain nothing at all. That premise is not entirely true. You'll see a few direct benefits:

- Your thin façade hides the details of the existing outbound interface. If the code it is wrapping ever changes, you can react to that change in the façade, leaving the other code intact.

- The façade is thin, and cheap. The code it is wrapping probably isn't. If you need to throw away the façade, you have not lost much.

You've probably seen other kinds of intermediaries as well. Rather than initialize a class with a new one, followed immediately by many sets, you can insert a constructor as an intermediary to enforce a policy for construction and consolidate several method calls. If you need to consistently call five methods to do a job, such as to establish a JDBC connection, you can wrap that code into a single method, or a class, like a connection manager.

Inheritance

Inheritance is one of the least understood mechanisms in modern programming. It is tempting to use the casual "inheritance is for is-a relationships," but this is just semantic handwaving. Everything "is-a" something else. Conceptually, there are two kinds of inheritance: *implementation* and *interface*. When a class inherits from another class and by doing so inherits actual implementation details (field values or code blocks), that is implementation inheritance. When a class implements an interface, thus promising to provide the services described there but without inheriting any specific values or code, that is interface inheritance.

In languages like C++, where multiple implementation inheritance is allowed, the problem can be quite severe. Classes that inherit from multiple direct parents can become logical Frankenstein's monsters, half-living beasts that don't quite look normal and never behave. Newer languages like Java solve part of the problem by eliminating multiple implementation inheritance. A Java class can have only one direct parent class (which in turn can have one direct parent, and so on). The chain is easier to follow and the results more predictable. However, classes can implement as many interfaces as they desire. Since interfaces do not impart specific implementation details to the implementer, just a public contract for services provided, the results are again easier to predict. Since any implementation code sitting behind an interface is living in the class itself, there is never the question of hidden conflicts and accidental overrides creating random runtime behavior.

In order to decide which kinds of ideas require which kind of inheritance, it requires a little common sense and a little Zen meditation. When two or more classes represent specific categories of a single idea (Employees and Customers are both a kind of Person), then implementation inheritance makes sense. Person is a good candidate for a superclass. All logical children of that idea share the data and methods abstracted back to the Person object.

Interfaces, on the other hand, are useful for identifying services that cross-cut the logical model of the application. Imagine you are writing an application for a veterinary clinic. You might have two classes, Employee and Customer, which both inherit from Person. You might also have three other classes, Cat, Dog, and Bird, all inheriting from Animal. If they should be persistent, you can implement the PersistentObject interface as needed. The key is that each kind of person must be a Person; they need not necessarily be persistent. Each kind of animal must be an Animal, but they only *may be* persistent.

Transitive coupling

Keep in mind that coupling is transitive. If A is coupled to B, and B is coupled to C, then A is coupled to C. This type of coupling often seems innocuous, but it can get out of control in a hurry. It's especially painful when you're dealing with nested properties. Whether you have something like this:

```
store.getAddress().getCountry().getState().getCity( )
```

or something like this:

```
address.country.state.city
```

you're building a whole lot of assumptions into a very small place. Dave Thomas, founder of the Pragmatic Programmer practice, calls this programming style the "Java train wreck." The worst form of the train wreck reaches into many different packages. The problem is that you're coupling all four classes together. Think of the things that might some day change. You might need to support multiple addresses, or international provinces instead of states.

Decouple this kind of code. You might decide to add some convenience methods for your customers or you might need to build a flatter structure, or even determine why you need access to the city in the first place. If it's to compute a tax, you might have a getTax method that isolates this coupling to one place. If it's because stores in certain cities have special attributes, you may add the attributes or methods to Store to loosen the overall coupling.

The role of transparency

Sometimes, you want to apply a little extra energy and completely focus certain pieces of code. For example, recall that we wanted to add security to our Account class without adding special security methods. We would do so with another layer. You would say that the Account class is transparent with respect to security.

Business rules often need special treatment, because they tend to be complex and tend to change with great frequency. Increasingly, leading edge Java developers look to find ways to isolate the business domain model from other concerns. Right now, the Java community is struggling to find the right way to package service layers, in order to keep business domain models fully transparent. Component architectures like EJB say that you should build your application as components and snap them into containers that provide the services. This architecture has tended to be too invasive and cumbersome. Instead, others say that services should be packaged as aspects, using a new development model called Aspect-Oriented Programming (see Chapter 11). As a compromise, many people are working to develop lighter containers that allow plain Java objects rather than special components. Pico and Spring (covered in Chapter 8) are two lightweight containers that are growing in popularity.

Testing and coupling

As you've already seen, your first defense against tight coupling is good, solid unit testing of bite-sized building blocks. As you code, you'll likely build an implementation, use that implementation in your code, and then reuse it again within your unit tests, as in Figure 3-5. Since you've built at least two clients into your development model and intend to test bite-sized pieces, you're much more likely to keep your coupling down to a level that's easy to manage. Further, your test cases will use each new class outside of its original context. With test-first development, you'll quickly understand where your coupling and reuse problems lie.

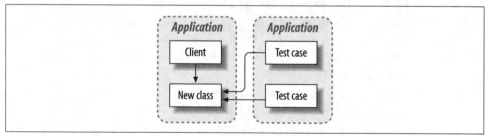

Figure 3-5. Testing offers the chance to have multiple clients for your new classes

Macrocoupling

Coupling at a higher level, or *macrocoupling*, is usually a much more serious problem than microcoupling because you want to keep each software layer as autonomous as possible. For years, distributed technologies forced significant coupling, making many kinds of refactoring nearly impossible. Communication protocols forced clients and servers to manage intricate handshakes even to make a connection. Later, remote procedure call technologies forced clients to bind directly to a named procedure with a fixed set of parameters and fixed orders and types. CORBA took things a step further, and forced clients to bind to a whole specific object.

Today, you don't usually have to couple as tightly. A variety of technologies help build and connect independent systems. You can fight macrocoupling on several different levels.

Communication model

Your communication model can have a dramatic impact on the degree of coupling between your systems. Early in your design process, make some painless decisions that reduce the coupling between your systems:

- Prefer asynchronous messages where coupling is a factor. A one-time message using something like JMS generally requires less coupling than synchronous technologies like session beans or RMI.

- Prefer established standards to reduce dependencies. If you build a standards-based communication interface, you're placing fewer restrictions on either end of the wire.

- To reduce coupling, use a flexible payload. If you fix the number, order, or type of parameters, you're going to increase your coupling. Instead, try to use a more flexible payload, like a system using name-value pairs (such as a JMS mapped message) or an XML document.

Each of these techniques can reduce coupling, but remember that sometimes coupling is good. If you've got strict control of both ends of an interface, and if you don't expect the interface to change, then a tighter coupling can possibly buy you better performance. For the most part, however, it's usually worth it to pay a small performance penalty to reduce coupling from the beginning.

Façades

Façade layers don't really reduce your coupling. Instead, they let you couple to something that's a little less permanent. In addition, façades have some other important benefits:

- You can change a lightweight façade much more easily than you can change your business domain model.

- A façade lets you adapt your interface. You may want to translate value objects to XML documents to have a looser coupling over a distributed interface. A façade is a logical place for that conversion.

- A façade can let you build a coarse-grained interface to a fine-grained model. For example, instead of forcing your user interface to read each element of your invoice, you could return an entire invoice, such as the one in Figure 3-6.

- A façade provides a convenient attachment point for services. Transactions and security work well within a façade layer.

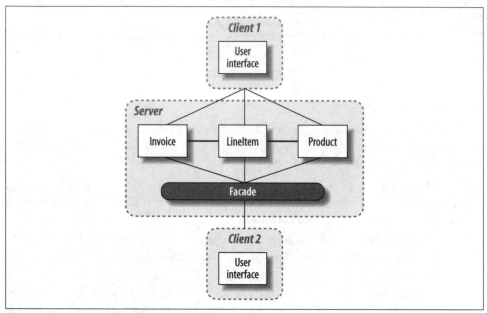

Figure 3-6. Client 1 must make four round-trip communications to the server; Client 2 reduces the total number of communications to one

Shared data

Applications that share interfaces usually need to share data as well. Whether you're using a buffer or a parameter list, the problem is the same. If you fix the number, type, order, or size of parameters, you're asking for trouble, because changes in the payload invariably force both sides of the interface to change. These strategies can help you to reduce coupling between subsystems that share data:

Allow optional parameters
> When you don't control both ends of an interface, you need to have features that allow both sides to advance at their own pace. Optional parameters let you support a new feature without mandating immediate support on both ends of the interface.

Use name-value pairs
> For interfaces that have a list of parameters, it's often better to name each parameter and pass them as a series of name-value pairs. Hash tables, maps, and

XML documents all let you build name-value pairs as input parameters. If you can support arbitrary text, you can handle XML. If XML seems to be overkill, JMS supports mapped messages, and you can use collections to handle this message type if you share memory addresses. The advantage of this approach is that applications need not depend on order, and optional parameters can be safely ignored.

Flexible data interchange formats are both a blessing and a curse. Your endpoints are more flexible in the face of changes to the payload, but it is more difficult to know exactly what is being shared. The more loosely typed your data interchange format, the more self-describing it must be. This is vital. If you pass name-value pairs, make sure that the consumer of the data can enumerate over both the values and the names. XML is a perfect format, since it is inherently self-describing.

Databases

The data access layer is one of the most problematic for Java developers to isolate. It doesn't need to be. Many good frameworks and solutions let you build an independent, transparent business model that knows nothing about persistence. Many persistence frameworks (such as Hibernate, JDO, and OJB) handle this well.

You must also ask whether you need a full relational database management system (RDBMS). Relational databases are large, expensive (in both resources and dollars) and complex. Sometimes, flat files are all that is needed. Make sure that you need what it is you are trying to wrap.

Regardless, you need not bite off a full persistence framework to solve a good chunk of this problem. You can build a lightweight DAO layer (like the one that we started for this chapter's example) to manage all data access for your application. There are a variety of IDEs and standalone tools that generate DAO layers automatically.

Configuration

Many times, you might want to avoid a particular standardized service to use a lighter, faster proprietary service. If you did so, you would have better performance and an easier interface, but you could be boxing your users into a corner. The makers of Kodo JDO faced that problem, and decided to make the service configurable. Increasingly, frameworks use configuration to decouple systems. Better configuration options invariably reduce coupling.

This list is far from exhaustive. If you want to excel at finding coupling problems, you've got to sharpen your observation skills. There's simply no substitute for reading code and watching the usage patterns, especially around the perimeter of a layer.

Summary

This chapter makes only one point: great software maintains focus on one task. To focus software, sharpen your ability to collect requirements and control your customers. If you're not careful, scope creep can confuse the basic theme of your software. When you've got a more complex problem, break each fundamental theme into a layer, or subsystem. In general, common layers are always evolving for Java technologies. Many of the accepted practices are sound, but others are suspect. Better layers share a common purpose and an effective interface.

Once you've designed effectively layered software and built clean software with a distilled purpose, maintain your clarity of purpose. To keep software focused on a central theme, you'll need to frequently refactor to loosen the coupling around tightly coupled components. Loose coupling is desirable at a lower level, and you can control it by testing and refactoring with techniques like interfaces. Also, pay attention to coupling at a higher level, so that each major subsystem is as isolated as possible. You'll improve reuse and isolate one subsystem from changes in others. In the next chapter, we'll discuss how to take the some extreme steps to reduce coupling between business domain models and services through increased transparency.

CHAPTER 4

Strive for Transparency

In the *Lord of the Rings* trilogy, the fate of Frodo Baggins is tied to the ring of power. The ring provides incredible power, but at a terrible cost. In the end, it invades his sleep, every hour of consciousness, and even his relationships. He is so possessed by the ring that he cannot drop it, although it is consuming him. I've suffered projects where our frameworks felt a little too much like that ring. In the beginning, the power blinds us, and near the end, it invades the core of our being, from the design philosophies all the way to the thoughts and mood of the whole team. In fact, I've even helped to build, and sell, such a framework, a demon disguised by the false name of CORBA. I'm not alone. I've been approached to rescue many an application from a cloud of doom, whether it's CORBA, VisualBasic, EJB, or even database stored procedures and user-defined functions.

In Chapter 3, our goal was to focus our software efforts on a central task. There weren't any earth-shattering techniques. You probably already do some kind of layering, and at least understand the value of decoupling. In this chapter, you'll see techniques to take the power of decoupling to the next level. In fact, it's often important enough to decouple critical layers like your domain model from all other services from the very beginning. You're looking for *transparency*, and this chapter introduces the techniques that you need to get there.

Benefits of Transparency

For most of this chapter, I'm going to explore the relationship between a service and a model. Your ultimate goal is to build a layer that's completely independent from the services that it uses. In particular, you want to keep all peripheral systems out of the domain model—persistence, transactions, security—everything. Why should the business domain model get such special treatment?

- Business models tend to change rapidly. Transparency lets you limit the changes to business logic.
- With transparency, you can limit changes to other parts of the system when your model changes.

- You can understand and maintain transparent models much more quickly than solutions with tighter coupling.
- By separating concerns of your layers, you can focus business, persistence, and security experts in the areas that make them the most productive.

You can also build completely generic services that know nothing in advance about the structure of your model. For example, a persistence service can save any generic Java object; a security service needs no additional code, but is based on configuration instead; a façade gets the capability to make a series of steps transactional just by adding a POJO to a container; a serialization service can turn any object into XML without knowing its structure in advance.

The core techniques in this chapter—reflection, code injection and other code generators—pack a punch, but they also add complexity and weight to your applications. My hope is that with a little supporting theory on your side, you'll be able to use these techniques to pry that ring out of your hand.

To be sure, none of these ideas are new, but I don't believe that they've received the weight that they deserve in the Java mainstream. I'll first talk about moving the control centers of the application to the appropriate place. Then, I'll give an overview of the tools that limit transparency, and wrap up with a few recommended tools to achieve it: code generation, reflection, and byte code enhancement, with an emphasis on reflection. If you're not used to coding this way, you'll find that it's going to warp your mind a little. Take heart. You've probably seen these techniques before, though you may need to rearrange the ideas a little. In the end, you'll find the ideas that percolated in the center of Smalltalk and around Java's perimeter have the power that you want, and even need.

Who's in Control?

Close to the center of my universe are my two little girls. One Christmas, we splurged a little and traded in our out-of-date 19-inch TV for a much larger model. We set the new television up. A little later, I looked around the room: one of my daughters was staring with a blank, passive face at frantic Disney images on the TV. The other kid had the cardboard box. With her mother, she had carved out doors and a window, and was actively jumping and dancing around the passive box. The contrast was striking. On one side, I saw an active toy, and a passive kid; on the other side, a passive toy and an active kid. Since then, I've repeated the experiment, albeit more intentionally. I've filled my house with passive toys that let the kids actively build, imagine, create, or act (at least, when I can pry them away from the TV).

Active Domain Models

Modern programming is undergoing a similar transition from active to passive domain models. Figure 4-1 shows the organization of classic services in a client-server

---

application. Designers put services on the bottom, so their clients could build applications that use the services directly. Essentially, active business logic invoked services as needed. The passive services presented an interface, and waited idle until invoked. Early programmers found it easy to build applications with active business layers. When they needed a transaction, they called a function like BeginWork. When they needed data, they asked for it directly from the database. Easy development gave way to complex maintenance and foiled attempts at extension, because the architecture muddied and entangled concerns between layers.

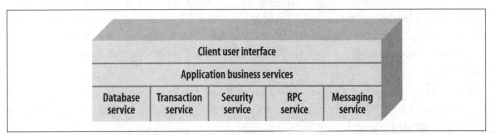

Figure 4-1. This client-server model lets service logic intrude into the business logic, increasing coupling and complicating code

The problem at the core of this type of design is the commingling of business *entities* and business *rules*. The entities themselves, representing the central concepts of the problem domain, manage their own state and their interactions with other entities. This makes changing them more difficult, since structural changes will at the very least entail wading through the logic, and usually involve editing it as well.

When your model actively reaches into other areas of your application, passive services like persistence, logging, and security tend to cut across all aspects of an application. Said another way, a crosscutting concern applies to every aspect of an application. Object-oriented technologies do not handle crosscutting concerns very well.

The Power of Passive Models

You've seen that active models tend to couple much more tightly to individual services. Lately, new object-oriented architectures make an improvement over the all-controlling domain model. Figure 4-2 shows that the business domain model can relinquish control and act like other passive services. The business domain model, if anything, is just another service, albeit an important one. Usually, peer relationships exist between the model and services. You should strive to diminish them. Using this paradigm, controllers marshal data between the model and other services as needed. Controllers model the rules of the application, while the domain model represents the entities. Whole frameworks, like Struts or JDO, solve this problem for user-interface development or persistence.

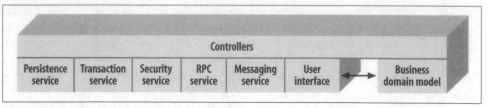

Figure 4-2. A better architecture has controllers dictating program control

Still, today's developers rely too heavily on hard-wired peer interfaces directly between the business layers and individual services. The next natural step in development evolution is to build a model with generic services that have no advanced knowledge about the model at all. It's a difficult problem that raises some complex questions:

- How can a service support a business object without explicit knowledge of it? For example, how can you save an Account object without knowing about the account in advance?

- How can you build a business model that uses services in a complex way, without prior knowledge of those services? For example, how can you make sure that the first four business rules execute in one transaction, while the next two occur in another?

- How can services react to events in a business model?

These are issues are about establishing transparency. If you haven't dealt with these issues before, it may sound like I am promoting anything but better, faster, and lighter Java. Stay with me, though. These techniques can help you dramatically simplify other areas of your architecture. They are worth the effort.

Alternatives to Transparency

Most people use the term *transparent* in a very specific sense, referring to code that does a job without explicitly revealing the details of that job. Distributed code with location transparency does not explicitly refer to the location of other machines on the network.

Consider a specific example. Persistence frameworks let you save Java objects. If you don't have to build in any support to get those benefits, then you've got transparent persistence. You'd think that you've either got transparency or you don't, but unfortunately, it's not always black or white. You may need to make some minor compromises:

- Your code may be transparent, but you may have to deal with minor restrictions. For example, some frameworks use JavaBeans API, and require getters and setters on each field (such as earlier versions of Hibernate).

- You may have to deal with major restrictions. Some frameworks don't support threading or inheritance, like EJB CMP.

- You may need to add special comments to your code. XDoclet relieves some limitations in other frameworks through code generation, but forces you to maintain specific comments in your code.

- You may have to make minor code changes, like supporting an interface or inheriting from a class.

- Your framework may generate your code, but you may not be able to modify that code and still support regeneration, like many IDE wizards.

- You may need to change the build process, such as in frameworks with code generation like Coco Base, or frameworks like JDO with byte code enhancement.

Some of these restrictions are minor, but some are severe. Before I dig into techniques that promote transparency, you should know about other available techniques, and their possible limitations.

Techniques That Compromise Transparency

In the area of persistence strategies, all frameworks must make serious compromises. The most successful tend to provide the best possible transparency within the business domain model, with respect to persistence. Some of the less-successful techniques invade your programming model in awkward ways.

Invading the model

You may suggest that transparency is not important at all, and you should just add code to the model itself. You could just hardwire create, read, update, and delete (CRUD) methods directly to the model. But keep in mind that persistence is not the only type of service that you'll likely need to add. You'll also have to consider security, transactions, and other enterprise services.

Many of my customers applied this approach before calling me to clean up the mess. The problem is that each class gets large and unwieldy, because code for each aspect invades each individual class. It's tough to get a consolidated view of any one particular problem. Additionally, you end up with a quagmire of redundant code. If you suddenly change databases from SQL Server to Oracle, you might find yourself editing each and every class in your model.

Subclassing

If you want to build something that's persistent, you could use a persistence framework that forces you to inherit that capability—for example, from a class called PersistentObject, as in Figure 4-3. This creates a problem: since classes can only support single inheritance, you are limited in your choice of inheritance hierarchy. You also do not support true transparency, because you need to make a conscious decision to inherit from PersistentObject. The result works, but it complicates your designs.

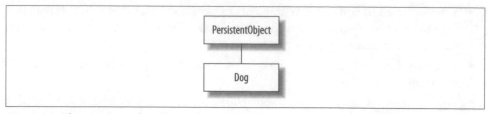

Figure 4-3. The persistent object Dog inherits from the class PersistentObject, but you can only add one type of service

Building a hardwired service

You could keep the model transparent, but build knowledge of each class in your model into your service layer. This technique is a brute-force approach. For example, you could build a data access object called PersonDAO that knows how to store and retrieve a Person object. That DAO would return Person objects so you could deal with the model transparently. That's often a workable solution. It's probably the preferred solution for simple problems, and for novice and intermediate developers. It's also the solution used in the Account example in Chapter 3.

This approach does have real benefits. It's easy to understand and easy to implement for smaller solutions. It leaves you with a transparent object model. The specific service approach does require you to do more work to implement each service. You can imagine how easy that it would be to load a simple object like a person, but loading a complex object with many parts, like a car, would be much more difficult. With a specific service, you have to manage complexities like this yourself. In this case, you need to add that persistence code to each class in your model, and hardwire each relationship by hand. As your requirements get more complex (such as adding caching or an ID generator to your persistence layer), you'll want to think of a more general solution to insulate you from these types of tedious details.

Code metadata

One strategy for persisting a model is to add metadata to pieces of the model that need special treatment, and then generate the code for persistence. For example, you may need to mark persistent classes, and mark each persistent field with a comment. If you're looking at this technique purely as a means to provide transparency, then it fails, because you need to change your programming model. It only provides an alternate means for coding.

Although these techniques do not improve transparency, I do recommend the combination of code generation and metadata, because it can relieve you from tedious implementation details. If you're not already familiar with persistence frameworks, here's a little background. Nearly all persistence frameworks make you build at least three things: the model, the database schema (the tables and indices), and a mapping between the two, often in XML. With metadata, you can automate two of the three artifacts. Using a tool like XDoclet, for example, you can add comments to your code that mark a field as persistent, and describe the relationships between the table and the code. In a pre-compilation step, XDoclet can then generate the mapping and schema based on these comments.

Be aware of what you're giving up, though. Inserting metadata actually moves some configuration details into your code. The line between metadata and configuration becomes blurry. For example, you may like metadata if you've got the responsibility for creating both the code and the schema, because it can help consolidate the mapping, code, and tables in one place. However, the approach tends to couple the concerns of the domain model and persistence, and that can bite you. For example, at some future date, you might not maintain the database schema. Then, you would prefer to keep a separate mapping, so when the schema changed, you'd often need to change only the mapping. The moral is to use the technique to save on redundancy where it makes sense, but be careful.

The metadata problem comes up regularly. Marking future requirements within code, marking persistent fields, and highlighting certain capabilities of a method, class, or property are just three examples. JDK Versions 1.4 and before don't have an adequate solution. For example, the Java language uses naming to tell the Java reflection API that a method supports a property—if get or set precedes a method name, then it's treated as a property. The XDoclet tool is growing because Java developers need this capability.

A committee is looking into adding metadata directly to the Java language in a specification request called JSR 175. For example, when you create a DAO, there's no good place to keep the JDBC connection. You can sometimes solve this problem through instrumentation. In order to define a metadata attribute called Persistent, create an interface like this:

```
@Documented
public @interface Persistent {
    public String jdbcURL();
    public String username() default "sa";
    public String password() default "";
}
```

In order to use the interface, add it to your class like this:

```
@Persistent(jdbcURL="jdbc:odbc:MyURL", username="btate", password="password")
public class Person
{
        // enter the rest of the code here
}
```

You can access the attribute through reflection. Then, you won't have to pass the JDBC connection through to each DAO. You could potentially use this technique the same way people use XDoclet today. The difference is that the Java compiler itself would be examining your attributes, not a third party.

Imposing an invasive programming paradigm

Many people have tried to solve the problem of crosscutting concerns. Some of those attempts actually improved our lives, but many were mediocre or downright awful. For example, Java's first attempt to solve crosscutting enterprise concerns used components. The idea makes sense. You can build a container that supports services. When you add a component to the container, it has access to the services, without requiring any code changes to the model. Your components are transparent (Figure 4-4). The devil is in the details, however. This approach depends heavily on how you define a component.

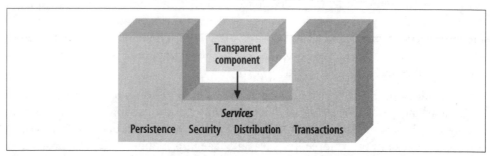

Figure 4-4. Components can theoretically access services without knowledge of the service

Java's most ambitious attempt at component-oriented development for the enterprise, EJB, has been in many ways a disaster. Here's how it works: the container accepts EJB components. To build a component, you define an interface that conforms to the specification and build a separate implementation. You then bundle deployment details in a configuration file called a *deployment descriptor*. When you deploy the EJB, the framework generates a component that uses your implementation and the interface you defined.

In this model, the container accepts frighteningly complicated components and the programming model blows away any notion of transparency. For example, to create a persistent component, a developer needs to build five Java classes, plus a deployment descriptor, plus the database schema. Further, the component model does not completely hide the service from the implementation. To use the persistence service, you must implement the `entityBean` interface and create a `primaryKey` class. This approach is not transparent. It's invasive.

Finally, you cannot readily extend or modify the services of the model. They are so integrated and coupled that it's nearly impossible to inject new services or modify the old ones in meaningful ways. Commercial vendors don't encourage you to even try. For example, RMI is the communication protocol for EJB. It's so tightly integrated with the container and other services that it's nearly impossible to replace.

Table 4-1 shows a summary of the alternatives that limit transparency. Notice it's not all cut and dried. Usually, generating transparent code takes time and effort, so save that technique for the problems that will benefit it most.

Table 4-1. Implementation techniques that reduce transparency

Technique	Advantages	Disadvantages
Invading the model	Easy to build	Model becomes too complex
		Maintenance gets tougher
		Combines concerns of services with model
Subclassing	Provides services without additional coding	It complicates introduction of new services
	Uniform interface	It abuses inheritance, leading to confusion
		It imposes code changes on the model
Hardwired service	The model remains transparent	Changes in the model also force changes in the services layer
Instrumentation	Reduces replication of code	Imposes code changes related to a service on the model
	Consolidates code and configuration, often easing implementation	Couples configuration and code, possibly complicating maintenance
Imposing invasive coding models	Subject to implementation	Subject to implementation

In general, as your domain model increases in complexity, insulating the model and services from one another becomes more important and you need to achieve better transparency. In the next chapter, we'll discuss techniques that take an extra step to achieve transparency.

Moving Forward

Now that you've seen (and likely used) many of the techniques that limit transparency, it's time to examine some of the preferred techniques. Think about transparency in more general terms. You want to perform a service on a model without imposing any conditions on the model at all. In other words, you want to isolate your passive model to its own box. You also want to build services that have no advanced knowledge of your model. Here are some basic assumptions about transparency (as I am defining it) to know before we continue:

The model consists purely of plain old Java objects (POJOs) or beans. The services cannot assume anything about the objects, and will need to deal with the model in the most general terms. That means the service will deal with the model as plain Java objects, or beans.

New services or model improvements must not force developers to make source code changes elsewhere. In other words, the service should not arbitrarily force changes on the model. Neither should the service need to change to support a different model.

All model and service code changes must be automated, and may happen no sooner than build time. If the user can't make changes, you've got to automate any coding changes. Further, you can make those changes no sooner than build time, meaning there should be no specialized preprocessor, macro language, or other type of nonstandard build step.

I intentionally allow two types of changes: first, I allow configuration, because it's not Java code, and it's flexible enough to change after build time. In fact, configuration is a preferred part of most solutions. I also permit controllers and impose no restriction on them. Controllers need not be transparent. This strategy makes sense if you think of controllers as clients of both the service and the model. It doesn't make sense to hide an interface from its client, so I allow unrestricted access to the model, or the service, from the controller.

Since so many people value transparency and work to make it happen, it pays to look at a few problem spaces and examine the solutions that have been suggested. Persistence frameworks, lightweight containers, and aspect-oriented programming frameworks all need transparency to function. These are the ways that other frameworks solve the transparency problem.

Reflection

The most accessible way to build a service that depends on model data is *runtime reflection*. I don't know why Java developers never have embraced runtime reflection the way that other languages have. It tends to be used by tool developers and framework providers but not general application programmers. You don't have to use reflection everywhere, nor should you try. Instead, apply a little reflection where it can have a tremendous impact. Here are some things to keep in mind:

General needs versus specific needs
> When you need to access an object's features in a general way, use reflection. For example, if you're moving the color field from an object to a buffer for transport, and you don't ever use the field as a color, consider reflection for the task, in order to reduce coupling. If you're reading the color and setting other objects to the same color, direct property accesses might be best.

Delaying decisions
> If you don't know the name of a method or class until runtime, consider reflection. If you already know the name, there's no reason to delay the decision—a simple method call is a better choice. For example, through configuration, you can frequently decouple code and delay decisions until runtime. Reflection gives you a tool to help this happen.

Bear in mind that although the performance of reflection has improved in recent years, postponing binding decisions until runtime has a performance cost. Jumping to a specifically named method or property is much faster than going through the reflection API by a factor of two or more. Reflection offers great power, but be judicious.

The Reflection API

The Java reflection API lets you access all of the elements that make up a class at runtime without requiring source code or any other advanced knowledge of the classes. Using reflection, you can:

Access a class's definition
> When you declare a class, you specify a class name and a set of modifiers (like synchronized, static, and public).

Get all field definitions in a class
> You can get the names, types, and modifiers for all of the fields in a class.

Get all of the method definitions in a class
> You can get the names, return types, parameters and types, and modifiers for all of the methods in a class.

Get the parent class
> Of course, since you can get a superclass, you can get all of the indirect methods and fields as well.

Access an instance's fields
> You can read or write directly to the fields or utilize any getters and setters the instance might expose.

Call an instance's methods
> Using reflection, you can also call methods on an instance.

In short, you can learn anything that you need to know about a class and directly manipulate an instance of that class. If you want to build a service that's independent of the structure of an object, that's a powerful combination of tools. You can inspect any method or field. You can load a class, call a method, or get the data from a field without knowing anything about the class in advance.

Further, reflection works well with a passive model because through reflection, the model already has all of the information that a potential service might need. That service can accept the whole model (or one class from the model) as input and use reflection to extract the data to do something useful, such as serialize the data to XML (like Castor), save it to a database (like Hibernate), or even wire together behaviors and properties (like Spring).

When you use the reflection framework, you must import the reflection libraries:

```
import java.lang.reflect.*;
```

The java.lang.reflection package contains everything you need, including four major classes: Class, Constructor, Field, and Method. These classes let you deal with each major element of a Java class. Java's runtime architecture makes it possible.

If you're like most Java developers, you probably deal much more with an instance of an object rather than the class object, but the class object is an integral part of Java's runtime architecture. It contains the basic DNA for a class. It's used to create classes and serves as an attachment point for static methods and members. It keeps track of its parent, to manage inheritance. You've probably used classes in these ways, but it's also the tool that enables reflection. Figure 4-5 shows a class instance at runtime. Each object has an associated class, which is the DNA for a class that determines its type. The class is the central entry point for the Java reflection API. Using it, you can access the fields, methods, and constructors for any class. You can also invoke methods and access the data for an individual instance of the class. The rectangles in grey represent the Java reflection framework.

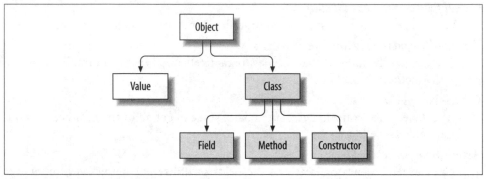

Figure 4-5. All Java objects have an associated class

Accessing a Class

The class is the entry point for reflection. Once you have the class, you can call specific methods to get the associated methods, constructors, and fields. Using the class, you can get a single method or field by name, or get an array of all of the supported fields or methods.

You can get the class in several ways. Sometimes, you don't have an instance. For example, if you're working on a factory, you might have access to only the name of a class. In that case, load the class like so:

```
Class c = Class.forName(aString);
```

Other times, you might have nothing more than an object. In that case, you'd get the class from the instance, like this:

```
Class cls = obj.getClass();
```

It's actually not quite that simple. But for now, you just need to understand that Java supports more than one class loader (though the architecture for doing so changed for Version 1.2 and beyond). Chapter 6 fills in the details about class loading.

Accessing Fields

You're probably ready to see a method that's a little more concrete. Let's use reflection to build a transparent service. Assume that you need a service to emit XML for a given object. Further, you want the model to remain transparent to the service, so you won't need to change any model code to support new objects. Given a target object, you're going to attack the problem using reflection:

1. Get the class for the target object.
2. Get the declared fields from the class.
3. Get the value for each field.
4. If the object is primitive, emit the appropriate XML.

I'll show you the code all together, and then we'll go through it in pieces. Here's the entire method to process an object:

```
        public static void doObject(Object obj) throws Exception {
❶           Class cls = obj.getClass();
            emitXMLHeader(cls);
❷           Field[] fields = cls.getDeclaredFields();
            for (int i=0; i < fields.length; i++) {
              Field field = fields[i];
❸             field.setAccessible(true);
❹             Object subObj = field.get(obj);

❺             if (!Modifier.isStatic(field.getModifiers())) {
                if ((field.getType().isPrimitive()) ||
                    ((field.getType().getName() == "java.lang.String"))) {
❻                 emitXML(field.getName(), subObj);
                } else {
❼                 doObject(subObj);
                }
              }
            }
          }
          emitXMLFooter(cls);
        }
```

That's it. Let's see how the individual pieces work.

❶ First, you've got to get the class object, given an instance. You need the class to emit the XML tags that bracket an entire object. You'll also get individual fields from the class. Since you're getting the class from a known instance, you use this method.

❷ Next, the class must declare the fields. The Class object lets you use several methods to access its fields. At times, you'll want to get a specific field, given the name of a property. You can do so with getField(*String name*), a method on class. Sometimes, you want to get only the declared fields for a class. Do this with getDeclaredFields(), which returns an array of fields. Other times, you also want to get inherited fields. You can do this with getFields(), which returns an array of all fields declared in a class and its parents. In this case, you'll get the declared fields, get back an array, and iterate over the array.

❸ Often, your service will need to access fields with a narrow scope, such as private fields. You wouldn't want to always package such a service with your model, so the Field class lets you step outside of the scoping rules for convenience. In this example, you'll want to make sure that the field is accessible, even if it's a private field. To do so, simply call setAccessible(true) on the field.

❹ Access the field's value by calling the get() method on your field object, to get the value for the individual field.

❺ Look at the modifiers to see whether the field is primitive or static. If it's primitive, emit the XML. If it's static, you'll want to skip it, because it's attached to the class instead of your object. The reflection API encodes all of the modifiers within an integer, so they'll take up less space. In order to read them, use a helper class called Modifier to check if a modifier applies to your class. You can access any modifier on a class, field, method, or constructor in this way.

❻ If it's primitive, emit the appropriate XML and complete the XML for the class.

❼ If it's not a primitive, call the method doObject again, this time with the field value.

The bulk of the work is done within the doObject method, as it should be. The code to emit the XML is surprisingly simple. Here are the methods to emit XML for the overall class, and for a field:

```
public static void emitXML(String name, Object value) {
  System.out.println("<" + name + ">");
  System.out.println(value.toString());
  System.out.println("</" + name + ">");
}

public static void emitXMLHeader(Class cls) {
  System.out.println("<"+cls.getName()+">");
}

public static void emitXMLFooter(Class cls) {
  System.out.println("</"+cls.getName()+">");
}
```

The nuts and bolts are all there for an XML emitter. You've probably noticed that I cheated and handled only the simplest case. In fact, you'll need to handle at least four types of fields for a general-purpose emitter:

Primitives
  With reflection, you deal with everything as an object. Since primitives are not objects, reflection wraps them in type wrappers. For example, to wrap the int 37 in a wrapper, you'd say Integer intWrapper = new Integer(37). To get the value from a wrapper, call a method on the Integer class, like intWrapper.intValue().

Objects

> If a field value is not an array or primitive, it's an object. You can deal with other classes recursively. Get the class from the object and iterate through its fields.

Arrays

> Reflection uses a special class to wrap arrays called Array. This class lets you access the type of the array and also provides access to each individual element of the instance.

Special classes

> Generally, you're going to want to treat some classes differently than others. For example, you may want special treatment for strings or collections.

We've only handled the first two types of fields, plus strings, but you can see how reflection works. You've supported a surprising number of classes without needing to alter model code at all. I must note that the emitter we've constructed here, though generic and useful, is not a full implementation. For a truly generalized emitter, our class would have to be able to handle circular references between classes, optional omission of referenced classes, logically transient fields, and some kind of optional name-substitution mapping pattern. Regardless, the point is no less salient: reflection can provide an enormous amount of power without any tight coupling.

You've seen how many transparent services use reflection: they simply access a list of properties, recursively if needed, and do the appropriate service. The types of services are unlimited:

- Hibernate, a persistence framework discussed in Chapter 7, looks at the value of your model before and after you change it, and then generates SQL based on your mappings to save the changes to a database.

- Spring, a lightweight container discussed in Chapter 8, populates fields in your objects based on a configuration file to wire your target objects to services.

- XML emitters like Castor scan an object's fields recursively to emit XML.

- Distributed messaging services can use reflection to scan an object's fields so that they can store compound objects without depending on a memory address.

So far, I've only told you how to deal with data. Fortunately, the reflection API also makes it easy to deal with behavior.

Accessing Methods and Constructors

You can use reflection to examine and execute methods. You can access methods through `java.lang.reflection.Method` and constructors through `java.lang.reflection.Constructor`. I'll describe the way that methods work; you'll find constructors work the same way.

As with fields, you can use `Class` to access methods in two ways: `getMethods()` returns an array with all supported methods, and `getDeclaredMethods()` returns only the declared methods for a class. You then can access the parameter types, modifiers, and return value from the Method class.

Here's an example that prints all of the declared methods in a class. It also prints out the types of each parameter, and the return value:

```
    public static void printMethods(Object obj) throws Exception {
      Class cls = obj.getClass( );
❶    Method[] methods = cls.getDeclaredMethods( );
      for (int i=0; i < methods.length; i++) {
        Method method = methods[i];
❷      System.out.println("Method name:" + method.getName( ));
❸      Class parmTypes[] = method.getParameterTypes( );
        for (int j = 0; j < parmTypes.length; j++) {
          System.out.print("  Parameter " + (j+1) + " type:");
          System.out.println(parmTypes[j]);
        }
        System.out.println("  Returns: "+method.getReturnType( )+"\n");
      }

    }
```

Here's what the annotations indicate:

❶ As with the field example, you'll use the class object to return all of the declared methods for the class.

❷ Once you have a method, you have access to its name and type.

❸ You can also access each of the parameters. This example simply iterates through them to print their types.

As you can see, inspecting methods works a whole lot like inspecting fields. All that remains is to invoke a method.

Invoking a method

Often, you'll want to invoke a method or constructor without knowing all of the details until runtime, such as configuring an object from a file. To do so, you'll need several things:

The name of the method
Remember, that's not enough to identify a method in Java.

The types of parameters
You'll also need an array with the parameter types, because two methods with different signatures can share the same name.

The parameter values
You'll need to build an array of parameters. If a parameter is an object, you'll place it in the array directly.

If a parameter is a primitive or array, you'll need to wrap it first. For example, call new Integer(59) to wrap a primitive integer. To wrap an array, you wrap it in an instance of Array. For example, to wrap an array of five Integers, a single parameter would look like wrappedArray below:

```
int a[]={1,2,3,4,5};
Object wrappedArray = Array.newInstance(Integer.TYPE, a);
```

The return type

The invocation returns an object or nothing at all. You'll need to cast it to the appropriate type.

Here's the code to invoke a method called sum on class Adder that takes two int parameters and returns an Integer:

```
// target object is called "target"
Class c = Class.forName("Adder");
Class parameterTypes[] = new Class[2];
parameterTypes[0] = Integer.TYPE;
parameterTypes[1] = Integer.TYPE;
Method m = c.getMethod("sum", parameterTypes);
Object parms[] = new Object[2];
parms[0] = new Integer(1);
parms[1] = new Integer(1);
Integer returnValue = (Integer)m.invoke(target, parms);
```

That's really the bulk of working with reflection. Compared to a simple method invocation or a simple field access, it does not look simple. When you consider the overall impact, though, the effort makes a huge difference.

Injecting Code

To get better transparency, you can always automatically generate code and add it to the model. To date, most frameworks use this approach. Of course, since most Java developers use Ant to build their projects, adding a simple code enhancer to your applications is relatively easy to do with little intrusion on your build process. You can use code enhancement in two ways:

Source code enhancement

This technique uses a program to read through your source code and make additions in the necessary places. For example, to make code transparent with respect to a performance tool that does performance profiling, you might run a precompiler program that injects code that takes a timestamp any time you enter or exit a method you want to measure.

Byte code enhancement

Since Java programs compile to a standard compiled form called byte code, you can inject byte code to add services and still maintain transparency. For example, most JDO implementations use a byte code enhancer.

Often, when you inject code, you're actually injecting methods that perform the work of your intended service, as with the source code enhancer in Figure 4-6.

Source code enhancement takes a class as an input and then generates code, typically method calls, to inject service capabilities into code, completely preserving transparency in the original class.

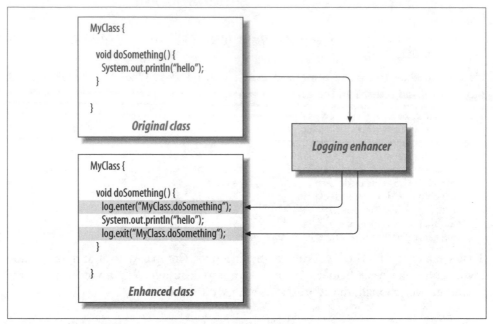

Figure 4-6. This source code enhancer addslogging to MyClass

JDO enhancers work this way: you create a class that's transparent with respect to persistence. The job of the JDO enhancer is to implement the `PersistenceCapible` interface. In order to make the class persistent, let your build process run it through a JDO enhancer. (Some of these use source code enhancement but most use byte code enhancement.) The enhanced class then calls the JDO framework to actually implement persistence. Some aspect-oriented programming frameworks use byte code enhancement, as well. The technique has many benefits:

- You don't have to make any changes to source code.
- You don't impose any restrictions on your class, so you completely preserve transparency.
- Code injection is fast at runtime. The additional steps occur at build time, so you pay any performance penalty once, at build time.
- This is a build-time technique. If you're using Ant or something similar, after a one-time change to your build scripts, you will not need to make other changes to your build process.

For the most part, source code injection works well for techniques that are easy to parse and inject with simple code. Tasks such as adding logging, instrumenting code for performance analysis, or intercepting method calls all work well with a simple code injector.

Byte code enhancement frameworks

Byte code enhancement is a little more difficult to pull off. You'll need a strong knowledge of compilers, the Java byte code specification, and finer issues like threading. For this reason, most people use byte code enhancement through other frameworks.

Some developers frown on byte code enhancement. It's been my experience that fear of the unknown drives this attitude more than practical experience. Knowledgeable teams can and do build byte code enhancers for commercial applications. Still, some perceive disadvantages:

- Some fear that byte code enhancement may be difficult to debug. If you're the type of programmer who needs to see the Java source for every line of code in your system, byte code enhancement is not for you. I've generally found that enhancements are little more than method calls into a services layer, so it's usually not an issue.

- Theoretically, two byte code enhancers applied to one class could possibly collide, causing some breakage. I haven't seen this happen in practice. In fact, not many byte code enhancers exist.

The framework you choose depends on the services you need. JDO uses code enhancement to add transparent persistence. Some tools that make understanding decompiled code more difficult, called *obfuscators*, also use byte code enhancement to help you protect your intellectual property. In addition, some AOP frameworks enhance byte code at runtime when they load classes. You'll probably wind up using byte code enhancement solely through one of these.

Generating Code

As you've probably noticed, many Java frameworks require a whole lot of tedious, redundant syntax. In his book *Refactoring* (Addison-Wesley), Martin Fowler calls such a design a "code smell." Since Java developers are a lazy and creative lot, they seek ways to automatically generate repeated bits of code. Further, they think of ingenious ways to configure their code generation engines. Take an EJB application, for example. In order to create the persistent model with a remote interface, you'll need to create at least seven files: the home object for lifecycle support, a local that serves as a proxy, the interface, implementation, primary key, deployment descriptor, and schema. With code generation tools like XDoclet, you can automatically generate at least five of the seven, and often six of the seven. You create an XDoclet by instrumenting your code with simple JavaDoc comments. While this technique doesn't make your code completely transparent with respect to persistence, it certainly makes it *more* transparent.

How Code Generation Works

While novice and intermediate Java developers see code generation as black magic, it's really quite simple. If you've ever used a mail merge program, you know how it works. You create a working piece of code. Then you mark the areas of the code that vary from instance to instance. Together, these form your template. Next, you provide data to fill in the variables. Like a mail merger, the code generator takes your template, fills in the blanks, and generates working code, as in Figure 4-7.

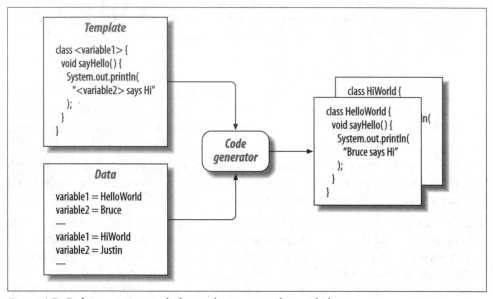

Figure 4-7. Code generation works by combining a template with data

Figure 4-7 shows the general concept, although it simplifies the problem in several ways. You can generate multiple targets. You can also generate code with complex structures, such as repeated or conditional blocks. In general, if you can describe the patterns in your code and clearly define areas of duplication, you can probably find or build something to generate it. There are several types of generation strategies:

Wizards
> Many an IDE uses wizards to provide data for code generation templates. Microsoft Studio is famous for these, but others use wizards prolifically as well.

Code inspection
> Some generators, like XDoclet, parse source code to understand what to generate. The generator may parse the Java application and look for specialized commands in comments or certain naming conventions. It may also use reflection to determine generation requirements.

Template engines

Some code generators work with a general-purpose template engine and let you generate targets from a variety of prepackaged templates. Perhaps the most popular is Apache's Velocity.

Alternative model transformations

If you're starting with a non-Java model (most commonly, XML), you can simply use XML's transformation stylesheets (XSLT) to generate your targets, or do a transformation in other ways.

Combined approaches

The MiddleGen open source project combines approaches, using Velocity, XDoclet, Ant, and JDBC to build a database-driven template approach to generate code for EJB, Struts, and a variety of others.

As you can see, code generation lets you minimize redundant data through a variety of approaches. The end result is a happier developer who's not a slave to tedious details.

Code Generation and Transparency

You can use code generation for much more than saving duplication. From a configuration file containing classes with properties and their types, you can generate a database schema, a transparent model, and a DAO layer. It's an interesting way to code, with several tangible benefits:

- You can have a completely transparent model.
- If you generate your services, your developers will not need to modify them to support your model.
- If your requirements of generated services change, you can change a template in one place and generate them all again.
- You can create a generalized domain language for your problem domain without writing a compiler for it. (You can solve problems in a specialized template language that generates Java, whose compiler you then take advantage of.)

Whenever you read a list of benefits like this one, keep in mind that there's always a big "but." Generated code does have its downside:

- When it's used to solve duplication in an application, code generation treats the symptom (retyping tedious redundant code) and not the cause (too much duplication). As such, it can remove your motivation for refactoring problem areas.
- When it's used with code instrumentation (such as XDoclet), it can couple your configuration with your code. You may be combining concerns that should logically be separated, such as your code and your schema designs.
- Code generators often create seriously ugly code. Even if you don't have to write it or maintain it, ugly code is hard to debug and understand. For example, a

wizard may not know whether a class has been loaded or not, so it's much more likely to generate code that looks like this:

```
cls = Class.classForName("java.lang.String");
str = c.newInstance( );
```

than code that looks like this:

```
String str = new String( );
```

- Developers may change generated code, even outside of protected areas. As a result, changes to the template will not make it into production code.

Code generation is just one of the tools in your tool box and with each application, you should look at it with fresh skepticism. In particular, observe these rules:

- If you can't read it, don't use it. A wizard may seem to help at first, but it'll spin out of control quickly if you don't understand every line that it generates. You want to know that the code will perform and that you can maintain it when the time comes.

- Try to refactor duplication before addressing it with code generation. In other words, put away that sledgehammer, and grab a flyswatter instead.

- Change the templates instead of the generated code. If you must change generated code, make sure that you've got a protected area to do so, and that you stay within it. To enforce this rule, don't check in generated code. Build it from scratch each time.

- Use respected templates and products. Treat generated code with the same skepticism that you reserve for human-written code.

As with the other techniques mentioned here, many readers of this book will never build a code generator. You don't have to. Instead, you can choose from a number of frameworks or products that enable code generation or use it under the covers. While code generation does not always provide transparency by itself, it can relieve you of many of the details when you're forced to use a framework that lacks transparency.

Advanced Topics

Now you've seen three tools for achieving transparency. If you're anything like my clients, you're probably wondering which is best. I'm going to carve that decision into three pieces:

- If I'm building a transparent service myself, I prefer reflection. I'd simply prefer to call a library than build a code generator or byte code injector. I prefer to have business logic within my domain model (instead of just data holders), and that eliminates code generation. Though the performance is doubtlessly superior, byte code generation is too difficult and risky for most small or inexperienced IT shops.

- If I'm buying a tool or framework, I like the idea of byte code enhancement. I like that you pay much of your performance penalty at build time instead of runtime and I like that after the build, I don't have to worry about the service. With tools like JDO, I've rarely had instances where byte code enhancement made things difficult for me to debug, and I've always been impressed with the flexibility of byte code generation over reflection. As a case in point, after coming down hard on JDO vendors in their marketing literature, Hibernate in fact added a byte code enhancement library, called CGLIB, to improve certain aspects (such as lazy loading).

- I don't mind code generators, but I don't lean on them for transparency. In general, better techniques get the same benefits without some of the drawbacks mentioned earlier in this chapter.

If you're gung-ho about transparency, keep an eye on a couple of evolving debates. The first is the concept of coarse- and fine-grained services. The second is the future of programming techniques that may enhance your experience.

Coarse- and Fine-Grained Services

Nearly all applications support two types of services: coarse- and fine-grained. You may decide that it makes perfect sense to attach all services to the same point. Be wary, though. Many early EJB applications used that design, God rest their souls. Your problem is two-fold. First, if you present an interface, your users may use it whether it's a good idea or not. Second, different services have different performance requirements.

Consider CORBA for a moment. The idea was to have very large object models, which could find and talk to each other whether they were in the same memory space or across the globe. If you bought into that notion (as I did), you know how damaging it can be. The problem is that interfaces often have fundamentally different requirements. If your user interface wanted to display every field on a distributed object, it would need to make a distributed method call for every field, which is very expensive. Let's take the problem one step further. Let's say that you wanted to display every line of an invoice from across the network. You'd have to make a call to every field of every object on line item on an invoice, as in Figure 4-8. Each call represents a round-trip across the vast network, and regardless of how efficient your code is, the speed of light is still immutable. You have to be intelligent about the way that you apply transparency.

Instead, you need coarse- and fine-grained interfaces. Your model provides your fine-grained interface, and a façade provides a coarse-grained interface. Think of a fine-grained interface as private. You only want to share the most intimate details of an object to a selected number of, ahem, clients. Your public façade will provide the entry point to the rest of the world.

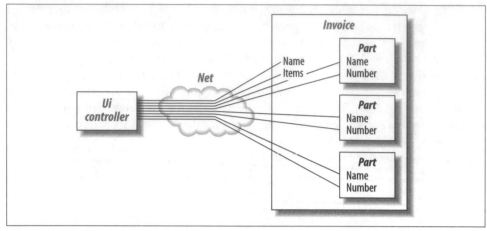

Figure 4-8. CORBA failed because it treated every service as a fine-grained service

You probably code this way already. If you don't, you're in for a treat. Facades make a convenient interface for providing a secure, transactional, or distributed service. You can offer these services transparently with many of the techniques in this book. Your façade need not be a session bean. You can achieve many of the benefits through lightweight containers and possibly RMI. The difference between this model and CORBA is striking: you don't sacrifice transparency, but you can attach coarse-grained or fine-grained services to the appropriate interfaces. Apply coarse services like messaging, distribution, transactions, and security to your façade, and your fine-grained services—such as logging and persistence—to your model.

A New Programming Paradigm

You might have noticed that object-oriented technologies do not handle services, like security or logging, that broadly reach across many objects very well. Academics call this problem *crosscutting concerns*. For this reason, many researchers and leading edge developers increasingly tout the *aspect-oriented programming* (AOP) model. While it's still in its infancy, AOP lets you insulate the issues of crosscutting concerns from the rest of your application. I'll talk more about AOP in Chapter 11.

It's my belief that new programming models evolve much more slowly than predicted. I also believe that once they succeed, they have a much bigger impact than we expect. Such was the case with object-oriented technology, which grew incrementally over 10 years through the adoption of C++, the commercial failure of Smalltalk, and finally the successful adoption of Java. You can find similar adoption patterns around high-level languages, structured programming, and even interpreted languages. While you might not see widespread AOP adoption by next year, you will likely see ideas that support an AOP move to the forefront rapidly:

Transparency

In this chapter, you've seen the impact of transparency across the Java language. The fundamental goal of AOP is to take crosscutting concerns out of your model.

Byte code enhancement

Many developers and decision makers reacted violently to any framework considering this technology, especially early versions of JDO. Increasingly, Java developers are recognizing the value of byte code enhancement. With each new implementation, support gets stronger.

Interceptors

Aspect-oriented frameworks intercept program control at critical places, such as when control passes into or from a method, when objects are destroyed, and when variable values change. Interceptors provide a convenient way of attaching behavior to an object through configuration, without forcing changes upon a model.

Lightweight containers

In Chapter 8, you'll see a lightweight container called Spring in action. Designers quickly saw that containers such as Spring, Avalon, and Pico make AOP easier.

Networking in person or online is the best way to deal with constant change. You need to be near the buzz so that you can respond to the ceaseless waves of changes as they break.

Summary

If you're trying to decouple that service from your model and you feel like you're standing half-dressed after pulling a single thread a little too far, take heart. If you put the effort into building transparency into your application, you're likely to get where you intended to go, fully dressed and on time.

Some other decoupling techniques don't go far enough. Inheriting a service leads to awkward models that are tough to extend in other ways. Hardwiring services has a place, but it starts to be limiting as an application grows in scope. New programming models such as AOP may help you some day, but others (like heavyweight invasive containers) can kill you.

Instead, if you've got an exceptional need to decouple a service from your model, strive for transparency. Effective frameworks seem to be divided across three camps. All have relative strengths and weaknesses.

- Reflection is the tool of choice if you're building a lightweight transparent service. It's relatively easy to use and doesn't require any changes to your build process. The downside is performance but if you don't overuse it, reflection is fast enough for many applications.

- Enhancement techniques directly modify the byte code in your application to perform the appropriate task. They do change the build process, and may theoretically be difficult to debug. In practice, though, it's a high-performance technique that's growing in popularity. Some frameworks to provide persistence, obfuscation, and aspect-oriented weavers all use byte code enhancement, either at runtime or build time.

- Code generators are relatively easy to understand and use. They merge a template and data to give you working code. Frameworks like XDoclet use code generation less for transparency than to eliminate repetition, but you can use other code generation frameworks like MiddleGen to create services and transparent models, often without any user intervention beyond creating a few JavaDoc tags or an XML file.

Use these techniques to build transparent services. Don't forget that complete transparency can often burn you, as with CORBA. Instead, create transparent services to handle coarse-grained interfaces, such as façades, and fine-grained services, such as your model. Keep an eye firmly fixed on the future. While AOP languages and environments may still be a ways off, AOP techniques such as lightweight containers and interceptors will creep into the mainstream very quickly.

In this chapter, our focus was on using transparency to decouple services from your model. In the next chapter, you'll learn to choose the right tool for the job. It may sound like a trivial detail, but using poor technologies or abusing good ones has sunk thousands of Java projects.

You Are What You Eat

I love short cuts. On a now infamous hike, my wife was 10 seconds from calling for a helicopter because I'd left the main trail to traverse a swollen Appalachian riverbed. I loved the experience; she was less enthusiastic. Just this week, I hammered in a 1-cent nail with a $30 electric screwdriver rather than climb downstairs to get a hammer. I told myself that in two years, no one will be able to tell what I used to drive that nail home.

Sometimes, short cuts are good. In every chapter of this book so far, I've repeated that you can try simple, even imperfect solutions. After all, you can always refactor them later if you are wrong. And that's mostly true. Be careful, though. Like anything else you build, decisions that affect your foundation last longer. I've spent a good number of years helping customers with deep pocketbooks unmake big decisions. Here are some areas to watch out for:

- Your choice of an RDBMS, and perhaps the persistence layer that sits atop, lasts for the life of an application. RDBMS data and queries may be transferred to a new platform, but usually a database decision is final. Database data and schemas can usually commute, but stored procedures, user-defined functions, and triggers are less portable. Some customers pick the wrong horse and then complicate a serious problem by betting everything on that horse, basing applications on stored procedures, user-defined functions, and triggers.

- Programming languages, and even dialects, dramatically affect your architecture, programming decisions, and even your available talent. For an obvious example, consider two languages as similar as C# and Java. They're alike in many ways but will take your design in dramatically different directions. Some customers naively take small sips of freedom with tools like Visual Basic. Eventually, those departmental tools grow and escape, forcing the customer to gulp from the Microsoft fire hose.

- Beware of tools that couple. Proprietary tools often make it too easy to make sweeping decisions on the fly, without considering consequences. A whole generation of tools, like PowerBuilder and OracleForms, coupled applications to the database in unnatural ways. Only the application and database vendors came away smiling. Often, when you make the decision to tightly couple two subsystems, you lose the practical ability to separate them soon after. One of my clients used a tool that encouraged imbedded SQL in their business tier. When the tool fell out of favor 10 years later, they paid a quarter of a million dollars to rewrite a tiny frontend because they couldn't extract the business logic.

In this chapter, I'll discuss decisions that have far-reaching implications. You are what you eat, and your application is exactly what you feed it. If you give it a steady diet of bloat, you'll build bloatware. If you feed it fad diets full of temperamental, experimental technologies, you'll build finicky, temperamental systems. If you feed it those sweet and sticky frameworks that goop everything together, you'll get applications stuck together in unnatural ways. If instead you feed your code a light, pragmatic diet of the right pieces in the right proportions, then your users will love you. Your applications will take on the personality of the frameworks that you use.

Golden Hammers

In my first and second Java books, I addressed *antipatterns*, patterns of solutions that break in systemic ways. By far the most common antipattern is the *golden hammer*. As a weekend builder, I know the metaphor well. Most carpenters have a tool in the box that's so beautiful that they want to use it for every task. I'm the poster boy. I've literally used a circular saw with a carbide blade to cut wire. Java developers are no different. All of us have developed favorites. In this section, I'll lay out a beautiful set of golden hammers for your inspection. Chances are good that you've used one to hammer the occasional screw.

The Allure

An antipattern is a bitter idea that seems sweet at the time. A golden hammer attracts a Java programmer like a box of Krispy Kremes and a bottle of Jolt. The power of bad frameworks over otherwise intelligent developers has sometimes bewildered me, but I guess it's good for business.

Sometimes, programmers do the damage to themselves. Past success can cloud your judgment. I learned XML while working on a very successful project and afterwards, I wanted to use it everywhere, from writing simple, four-line configuration files to building an alternative programming language. Others have had the same experiences with CORBA, persistence frameworks, web services, and even Java itself.

The sales process

Other times, aggressive marketing or sales can do you in. Understand that the stakes are high, and this industry spends millions of dollars at the drop of a hat to get you to like and use something. If you're making a major buying decision with the help of a sales staff, be very careful. If you don't know how the process works, you can't make the most informed decision. Since I've worked in sales, I can tell you how that process works from the inside. Figure 5-1 shows a combined version of all of the technical sales processes that I have seen from the inside.

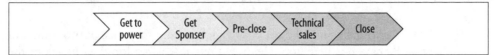

Figure 5-1. *Knowing the typical J2EE sales process helps you buy smarter*

Here's a little more detail about each step:

Prospecting

The best salespeople make hundreds of phone calls and mine their customers for leads. The goal is to establish an interest in their product. Once the salesperson has established interest, she'll try to get to the decision maker. That's called getting to power. The final step is to establish that the customer has the budget to buy the product. If you're a serous buyer, don't share your overall budget with your vendor! They'll use that information against you.

Securing sponsorship

Sales reps know that sales involving an inside sponsor (usually called a *power sponsor*) are more successful because there's no trust barrier to overcome. It's often a good relationship for both parties. If you've already decided on a technical solution and you're trying to sell a technical solution to your management, you can use your role as a power sponsor to get your vendor to do a lot of your legwork for you. Chances are good that they have much more information.

Getting agreement (pre-close)

The sales rep comes in, buys lunch, and slings around some nice coffee mugs and cool pens. In the relationship stage, the salesperson wants to build up a level of trust. In the relationship building stage, the sales rep tries to get a list of objections. Their goal is to get you to agree to buy the software once they overcome all of your objections.

Execute (technical sales)

Armed with a set of objections, the vendor passes control of the sale from the rep to the technical sales team. The sales team can take a number of different approaches, all designed to overcome your objections and make the sale. They may include one or more of these elements:

- *Technical presentations*. Use these to your advantage. Let your vendor answer critical questions about their product. Be careful, though: the vendor is not the best source of information about their competition. (In fact, while I was at IBM, I found that certain vendors were notoriously bad.)

- *Proof-of-concepts (POC)*. This is the sales job that I did at IBM. POC engagements are expensive. A vendor may do a POC if you say you'll buy if it's successful, if they believe that it will improve their odds of closing the deal (usually, based on some competitive advantage), or if they believe that you won't buy without one. Once you've come to a tentative decision about a vendor, get proof that the product works. Pay if you must.
- *References*. Reference selling is increasingly taking the place of proof-of-concepts. Be cautious here, too. Hearing a name at a vendor meeting is not the same as talking to the customer. You'll also want to know if the customer received any special consideration in exchange for the reference, and if they got any special support to make a project go smoothly. Unless you also agree to be a reference, you may not get the same support, so take references with a huge grain of salt. Further, don't buy without a reference that you trust.

The close

Once you're at the end of the process, the vendor closes you. If you've got special negotiators at your company, it's best to take advantage of them. If you don't, then it may pay you to take advantage of a negotiating class. Your sales rep probably has.

That's what you're up against. You can use the sales process as a source of information to make a knowledgeable decision. You should use them to help you fully understand a particular product and areas in which the vendor believes it has an advantage. Just don't use the sales process as your *only* source of information. And above all, don't make buying decisions based on friendships with sales reps! If you do either of these things, you'll find a toolbox full of shiny, expensive golden hammers.

Some Examples

Project teams across the nation have shown me many examples of golden hammers. Few of them knew that they were making bad decisions at the time. My favorite early examples include C++ for a team of COBOL retreads, Visual Basic for an inventory and control system, and Lotus Notes for a transactional airline reservation system. With Java, we've got a whole new collection of potential golden hammers.

Java

Java is one of the biggest golden hammers that you're likely to wield. You should have many other tools to choose from, including scripting languages and competing languages. Yet choosing alternatives often carries a stigma that it doesn't deserve.

Some industry dynamics are hard for me to understand. Microsoft technologies build richer interfaces with much less effort than their Java counterparts, and many enterprises support nothing but Microsoft clients. Yet even in this restricted environment, most developers would rather wade through the neck-deep quagmire that Swing has become rather than inject any Microsoft development where it makes sense. On the other side of the fence, Microsoft bigots would prefer to tune up that rusting clunker that Microsoft calls their message server and tie it together with 10-year-old transaction code in an unmanaged environment, duct tape, and bailing wire rather than use a better middle-tier technology like one of dozens of Java application servers.

J2EE

Most applications don't need J2EE. Sun has effectively carried the J2EE brand into the mainstream. It's hard to find a simple, standard-edition application server and few customers consider deploying that way. If you've ever been tasked with getting a J2EE server off of the ground, you know: it's a tedious, demanding process under the best of circumstances. On the other hand, if you've been fortunate enough to lay out a lot of money to buy a whole fleet of these things, you may have had your vendor install it for you. When you lay out a ton of cash, they work hard to keep you happy.

But J2EE is not the lowest common denominator! Many applications should deploy with nothing more than a servlet container, a web server, and a database connection. Some of the finest and fastest commercial web sites use nothing more than Tomcat on Apache.

Distribution

When you're reading about web solutions, you probably see all kinds of potential clustering strategies in the name of scalability. Customers with larger applications often settle on deploying a cluster of presentation servers, a cluster of business servers, and resource servers. It's a tried-and-true formula that scales well for large loads, but it's not the *only* formula.

Increasingly, experts are thinking about how to consolidate these systems to save complexity and communications costs. Often, you can get away with one middle tier cluster. The motivation is simple: when you begin to add distributed nodes, you're inviting complexity and overhead into your door. You frequently invent the need to connect to named services, manage distributed transactions, and create synchronous and asynchronous messages. I have seen any number of middle tier applications designed with arcane multiobject hierarchies wrapping a *single, local database transaction*. It pays to occasionally look at every distributed tier with fresh skepticism. You can frequently consolidate individual tiers with potentially significant gains. Figure 5-2 shows two alternatives for consolidating a typical architecture. One alternative is to deploy static content and the MVC framework with the business tier, eliminating the need for a distributed façade. Another alternative is to deploy the CPU-intensive business tiers with a RDBMS, which often underutilizes CPU cycles.

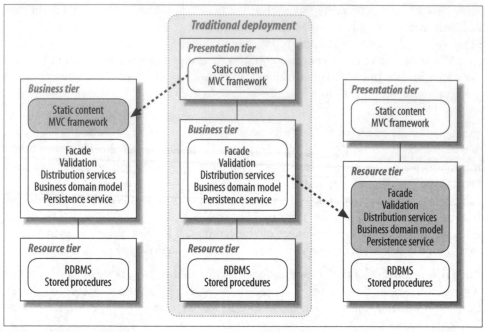

Figure 5-2. Sometimes consolidation of tiers reduces overhead and complexity

The image in the center of Figure 5-2 represents many typical deployments. However, by deploying the façade layer next to your MVC framework, you can eliminate the need for a distributed façade. One client of mine did so and at the same time eliminated the need for a J2EE server by eliminating the need for stateless session beans.

Another strategy (the right-hand side of Figure 5-2) shows the deployment of business-tier logic with the RDBMS. This deployment solves three major problems:

- Typical well-tuned RDBMS servers rarely use more than a small percentage of CPU cycles. Deploying a CPU-intensive business tier can take advantage of those extra cycles for intensive data marshalling.

- The communication costs between a database tier and a business domain model can be among the most expensive in an entire application. Deploying them together alleviates this concern.

- Security is harder to manage across a wire than locally between processes.

Think about it like this: it takes a great deal of energy to confine your business domain model to the middle tier. Some of the logic inevitably wants to fight its way to higher or lower tiers. Presentation logic needs frequent access to validation; a persistent domain model has a tight affinity with the database; façade layers are much simpler to code and deploy as local interfaces. If your situation seems to require a deviation from the norm, don't fight it.

EJB

EJB is not so much of a golden hammer as a glass hammer. The idea may be pretty to look at, but it's much less impressive in practice. Perhaps no other Java API has been as hyped or oversold as EJB. I've written a whole book on the topic; I won't rehash it here. As the years go by, I spend less time talking about EJB pitfalls and more time talking about when EJB should be used at all. This book is about moving away from EJB in its entirety. Still, certain elements of that framework have a limited value. If you're going to use EJB, use it appropriately in situations like these:

Façades
> If you have a distributed, transactional façade that needs to be highly scalable, consider EJB. In fact, in its original incarnation EJB supported only stateless session beans, with plans to quickly add message-driven beans. The EJB framework was to provide scalable pools of stateless resources, to control access to scarce resources on higher tiers.

Thin wrappers
> Don't put too much of your logic inside of the EJB itself. Use the EJB as a façade or a thin wrapper around POJO objects that do the actual work. This design is much more testable and easier to manage.

Multiple services
> Use EJB only for transactional, distributed problems. If you find that your façade layer no longer needs to be distributed, don't use session beans for it. They're overkill for a local call. Similarly, don't use EJB when you only need one token service. Whenever possible, adopt a simpler solution.

No entities
> Avoid entity beans and CMP altogether. Entity beans are unwieldy albatrosses that take tremendous energy to understand, code, tune, and maintain. Better solutions are out there; find them.

No stateful session beans
> Avoid stateful session beans. You're better off using HTTP sessions or databases, depending on your solution. Those solutions are more broadly adopted and won't tie you to EJB for the long term.

Experienced team
> Consider EJB only when you've got enough experience and skill to deal with the inevitable issues. Don't kid yourself. EJB requires a lot of knowledge and finesse to pull off. If you don't have it on your team, get it or use another framework.

These are just a few guidelines for using EJB appropriately. But just to reiterate, I strongly believe that the best way to win the EJB game is not to play.

XML

Few will argue that XML has changed the face of Java programming forever, but not all of the changes are for the better. XML does solve some problems very well, but it also has serious limitations.

XML is hard. If you're a great programmer, you probably think that "hard" is over-stating it. You might prefer "tedious." If you're new at programming, you may wish that I'd chosen a stronger word: the syntax is awkward, and the many versions often collide. If you've ever needed a different version of your XML DOM classes than your JDK provides, you know exactly what I'm taking about. XML does seem to be getting more difficult. As it becomes more sophisticated to solve the demanding problems of the few, it's rapidly succumbing to the bloat. XML can also be slow. Depending on what you're doing, it can take a whole lot of time to move those bytes around. Since it's so verbose, XML takes longer to marshal than other, more limited message formats.

XML sometimes forces you to define your data structures too early and too defini-tively. DTDs and Schema are hard to write and often you end up writing them once, too early in the process, and bound to them for the rest of time. This is one of those coupling-by-decoupling paradoxes: XML Schema is supposed to free us from long-term coupling to a data definition, but in practice, it usually ends up just as restric-tive as all other data definition mechanisms.

Still, XML has its place. If you value decoupled software and think that messaging models are undervalued and underused, you'll recognize the incredible benefits XML delivers. It's flexible, self-describing, and broadly adopted. There's nothing out there that comes close to it. (Can you see the gold on that hammer beginning to gleam?) These advantages drive XML everywhere, including some inappropriate places. You don't have to drop that tool like it's heated up to 400 degrees. Just be careful.

XML is just the input, or output, for an interface. To use it appropriately, consider the nature of the interface. XML works well to reduce coupling by providing a stan-dard, self-describing payload for some type of interface. It provides power and flexi-bility at the cost of complexity and performance. To decide whether to use it, ask these questions:

What will a tighter coupling cost?
> If you're building a very specialized interface with high performance require-ments, it's perfectly valid to live with tighter coupling in order to reduce complexity.

How complex is your message?
> If it's not complex, something simpler may serve you well. You wouldn't con-sider XML to specify command-line parameters—it's overkill. You may only need a simple text string, or a map of name-value pairs. Both of these message types can be quite flexible and dynamic. On the other hand, your message may be deeply nested, with rich schema requirements.

For messages, do you control both ends of the interface?

If you do, consider a lighter message payload. If not, XML may allow you to have a message format that's self-describing, extensible, and neutral.

Do you need to bridge programming languages, or enterprises?

If you're working across very different platforms, XML can provide a convenient intermediate representation to let the platforms communicate.

Are your performance requirements relaxed?

XML requires significant data marshalling. Be sure that your infrastructure and application can afford the increased requirements. If it's a borderline situation, do a brief proof-of-concepts to be sure.

Are you trying to support possible future requirements?

If you are, stop. It's usually better to adopt a simple solution and make sure to build a loosely coupled service that you can adapt to future purposes.

On the topic of XML, I'm not religious. I'm a pragmatist. XML is a fact of life. Use it when it makes your life easier; leave it behind when it doesn't. If you're a Java programmer, you probably need XML within your bag of tricks somewhere, but you don't have to reach for it at every opportunity.

Persistence frameworks

As the programming craft advances, developers need to think in progressively more complex abstractions. Half of everything that you know will be obsolete in seven years. Your brain is like any other computer: space is limited. When you push a new piece of data in—such as aspect-oriented programming—something else is discarded. One of the skills that's getting progressively harder to find is good database application programming. As a result, many developers tend to reach for persistence frameworks and expect them to hide all of the database details. In fact, that's what persistence frameworks are designed to do. The problem is that reality gets in the way. Real persistence frameworks eventually create good or bad SQL. Real applications are either good or bad citizens of the database realm. It's hard to build a persistence framework that solves general problems well for every instance and it takes a knowledgeable database developer to know the difference.

Persistence frameworks do have a major tangible benefit. They let Java developers deal with an application in comfortable terms. Java classes, instances, and idioms replace database tables, indexes, and records. Persistence frameworks also have a cost: their abstractions can hide problems, they can be hard to tune, and they may get inexperienced developers into trouble.

If you have a complex data model and you're spending a lot of time wading through endless persistence details, a persistence framework can save you a whole lot of time if someone on your team knows what's going on under the hood. But don't use what you don't understand. If database access is working and the details aren't overly tedious, you probably don't need a persistence framework.

Web services

The web services standard is the latest in a long line of technologies that promise to tie disparate systems together. It was supposed to be simple, fast, and intuitive. One look at the list of acronyms for associated technologies tells us something has gone horribly awry (SOAP, XML-RPC, WSDL, Disco, UDDI, WS-I, WS-Eventing, and WSA). SOAP originally stood for Simple Object Access Protocol but tellingly, they've dropped that acronym.

Yet you can't simply ignore web services. With the potential to tie together Java and Microsoft technologies and the strong backing of most of the players in both spaces, web services has a meaningful niche to fill. So far, I've had a difficult time understanding what that niche should be. If you look at the basic characteristics of the technology, some ideas begin to crystallize:

Relaxed performance requirements
> The web services API is heavyweight and relatively slow. It's tough to imagine a credible use for web services with demanding performance requirements.

Spanning languages or platforms
> Java has many better native options. If you're trying to wrap a Java service for a Java consumer, it pays to check one of the excellent native APIs first, such as a lower-level API like JMS or even RMI, depending on what you're trying to do. Web services do have strong supporting tools on many platforms, most notably Java and .NET, as well as several others. It's a strong alternative to link disparate systems, since it's relatively simple compared to the alternatives.

Service model
> Web services encapsulate a loose-grained client/service model. It should be used accordingly. Trying to use web services for fine-grained communications is asking for trouble.

Table 5-1 is a list of the most frequently used golden hammers. It is by no means complete. If you look closely, you can see a pattern begin to emerge. A golden hammer can definitely drive in a screw if you strike it often enough and hard enough. Most of the golden hammers that I've listed can do a job—just not efficiently or well.

Table 5-1. Java's most common golden hammers

Tool	Suitable for	Not suited for
Java	Object-oriented programming	End-user scripting
	Web-based development	Rich user interfaces on homogeneous platforms
	Server-side development	
J2EE	Distributed transactional programming	Lightweight applications
	Heavyweight enterprise applications	
Distribution	Scalability	Simple, lightweight applications
	Controlling access to scarce resources	Performance improvement

Table 5-1. Java's most common golden hammers (continued)

Tool	Suitable for	Not suited for
EJB (stateless session beans, MDB)	Distributed, transactional façades	Lightweight applications
	Secure, distributed transaction monitor	Applications where transactions are limited to one database
		Façades that are not distributed
EJB entities	Nothing	Sane applications
Persistence frameworks	Sophisticated domain model	Relational problems (e.g., reporting)
	Relational database	Simple problems
	Moderate performance requirements	Problems that do not present a domain model
		Teams without database experience
Web services	Heterogeneous platforms and languages	Java to Java applications
	Coarse-grained communications	Demanding performance requirements
	Moderate performance requirements	Fine-grained communications
XML	Self-describing data	Message format when one team controls both the producer and consumer
	Standardized data format	High performance requirements
	Heterogeneous messaging	Simple, lightweight applications

The list of golden hammers is not complete. They do have a few things in common, though:

Sweeping integration

Integrated frameworks and platforms claim much, but don't always deliver. Attempts to solve more than one problem can break down if a framework is not easy to extend or adapt. It's just too hard to predict in advance exactly how a multifaceted framework will be used in every instance.

Design-by-committee

EJB, web services, and CORBA were collaboratively designed frameworks. They were also released before anyone had any real practical experience with them. Frameworks designed by committee are especially prone to problems. The open source model works because visionaries prove their designs under the strain of real-world problems. Most people don't understand that most open source projects fail. This is natural and healthy.

Older frameworks

In the early stages, even sound frameworks can become bloated and lose their value. While XML has unquestionably added some useful capabilities, its practical utility is diminishing because it's getting too hard for the everyday programmer to use. Web services seem to be taking this path as well.

Complexity

There's a time and place for complexity and you've got to balance a healthy tension between power and complexity. As a rule, watch out for increasing complexity.

It isn't always true that where there's smoke there's fire. In fact, you can come up with counter-examples for each of these warning signs. My point is that frameworks and platforms, like code, can also smell bad. Develop your instincts, hone them with data beyond the latest marketing hype, and develop sources that you trust.

I've given you a few examples of golden hammers and other frameworks that I don't like. While these warning signs might steer you away from bad decisions, they can't help you make good ones. In the remainder of this chapter, I'll tell you some techniques I've used to help my customers choose a good foundation.

Understanding the Big Picture

It probably won't surprise you to learn that many—even most—decisions in our industry are not based on the requirements of one or more applications. They're made for a variety of emotional, political, and social reasons. Some are valid and others less so.

I specialize in design reviews, at all points in the development process. My customers typically understand the need for a good foundation. They usually want to know the best frameworks for a category—or more rarely, the best integrated middleware suite for Java—and I can certainly take a shot in the dark, for a fee. Sometimes, there's a pat answer. For example, hands down, you should be building with Ant and unit testing with JUnit. Other decisions are not so cut and dried. You've got to take inventory of all of the factors that affect your project. For most projects, I don't recommend putting these into a giant, formal document. Email or simple text documents are usually enough, with the occasional very simple diagram. Think low-tech first.

However you record them, environmental and political concerns weigh heavily in the initial decisions. The best software architects effectively balance these concerns and still exert some control over a technical architecture. In particular, application requirements form only a small part of the overall landscape:

What has already been decided?

Certain decisions may be made for you. If you've already had standards set, you'll likely have (or want) to work within that framework. You may not have to make all of the same decisions, but you certainly don't want your decisions to isolate you, either. Consider decisions that ripple, such as a mandated application server that only supports certain middleware components.

Who will build it?

More than any other factors, the experience, talent, and skill of your team determine your success. You can make the best of each by choosing a familiar set of technologies and languages. You can also render experience obsolete by ignoring the makeup of your team. Finally, you can mitigate skill shortages by getting qualified help to review a design or mentor and train your team.

When will you need it?

It seems obvious, but your schedule, process, technologies, and tools must be in harmony. A heavyweight process takes longer. New or complicated frameworks take longer to learn or use. Certain tools make it easier or more difficult to shorten schedules through continuous integration, unit testing, and performance profiling.

How will you build it?

Your process may dictate your toolset and as a result the frameworks that you have available. If you've got a choice in this area, make sure to tailor your process to your goals. Don't try to build space-shuttle software with extreme programming. Don't try to build a departmental calendar with the Rational Unified Process, as hard as the marketing collateral or sales rep works to convince you otherwise.

What are you trying to build?

Note that technical requirements form only a small piece of the landscape. Once you've worked through your environment, need, in the form of at least one technical requirement, should drive all of your technology choices.

Figure 5-3 shows another view. Many high-level external factors come into play before you ever weigh the technical merits of a middleware stack or even a single framework. Your goal is to put the appropriate weight on each of the factors. Many external, often conflicting influences work to determine the best set of foundational technologies for a given project. Before I move ahead to technical concerns, allow me to rant about factors that don't belong in the decision-making process.

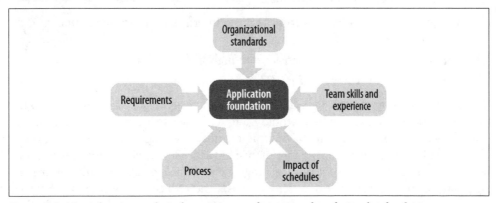

Figure 5-3. More than just technical requirements shape your foundational technologies

Modern Cathedrals

Smart people without enough common sense have an unfortunate tendency to build beautiful, massive cathedrals without pews, bathrooms, or emergency exits. There's a healthy tension between a purist and a pragmatist, and good teams need both. If I've got to choose between the two, though, I'll take the pragmatist every time.

Aligning your goals

Many programmers have developed an unhealthy fear of management, especially managers who hold the purse strings. "Dilbert" cartoons with the pointy-haired boss hang on thousands of cubicles around the world. It's ironic, because developers and management should fundamentally want the same things. If you're a developer who fears management, you've got a decision to make when you're choosing your foundation. Are you building a cathedral, or are you building software? If you're building software, then your philosophy should be unequivocal: business decisions rule.

A hypothetical example

Here's a real-world scenario. A director wants to build an application in Visual Basic because the company already owns the software licenses and new developers will be cheaper. The team would rather do it in Java because it's a more complete development environment and they trust the Java community more than Microsoft. If you're a developer on that team, you need to look at the issue as a business decision. For a small, departmental application, you'll establish one set of criteria. For example, consider a complex user interface on purely Microsoft operating systems with a relational database backend, and low-volume, read-only access. Even with heavier Java skills on the team, the most pessimistic Visual Basic schedule is shorter than the most optimistic Java schedule. It would be hard for any developer to justify J2EE for this scenario.

A medium-sized application with more intense requirements may provoke a different answer. Let's assume the following:

- The application requires a web-based user interface for customers outside of the corporate firewall.
- The backend is an Oracle database with high transaction volumes.
- Schedules slightly favor the Visual Basic application.

Under these conditions, the Java developers could easily make a case for an application with looser coupling, which would be much easier to support and extend. Further, Java provides excellent MVC frameworks, creating a cleaner design that dramatically reduces long-term maintenance burdens. The trick is communication. If you want to push a Java solution, use language and goals consistent with your management team. You will save maintenance costs and reduce long-term risks. You will increase quality with automated unit testing (which is supported better on the Java side). You will offset marginally higher short-term costs with dramatically reduced long-term costs. You'll support a broader user population. You can use technical arguments, but only to the extent that they bolster business arguments.

It's all business

In either case, I say again, it's a business decision. If you find yourself frequently at odds with management decisions, part of the problem is likely on your end. You need to learn to think and negotiate on their terms. Know their language and understand their hot buttons. Leadership likes reduced costs, better availability, fewer bugs, and more customers.

I recently visited a customer who had availability problems. They said their management would not let them unit-test. I thought about it and wondered why a management team would willingly slit their own throats. It turns out the team had pitched the idea weakly, asking, "Can we take a break from fulfilling our mission to build in features that our customers won't ever see? Oh, by the way, it's going to cost a whole lot of money."

I simply asked for the same resources, using the same schedule, with the same cost. I just reframed the request: "What if I could improve your availability and do it with less than it costs you in downtime today?" When availability suffers, your customers make you feel the heat. It did not surprise me that I piqued the customer's interest. Of course, they saw the revised schedules and asked why some medium-priority user requests slipped. I told them the team slipped those features to move up availability changes. I further told them that customers helped me make that decision.

I often find that I'm a high-paid intermediary between teams and management. You'll be more successful if you can do it yourself. I promise that there's more than enough strife out there to keep me busy. Simply align your goals with those of your management. If you've got poor managers, go find better ones. Life's too short to put up with unnecessary stress every day. You need to work in a place that fuels your personal passion.

Passion and software

Passion fuels the best and the worst of software development. Good passion fuels healthy debate, which leads to better decisions and software. It fuels quality and can be a catalyst for good change or a balance against unnecessary change. It's driven from the inside by your core work ethic, values, and goals. It's driven from the outside by people: your peers, leadership, teachers, and mentors. Good passion, more than any other attribute, determines the success or failure of a career. Great passion alone is not enough to build good software, but it's hard to build great software without it.

There's an ugly side to passion, too. When it's misguided, passion cripples projects and even whole companies. Bad passion fragments a team and limits good passion. You'll often hear words like "religion" used to describe bad passion. Drivers for bad passion are egotism and fear. The longer you think about it, the more it makes sense. We're no different from other artists. Great artists throw away a whole lot of work. We need to do likewise. When you wrap your ego around a piece of software, you get too attached to it to make good decisions. Teams crippled by bad passion may still build software, but it's rarely as good or as fast. They'll usually fail over the long term.

A great team is a mix of missionaries on the one true path and nonbelievers casting stones from the side of the road. If the company is overloaded with the former, chances are good that the one true path leads right off the one big cliff. If the company has too many of the missionaries, you may never even get started. Find the right mix of missionaries and pragmatists to get you to your destination. People drive good passion. Ego and fear drive bad passion. It's hard to make good decisions with too much bad passion.

Considering Technical Requirements

With some of the external factors out of the way, it's time to form a plan to find the best possible foundation, from a technical perspective. You'll be tempted to get a standard middleware stack and build from there. In fact, just by starting with the gargantuan J2EE platform, you're probably making far too many assumptions.

After you've taken stock of external influences, start with the most basic question: what are you building? Without gathering a full set of requirements, you can still probably answer some basic questions. You don't have to have all of the answers from the beginning. In fact, you'll find that you create additional questions as you spiral inward, as in Figure 5-4. That's perfectly normal. The important thing is to consider the questions that will have the biggest overall impact on your designs. The outer-most questions tend to disrupt designs more. Inner questions tend to affect fewer systems.

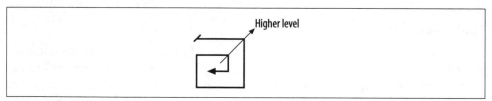

Figure 5-4. As you explore foundational decisions, the process tends to spiral from the outside in

Your goal is to avoid over-designing out of the gate. (In fact, you'd prefer to under-design out of the gate.) You just want to avoid questions like, "So, isn't passing SQL input directly from the user interface going to murder security?" 10 minutes before you're supposed to be in production. Higher-level questions—the outer questions—prompt more detailed questions. This is natural, and helpful.

Outer Questions

Outer questions are the higher-level issues that shape your foundation quickly. You may be able to make a rough cut at your overall design without writing any code, but it's not necessary. Just nail down enough details to get some code rolling. Early code then helps to shape your requirements and thus your design. Here are some outer questions:

What are your external interfaces?
> External interfaces make an excellent starting point when you're trying to iron out early decisions. An external interface is one that you don't fully control. Interfaces that cross major boundaries (such as programming languages, networks, firewalls, or JVMs) may need special consideration. You need a strategy for dealing with each before moving forward.

Who is your user?
> In the early design stages, look at your user interface as one more external interface. A professional data entry clerk has more demanding requirements than an occasional departmental user. Supporting external clients over the Internet also dictates requirements.

What are your physical deployment restrictions?
> Firewalls and existing deployment hardware or software shape your solution. You want to sanity-check compatibility at every turn. For example, if you deploy a new message board discussing products with your existing e-commerce application, make sure to use a compatible JVM, servlet engine, and other software.

What are your database requirements?
> Depending on your application, you may or may not decide to treat a database as just another distributed interface. Since databases form the core of many applications, I prefer to treat them separately. You'll need to decide on a persistence strategy fairly quickly. Is JDBC enough? Will you need a persistence framework? Do you expect to cache? Who owns the schema? These questions can make or break a project.

What components must/might you reuse?
> You may have inherited some business components that you think might be useful. They'll come with some baggage, including programming languages and styles, an interface, and an overall philosophy. If developers err in this area, they often work too hard to reuse a component that doesn't fit. It's far better to steal some of the best ideas of the inherited components and start from scratch. However, if one of the components is a tax rules engine with an investment of 30 million lines of code, you'll have to use it. Your most critical task in that case is to wrap it in a way that's consistent with your architecture.

What's your security policy?

Most developers treat security as an add-on service. Unfortunately, that technique extends to most operating systems and programming environments. Fortunately, the news about Java and .NET is slightly better. If you decide on a consistent security policy before you start coding, you'll avoid some common problems. In this area, you can't guess; you need to know. If you've never heard of a SQL injection attack, call an expert. Then form a cohesive policy and follow it for all of your applications.

How fast does it need to be?

I can't think of many applications that were designed correctly for performance out of the gate. Most were either over-designed or under-designed. It's likely that yours will be, too. The critical point is to make decisions that will not paint you into a corner later. If you may need to cluster, don't build in dependencies that make clustering more difficult. You don't need to (and shouldn't) optimize prematurely, but understand the possible design implications of your expected load.

You can draw some rough lines in the sand by looking for the core requirements of your project. That's the purpose of the outer questions. You'll find that you've only got partial answers, but you may have enough information to understand your security model, the potential software layers, and potential deployment scenarios.

Inner Questions

After you've asked the outer questions and done some further development, you're going to need to fine-tune your architecture. That's the purpose of inner questions. Inner questions drill down into specialized problems; their goal is to refine your design, middleware requirements, and the interfaces between layers. Think of an inner decision as a major fork in the road. It's a detail that will definitely force a foundational architectural decision. Answering an inner question permits you to refine your design. Here are some examples of inner questions. As you can see, they depend almost entirely on your application:

- Will we support stored procedures? And which persistence frameworks support stored procedures?

- Does my façade layer need to be distributed? If not, do we still need to use session beans in the façade layer? If not, can we replace the J2EE application server with a simple servlet container and a web server?

- Would a persistence framework simplify things? Am I spending too much time coding and debugging JDBC and raw SQL?

It's best to ask and answer these questions after you've had some experience with the problem. It's also best to put time and energy into answering the questions and then live with your first answer until something fundamental breaks.

Prototypes

Sometimes, you'll find that you need to write code to answer an inner question. That's expected and healthy. For example, you wouldn't want to use a persistence framework without trying it first. And you wouldn't want to use a persistence framework until you've established a need. (I tell my customers to push a POJO solution until it breaks, and only then get a persistence framework.) When you do decide to prototype, write just enough code to make your decision. Try to use production-coding techniques so you'll have a firm grasp of the shape of the solution. It's best to carve out a small but technically demanding scenario, one that proves a representative business requirement. If you're going to be paying for a product, consider getting a vendor's assistance.

Regardless of the technique that you use to answer the inner questions, make sure the team understands that once the decision is made, there's no going back. Technical decisions can fragment vulnerable teams. It's been my experience that in order to keep everyone pulling together, it's usually easier to get the entire team to agree to abide by a decision once it's made.

Documentation

When you think about it, what I've described is classical iterative development. Each iteration lets you know more about the system and solve more of your target problem. The primary way that processes differ in this area is the style and weight of documentation. You need to collect just enough documentation to do your job. Minimally, you've got to update your requirements to reflect any new, needed functionality, based in a foundational decision. The rest is entirely up to you. I prefer to keep it light. Frequently, I'll handle outer questions in meeting notes. For inner questions, if I need to get teammates to agree to a decision in a meeting or after a prototype, I'll try to follow the meeting or prototype exercise with a simple email that covers:

- What we were trying to learn
- What we decided
- What contributed to the decision

Then I'll copy everyone who needs to sign off and say, "Does everybody agree?" This informal process has served me well as a developer. It's fast, to the point, and has just enough process to get the job done. In fact, as a consultant, most of my major agreements are not formal contracts. I also follow up with my clients, describing what I learned and letting the customer sign off. I find email organization services like listservs to be invaluable in this respect. You can create a distribution list for "architecture and design," for instance. Then, for all decision-making emails, simply copy the "architecture and design" listserv, making a threaded repository of all decisions publicly available to the whole team.

Summary

In the end, your goal is to establish a good foundation. Since your application consists of what you start with (your middleware) plus everything that you add (your code), you've got to be careful to add only the things that you need, and only pieces that make your life easier. The Java community is becoming infamous for choosing bloated, cumbersome foundational technologies like J2EE (especially EJB) and growing functional standards until they're so complex that they are near worthless. You can learn to recognize and avoid these types of frameworks, though.

To make good decisions about your foundations, you need to consider many factors beyond technical requirements. All organizations have biases and many adopt standards that shape the solution before you even write a single line of code. Carefully evaluate your team's skills. When you're considering technical requirements, I recommend iterative development. Separate questions that affect your foundational technologies into two sets: outer questions, which can be answered immediately (at least in part), and inner questions, which come up as you're coding. In each case, communication plays a key role. In the next chapter, you'll see techniques that you can use to allow for extension.

CHAPTER 6

Allow for Extension

Nearly every extreme sports junky has one tool in common. It's a tool that you can't always find at an outdoor shop, although it's the first one you pack for extended river trips or mountain biking journeys. A close friend has used it as a first aid kit for major cuts and others have used it to splint broken bones. I've repaired major gashes in my boat, tightened up my cockpit, and even splinted a broken paddle. I've heard tales of amazing mountain bike repairs, from tires to gear systems.

Of course, the magic tool is duct tape. Like any other aspiring engineer, I stretch duct tape far beyond its intended use. In this chapter, you'll see some techniques that allow your applications to stretch in the same way. Enterprising users apply great code for a variety of purposes, including many the author never considered. If you want to build simpler software, extensibility can keep it from being too simplistic. If you don't allow for extension, you don't have a prayer of meeting the needs of today's sophisticated and rapidly changing customers. Give your customers room to be creative and they'll always surprise you.

The Basics of Extension

Extension is in many ways an awkward topic to write about because it encompasses so many different design principles. I've included it in this book because it's a fundamental capability for good applications. You need extensibility if you decide to apply the first four principles outlined in Chapters 2 through 5 because simplicity without flexibility is worthless. I'll define extensibility like this:

> Extensibility is the ability to quickly adapt code to do things that it was not built to do, in ways both planned and unplanned.

With this definition, I'm deliberately painting with a broad brush. It's important to do so, because you'll find value in many different types of extension. Some please your customers by letting you efficiently address short-term change. Others ease the burden of maintenance by allowing sweeping refactoring—even late in the application life cycle—with minimal effort. In this section, I briefly review several core concepts that lead to better flexibility.

Inheritance and Interfaces

The two most basic means of extension are *inheritance* and *interfaces*. If you were creating an interface for an electrical component, you could either attach your implementation to a ready-made plug or design your component to meet the specifications of the interface. With OOP, you have two similar alternatives (among others): first, you could think of a superclass as a working plug extended by a subclass; secondly, you could implement a Java interface. Each technique has strengths and weaknesses. Most beginning programmers automatically reach for inheritance, because it requires fewer files and less code, although most of the evil in this world happens because someone wanted to save a few keystrokes.

In OOP's earliest days, inheritance was the tool of choice for reuse and extension. As you might expect, many programmers abused inheritance badly. Still, there's a place for inheritance and abstract classes, in particular. If you're trying to preserve a default behavior with a common API, an abstract class is often the best way to go. Keep in mind that you want to use inheritance to capture some kind of is-a relationship, and not extend some form of service or capability to all classes. You've probably run across limiting code that's been written in this way. For example, consider a Person class that inherits from PersistentThing. How might you extend Person to also be transactional? Figure 6-1 shows three options, although none of them are good. Option 1 doesn't work if you want to add an entity that's persistent but not transactional. Option 2 won't allow only persistence. Option 3 does not support existing subclasses of Person.

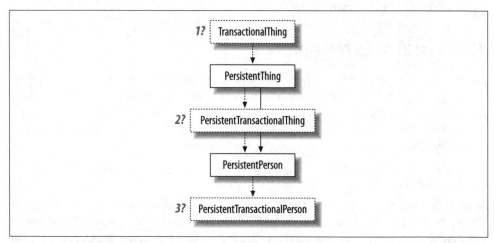

Figure 6-1. Inheritance can be a dangerous tool for adding services

A rough rule of thumb is to prefer interfaces to concrete inheritance, especially when you're trying to present a capability rather than an is-a relationship. Interfaces allow you to extend a class along more than one axis, as in Figure 6-2. You are not limited to a single service, and each service is independent and adaptable independently.

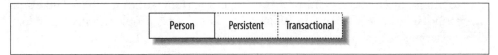

Figure 6-2. Interfaces let you extend a class to implement additional services

It's only a rough rule of thumb, though, and it can be taken too far. Interfaces can be abused as well:

- You don't need an interface for every class—only those that implement special abstract concepts. After having success with interfaces, some rigid managers go too far and demand all classes have an interface. This process leads to poorly designed interfaces and frustrated developers.

- An interface should not expose every method in a class—only those that relate to the concept that you're presenting. Beginning programmers who've just discovered interfaces make this mistake often, either because they can cut and paste or because they don't understand fundamentally what interfaces are trying to do.

When you're deciding between interfaces and abstract classes, the acid tests are type of relationship and behavior. If you need to capture default behavior, lean toward the subclass. You must also consider the abstraction that you're trying to provide. Remember, inheritance is most appropriate for capturing an is-a relationship, while interfaces seek to expose a basic capability. Abusing these rules leads to complications down the road, such as the one in Figure 6-1.

Planned Extension

In some cases, you can explicitly allow customers to extend your framework in predetermined ways. For example, Ant allows plug-ins in the form of Ant tasks. Plug-ins anticipate your customer's need for extension. Planned extensions often take effort and foresight: don't invest in them lightly. Listen to your instincts and know your customer.

Let's say that you've decided you need a specific extension. Further, it's a specific, difficult, tedious area to expose to your customer. It helps to look at the problem in a different way. You could break it down, which often allows two or more easier extensions. You could also try to generalize the problem.

The Inventor's Paradox

When you're solving a problem, you often decide to limit yourself to something that's as specific as possible. When you do so, you usually place awkward limits on developers who wish to use your framework and customers who would use it. General solutions often solve more problems than a specific solution does. There's an interesting side benefit. You can often solve the general problem with less effort, cleaner designs, and simpler algorithms. That's the *Inventor's Paradox*.

In *How to Solve It* (Princeton University Press), a book that's quite famous in mathematics circles, George Polya introduces the Inventor's Paradox: "The more ambitious plan may have more chances of success." In other words, you can frequently solve a useful general problem more effectively than a highly specialized one. It's a principle that works often in math. For example, try totaling all of the numbers from 1–99, in sequence. Then, think of it in this way: $(1 + 99) + (2 + 98) + ... + (49 + 51) + 50$. You can probably solve the second equation in your head. Once you generalize the problem in this way, you can quickly sum any sequence of numbers. The general problem is easier to solve. It works in industry, too, as you saw in my duct tape example.

There are many examples of the Inventor's Paradox in programming. Often, the most successful frameworks are simple generalizations of a complex problem. Apache web server plug-ins, Visual Basic custom controls, and the Internet are but a few examples of simple generalizations. Closer to home, Ant and Tomcat surpassed the wildest expectations of their author, James Duncan Davidson. Both of these frameworks allow exquisitely simple, elegant extensions. You don't have to have the luck of James Bond or the intellect of Albert Einstein to make the Inventor's Paradox work for you. Simply train yourself to look for opportunities to generalize. Start with this list of questions:

What's likely to change?
> You can't spend all of your time generalizing every block of code, but you can identify areas that you may need to future-proof. MVC is a famous design pattern because views and models change. It's important to generalize the way you deal with your views so you can change at need. If you intentionally identify and generalize these interfaces, you'll often be much better off. I'm not arguing for more complexity. You are looking for ways to generalize and simplify at the same time.

Is there a different way to solve this cumbersome problem?
> When I get in trouble, I usually step back and ask myself, "Why this way?" For example, many open source projects read configuration files as XML DOM (Domain Object Model) trees. Many developers begin to look at configuration as a Java representation of an XML file. It's not. Instead of looking for ways to efficiently lob DOM trees across your application, look for the reason that you're doing so. Maybe it's better to read that configuration file once, and translate it to a smaller set of concrete objects representing your configuration. You can share those at will.

Have I seen this problem before in another context?

Simple generalizations often show up in dramatically different contexts. For example, it took me a while to see that the model-view-controller concepts are not limited to views. You can generalize a view as just another interface. You can apply MVC-like ideas to many different types of services, including persistence and messaging.

In the next couple of chapters, you'll see these principles in action. Spring generalizes a concept called *inversion of control* and uses a generalized architecture to assemble and configure entire applications—from the database to the user interface and everything in between. Rather than including a stored procedure framework, Hibernate exposes the JDBC connection, allowing users to extend Hibernate in ways that the inventors often never considered.

The Inventor's Paradox represents all that's fun about programming: finding simple, elegant solutions to difficult problems. When you do, you'll find that patterns that seemed tedious in books emerge as new creations. But it's only the first step in allowing for extension.

Unplanned Extension

Not all requirements can or should be anticipated. Building simple software often means waiting to incorporate future requirements until they're needed. You don't have to completely write off the future, though. By making good decisions, you can make it easy to extend your frameworks in ways you might not have originally intended. You do so by following good design principles:

Expose the right methods, with the right granularity

Methods should be fine-grained and handle a single concept. If your methods bundle up too many concepts, you won't be able to extend the class by overriding the method.

Use Java interfaces

Providing general Java interfaces separates the interface from implementation details. If you see a service or capability that's buried in a class definition, break it out into a separate interface.

Loosen coupling between key concepts

This concept always comes up in good Java programming books for a reason. It works.

Keep designs clear and simple

Code that's hard to read and understand will be hard to extend.

Publish the code under an open source license

An application with source that can be examined and modified is much easier to extend then a closed-source application.

The key to extensibility has always been the same: build an architecture that separates key concepts and couple them loosely, so any given concept can be replaced or extended. You can see that the earlier concepts in this book (like transparency, focus, and simplicity) all come into play, especially for unplanned extension. For the rest of the chapter, I focus on planned extension and the tools that achieve it.

Tools for Extension

When I worked at a startup called AllMyStuff, we researched reporting tools. We wanted a tool that our users could drop into our framework and report on data that we gathered. We wanted to be able to work the reports into our user interface and we wanted the tool to use our existing data structures. Sales reps from various companies all said, "No problem. Our framework is completely extensible." As you might expect, that wasn't the case.

Of course, we wanted to extend the reporting tools in a variety of ways. Some of the extensions were minor. We needed the product to support our customers' databases. Most supported JDBC and all supported major database vendors. In other cases, we wanted to extend the reporting packages in ways that the original designers had not intended. We found that supporting a Java API was not nearly enough. We needed the user interface to live with ours without source code changes. We needed to integrate the security of the reporting package to the security of the application. We wanted our customers to be able to access extensions through configuration rather than coding changes.

When you're planning to build an extensible framework in the Java environment, you've got an incredibly broad selection of tools to choose from. The continuum of techniques ranges from requiring massive, invasive change to nothing more than configuration changes. In Figure 6-3, I identify four types of extension based on the level of effort it takes to extend the framework. The hardest—and most useful—type of extension to provide requires no code changes or installation. The application automatically recognizes the need to change and does the work. Norton Antivirus auto-update provides this type of support. The next-most stringent model requires only scripting or configuration. All other support is included or retrieved automatically. The next option, the plug-in, requires the user to provide and configure a compatible module. That's a very useful and common design for enterprise programming, and the one that will get most of our focus in this chapter. Finally, other modes of extension require coding changes. I won't spend as much time with these. The tools that you use to provide each type of support overlap but are different.

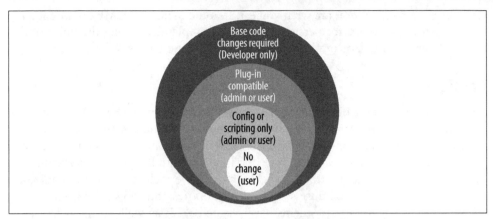

Figure 6-3. Different models of extension place different burdens on the user

Standards

Your first tool is a clear understanding of the key standards that improve extension. Using these and exposing relevant configuration can give you an important head start. This is the paradox: by choosing standards, you will limit your own choices, but you'll dramatically improve the choices that your customers can make after deployment time. The most critical standards for you are external touch points, like user interfaces, databases, transactions, or communication. Table 6-1 shows some important standards that you may choose to support. If you need a service in one of these areas, consider the corresponding standard.

Table 6-1. Java standards

Acronym	Meaning	Purpose
JAAS	Java Authentication and Authorization Service	Security of applications
JCA	Java Cryptography Architecture	Encryption of Java data
XML	eXtensible Markup Language	Structuring and representing data
JMS	Java Messaging Service	Messaging
JTA	Java Transaction API	Transactions
JCA	J2EE Connection Architecture	Connections management
JNDI	Java Naming and Directory Interface	Naming and registration of core Java services and components
JDBC	Java DataBase Connectivity	Relational database API
JDO	Java Data Objects	Transparent persistence for Java
RMI	Remote Method Invocation	Remote procedure calls in Java
IIOP	Internet Inter-Orb Protocol	Java-to-CORBA connectivity
Servlet		Server-side component, invoked via HTTP
JSP	Java Server Pages	A markup language for user interfaces that accepts dynamic content and compiles to a servlet

Be careful: remember, you are what you eat. If you choose EJB CMP because it's the most pervasive standard for persistence, you're completely missing the point of this book. Choose an implementation that works for you and works well.

Configuration

Configuration has long been the bane of Java developers everywhere. Most developers focus on reuse strategies that involve coding changes, such as introducing an API. If you're like most developers, you probably save configuration issues for the end of a project—but if you don't want to force developers to handle all possible extensions, you must address configuration early. Many developers choose to write configuration libraries themselves because so many Java libraries and tools have been so poor for so long. Configuration problems have plagued J2EE as well. In the recent past, EJB, JNDI, and J2EE security have all had vastly different configuration strategies, formats, and models. Recent Java developers have faced these problems:

Inconsistent strategies
> Java frameworks and applications had no consistent API for configuration. On the server side, that's still true. The Preferences API is strongly oriented toward client-side configuration.

Inconsistent formats
> Java frameworks have had no consistent format for configuration. The Java properties file used simple name-value pairs and other frameworks used ad hoc XML configuration strategies.

Inadequate tools
> The default configuration tool, the Java properties API, did not meet the most basic needs of configuration. (For example, it doesn't support multipart properties.) JNDI, on the other hand, is much too heavyweight for many applications.

Recently, developers have learned more, and other options have surfaced that allow much better control. Although they're not perfect, there's a much broader set of choices. You can choose from several strategies. There are too many solutions to count, but at least three look promising:

Java Preferences API for client-side configuration
> The Java toolkit provides a good library for client side configuration, called the Preferences API. It doesn't fully support the most common server-side configuration format, XML, but it does provide enough power and flexibility for client-side applications.

Apache Digester subproject for server-side configuration
> Apache projects broadly use a configuration tool called Digester, which takes XML configuration files and translates them to lightweight objects for configuration and also provides many services to assist configuration. This tool is probably the preferred way to deal with generic server-side XML configuration files.

J2EE still does not have a cohesive strategy or API for configuration, so I choose a reliable open source alternative.

Spring for framework-driven configuration

Often, you want all configuration driven by a central framework. At its core, the Spring framework provides a set of application configuration and assembly tools. It's a unified approach that's freely available to components across all layers of the application. We'll talk more about Spring configuration in Chapters 8 and 10.

Study every solution with the same diligence that you'd use for choosing any other major framework. Without effective configuration, your only option for extension is programming intervention. In this chapter, I look briefly at two possible solutions: the Java Preferences API and to a lesser extent, Apache Digester.

Client-side configuration with Java Preferences

The standard Java API for configuration is the Java Preferences API. As you'll see, it's designed primarily for client-side use, but lightweight server-side applications may make some use of it as well. It's designed independently of the backend data store. It lets you store system level properties and properties for individual users—thus, then name *Preferences*.

Preferences databases are stored in two different trees: one for the user and one for the system. Your primary window into a preferences data store is the node. You could decide to read the top node out of either preferences store, the system, or the user, but if you did so, different applications would potentially step on each other. The customary solution is to group preferences together under a package, as in Figure 6-4. You can get the top-level node for the user tree, for any given package, like this:

```
Preferences node = Preferences.userNodeForPackage(getClass());
```

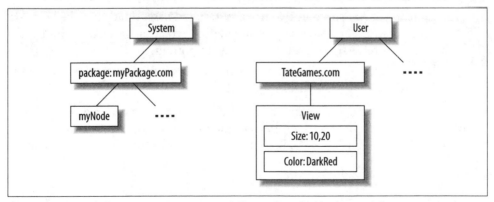

Figure 6-4. The Preference API supports two different trees, for the user and the system

Then you can use the Preference API to load and save preferences. You can always create additional tree nodes to organize things further but for simple applications, just store preference properties directly at the package level. For example, to get the "BackgroundColor" preference to "White":

```
node.putString("BackgroundColor", "White");
```

Preferences are simply name-value pairs. The first parameter is the key and the second is the value of the preference. You can use Strings, other primitive types, or byte arrays. The Preference API does not support complex objects. You'll read a preference in much the same way. As you'd expect, you look up a preference by its key value. For example, to read the default high score for a game:

```
node.getInt("HighScore", 0);
```

Here, the first parameter is once again the key but the second is a default, just in case the backend data store is not available. By default, the data is stored in different places on different operating systems. The Windows system (Windows 2000 and beyond) uses the registry. The Linux version uses a file.

You can also import or export a preference file as XML with exportSubtree and exportNode. Exporting a subtree includes children; exporting a node only exports a single level. For example, to dump the current user's node for a package:

```
Preferences prefs = Preferences.userNodeForPackage(getClass());
FileOutputStream outputStream = new FileOutputStream("preferences.xml");
prefs.exportSubtree(outputStream);
```

I haven't shown the whole API, but you have enough to get started. You may be wondering why the preferences may be appropriate for the client, but less so for the server. Here are the most important reasons:

- For the Windows operating system, the Preferences API default storage is to the registry. That's not the most appropriate place for all server-side configuration because administrators need to carefully guard the registry from corruption.

- The Preferences API specifies two trees, *system* and *user*. That's not the best possible organization for server-side configuration, which must also support other concepts like clusters, and user trees are less important.

- While the Preferences API supports XML import and export, there are more direct and efficient ways to deal with XML.

If you want to use a configuration service for a more sophisticated server-side application, I recommend that you look beyond the properties and Preferences APIs. In the next section, you'll see a high-level overview of the solution used by many Apache projects.

Server-side configuration with Apache Digester

The Apache project has a set of common Java utilities grouped into the Commons project. One of the tools, *Digester*, pareses XML files, helps map them onto objects, and fires rules based on patterns. It's helpful any time you need to parse an XML tree and especially useful for processing configuration files. Figure 6-5 shows how it works. You start with a configuration file, then add patterns and associated rules to Digester. When Digester matches a pattern, it fires all associated rules. You can use the prepackaged rules provided by Digester, or you can write your own.

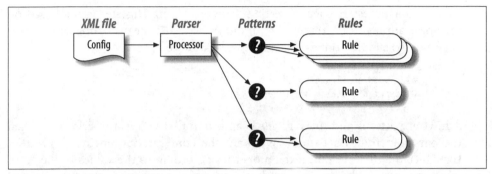

Figure 6-5. Apache's digester makes it easy to parse configuration files

For the most part, you're going to want Digester to create objects that correspond to your configuration tree. You also might want it to do special things to your objects when it encounters them, like open a connection or register a data source. Here's how to process a configuration file with Digester:

1. Create a configuration file. Your configuration file is a simple hierarchical XML file. For example, this application requires an output file for a log:

```
<config>
  <logFile>
    <fileName>myfile.txt</fileName>
    <path>c:\logfiles\</path>
  </logFile>
</config>
```

2. Create any objects that map to the configuration file In this case, the logFile XML node maps onto a class called LogFileConfig. It looks like this:

```
public class LogFileConfig
  private String fileName;
  private String path;

  public String getFileName() {
    return fileName;
  }
  public void setFileName(String name) {
    fileName=name;
  }
```

```
        public String getPath( ) {
          return path;
        }
        public void setPath(String name) {
          path=name;
        }
      }
```

Notice that you need to use the JavaBeans specification because Digester uses the JavaBeans API to populate the new classes the configuration creates. This structure mirrors the structure of the XML tree.

3. Create your Digester object. Creating and configuring Digester varies based on the application you're configuring. In our case, it just means configuring a new Digester. To simplify things, I'll also set validation to false.

```
class ConfigManager {
  public void configureIt( ) {
    Digester digester = new Digester( );
    digester.setValidating(false);
```

4. Add your patterns and rules. A *rule* is an action that you want performed when the parser identifies a pattern. We want the configuration engine to create a LogFileConfig object and set the properties according to the values in the XML input file. Apache has prepackaged rules to create an object and set the properties. The rules look like this:

```
digester.addObjectCreate( "config/logFile", LogFileConfig.class );
digester.addBeanPropertySetter( "config/logFile/path", "path" );
digester.addBeanPropertySetter( "config/logFile/fileName", "fileName" );
```

The rule to create a new object is first. The method name has two parts: add means we're adding a new rule to Digester and ObjectCreate is the action the rule performs. The first parameter is the pattern and the second refers to the class for the new object. In other words, when the parser encounters an XML <logFile> underneath <config>, it fires the rule to create an object of class LogFileConfig. Similarly, the second and third rules set the properties from the values specified in the XML file.

5. Run it. All that remains is to run the configuration file:

```
myLogConfig = digester.parse( );
```

I like the Digester framework because it's simple and lets you create a transparent model for your configuration—you can separate the configuration from the configuration implementation. That means you're not lobbing DOM trees all over your application.

Class Loading

Configuration lets administrators rather than programmers specify what an application should look like. Often, you'll want to allow the administrators to configure classes that you might not have anticipated when you build your application, or even classes that don't exist yet. In fact, that's the whole point—giving the users the ability to extend a system in ways you might not foresee. It's called *delayed binding*.

The problem with delayed binding is this: if you don't know the name of the class, you can't create it with a constructor. You'll need to load the class yourself or use a tool such as Spring or Digester that will do it for you. Fortunately, class loading and reflection give you enough horsepower to get the job done.

Many developers never use *dynamic class loading*, one of the Java language's most powerful capabilities. It's deceptively simple. You just load a class and use it to instantiate any objects that you need. You're free to directly call methods that you know at compile time through superclasses or interfaces, or methods that you don't know until runtime through reflection.

Loading a class with Class.forName

Sometimes, loading a class is easy. Java provides a simple method on `Class` called `ForName(String className)` that loads a class. Calling it invokes a class loader to load your named class. (Yes, there's more than one class loader. I'll get into that later.) Then, you can instantiate it using `newInstance( )`. For example, to create a new instance of a class called `Dog`, use the following lines of code:

```
Class cls = Class.forName("Dog");
```

Invoking methods

Now you've loaded a class; the next step is to use it. You've got several choices. First, you might invoke static methods on the class, like `main`. You don't need a class instance to do that. Invoking the `main` method looks like this:

```
myArgs = ...
Method mainMethod - findMain(cls);
mainMethod.invoke(null, myArgs);
```

Your next option is to create an instance and then call direct methods of known superclasses or interfaces. For example, say you know that you've loaded an `Animal` class or a class that supports the `Animal` interface. Further, `Animal` supports a method called `speak`, which takes no arguments. You can cast your new instance to `Animal` as you instantiate it. Understand that your class must have a default constructor that initializes your object appropriately, because you can't pass constructor arguments this way. Here's how you would create an instance of `Animal` and access its properties:

```
Animal dog = (Animal)cls.newInstance( );
dog.setName("Rover");
dog.speak( );
```

When I'm doing configuration of a service, I like to use the interface approach. An interface best captures the idea of a service. Other times, you're instantiating a refined concept, like a servlet (Tomcat) or component (EJB). For these purposes, subclasses work fine. Many Java services use a simple class loading and an interface or abstract class:

- The Tomcat servlet engine loads a subclass of a generic servlet.
- JDBC applications may know the name of a driver in advance. Still, they often load a class and invoke static methods on the class object in order to preserve portability.
- EJB containers load a class supporting the interface EJBObject.

Your next option is to use reflection to access fields or call methods, as in Chapter 4. Using this technique, you'll need to know the name and signature of the method that you want to call. Remember, Java allows overloading (methods that have the same name but different signatures).

For the most abstract configuration possible, you may well need reflection to invoke methods or access properties. For example, Hibernate and Spring both use configuration and reflection to access persistent properties. The Digester framework also uses reflection within many of its rules. All of these techniques depend on dynamic class loading to do the job. It's time to dive into some more details.

Which class loader?

Java 2 recently added a lot of flexibility to the class loader. The changes also added some uncertainty. Here's how it works:

- Every class has its own class loader.
- All loaders are organized in a tree.
- The class loader uses a *delegating parent model* that works like this:
  - If a class loader hasn't seen a class, it delegates the task of loading the class to its parent before trying to load itself. That class in turn delegates to its parent and work its way up the chain.
  - If the class loader has not loaded the class at the top of the tree, it tries to load the class. If it fails, it returns control back down the chain.
  - A class remains associated with the loader that succeeded in loading it. You can see the associated class loader with a Class.getClassLoader( ).

That sounds easy enough. The problem is that Java 2 supports more than one class loader, as shown in Figure 6-6. Three different hierarchies load three major types of files. The system loader loads most applications and uses the class path. The extension loader loads all extensions, and the bootstrap loader loads core Java classes in *rt.jar*.

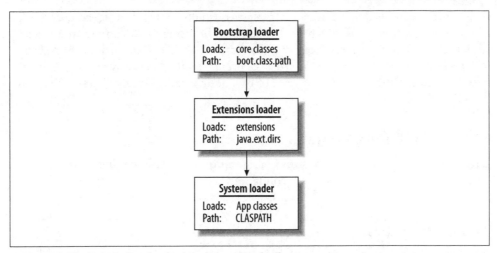

Figure 6-6. The Java 2 class loader has three major loaders

The Java runtime obviously needs special treatment. Since the Java runtime is not yet alive when it starts, Sun provides a basic bootstrap loader to load the Java runtime. It does not load any application logic at all. Only the most basic Java classes—those in *rt.jar*—are loaded by the Bootstrap class loader. It doesn't have a parent.

Many users complained that class paths were getting too long as the number of Java extensions grew. To simplify Java extensions, Sun provided an environment variable that pointed to a set of directories (specified in the environment variable *java.ext. dirs*) to hold all Java extensions. That way, when you want to add a service, like JNDI, you can just drop your *.jar* into Java's extensions directory.

The system loader is often the loader that your applications will use. If you don't specify a loader and you are not a Java extension, you're likely going to get the system loader as your ultimate parent.

The most important thing to keep in mind is that your classes may not have the same parent. If you're loading an extension, it may well use a different loader and check a different class path. If you're loading extensions from an application, for example, your class loader will have a different ancestor chain. You may have also run across similar problems when using applications like Tomcat or Ant, which rely on class paths and environment variables other than the CLASSPATH environment variable. You don't have to rely on luck. If you want to be sure that the new class will use the same class loader chain as your current thread, specify a class loader when you use `Class.forName`. You can get the context class loader for your current thread like this:

```
cl=Thread.getContextClassLoader( );
```

You can even set the current thread's context class loader to any class loader you choose. That means all participants in the thread can use the same class loader to load resources. By default, you get the app class loader instance.

The short version is that Class.forName(aName) usually works. If it doesn't, do a little research and understand which class loader you're using. You can get more details about class loading in an excellent free paper by Ted Neward at *http://www.javageeks.com/Papers/ClassForName/ClassForName.pdf.* Alternatively, some of the resources in the Bibiliography chapter of this book (Halloway, for instance) are outstanding resources.

What Should You Configure?

After you've mastered the basics for configuration and class loading, consider what pieces of your applications need configuration. Several important decisions will guide you.

Fundamental concepts

The first step in deciding what to configure is to understand the fundamental concepts involved. You might just use them as an aid to your planning or you might use them to help you organize your configuration implementation. After you've decided on the fundamental concepts of your system, begin to choose the ones that you'd like to try to configure.

Chapter 3 emphasized the principle "Do one thing and do it well." For extensibility, the key is to keep orthogonal concepts separate—not just in code but in configuration. If you're working from a good design and a good configuration service, it will be easy to organize and expose the most critical services. Keep the code for individual concepts independent so you can consider each concept individually. For example, if you're considering your data layer, you may decide to expose your data source, a database name, a schema name, and your database authentication data. You may decide to separate your transaction manager, since that may be useful to your user base should they decide to let your application participate in an existing transaction.

Keep the Inventor's Paradox in mind. It will help you separate important concepts in your configuration. You can often generalize a configuration option. The Spring framework discussed in Chapter 8 supports many examples of this.

External touch points

All applications access the outside world. You were probably taught very early in your career to insulate your view from the rest of your application. Often, you can get great mileage out of insulating other aspects of your application, as well. For example, you may link to proprietary applications that manage inventory, handle e-commerce, or compute business rules. In any of these instances, it pays to be able to open up the interface to an application. One of the most useful configuration concepts is to allow your customer to tailor external touch points. In order to do so, define the way you use your service. You don't always need to explicitly configure the service. You may instead decide to configure a communications mechanism for an XML message or wire into a standard such as a web service. The important thing is to allow others to use your application without requiring major revision. Whether you enable JMS or some type of RPC, you'll be able to easily change the way your clients communicate with your system. Frameworks like Spring handle this type of requirement very well.

External resources

Nearly all enterprise applications need resources. It's best to let your clients configure external services whenever they might need to change them. Data sources (especially those with connection pools), transaction monitors, log files, and RPC code all need customization, and it's best to do so from a central configuration service.

Sometimes, configuring external touch points requires more than just specifying and configuring a service. Occasionally, you must build a custom architecture to plug in specialized services with special requirements. These types of services require an architecture called a plug-in.

Plug-In Models

Many applications that need to be extended use a model called a *plug-in*. Both web browsers and web servers use plug-ins to display specialized content. A plug-in is an application component that can be installed into an existing application and configured by nonprogrammers. These are the key elements of the plug-in:

Interface
> The plug-in must have a well-defined API. Within Java, you can expose the API through a Java interface or abstract class. You need not expose the API through all classes in your component—only the classes that the base application will call.

Component
> The implementation is a component or a group of Java classes that work together.

Configuration
> Usually, plug-ins require specialized configuration by the base application.

Installation strategy
> With Java, installation can be surprisingly easy. Usually, an archive (WAR, JAR, or EAR file) is placed in the appropriate path.

Most applications hard-wire services to objects or components that use the service. You can't do that with a plug-in. The calling application needs to know to look for the plug-in without any compile-time knowledge about it. Let's put the Inventor's Paradox into practice and generalize the problem to include any service.

Plug-Ins at a Lower Level

You can generalize the plug-in model to most configurable services. For example, think about a typical J2EE application with a data access object. For the DAO to work, you need to supply a data source. You probably don't want to create and manage the data source within the DAO because you've doubtless got other DAOs and you'd like them to work together. Within your application code, configure a data source and use it to get a connection. Your application code will then somehow get the connection to your DAO. Most developers choose a hard-wired approach:

- J2EE developers love *singletons* (static classes with one instance). You might store the data source in a singleton and let your DAO get a fresh connection through the data source stored in the common singleton. Like global variables, the singleton approach can backfire by building dependencies between major components and harming testability.

- You might designate application code as a data manager to manage that data source. Then clients of a DAO can access the data manager to get a connection and pass it directly to the DAO as needed.

Either way, you have a hardwired connection. The application code drives implementations of a DAO, data source, and connection (Figure 6-7). This approach is sound but limited.

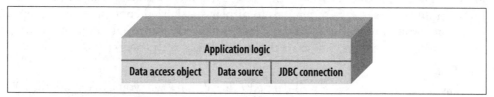

Figure 6-7. Some traditional J2EE applications have application logic that controls implementations of a DAO, a data source, and a connection

Both solutions have fundamental drawbacks. You must couple ideas that do not belong together. In this case, you couple the ideas of a data source, a connection, and a DAO together. You leave it to the application programmer to tediously manage and coordinate the resources. For example, the application needs to open and close connections appropriately. Further, the application is now hardcoded to use specific implementations of each of these three ideas. You need to change code to change the services that the application uses.

Good developers solve this problem with one or two mechanisms: the *service locator* or *dependency injection* (also called *inversion of control*). Both approaches work, but one does a better job of insulating configuration and extension from the developer.

Service locators

The most common J2EE solution is to add a layer of abstraction called a service locator. As you've probably seen, this design pattern lets you register a data source in a

---

hash table, database, or other data store. Applications combine the managing code to find and configure it into a single service called the service locator. Service providers can implement similar services at the interface level so that users can potentially replace like services with less impact. This idea does save some of the administrative burden and decouple your application from other concepts. But instead of completely decoupling the concepts, the burden simply shifts to a different component—because the application must still register services with the locator.

This design pattern is the fundamental driver behind JNDI. As with most design patterns, the service locator is a workaround for limitations within J2EE. It's an often-cumbersome way of solving the problem that relies on code rather than configuration, which is potentially limiting.

Inversion of control

Another possibility is an inversion of control container. Figure 6-8 shows the implementation. You can have the application programmer code an individual Java bean for the DAO and identify key services. The programmer identifies necessary services and specifies individual fields for those services, such as a data source. The programmer can then build a configuration file, describing how to create and populate individual instances. The configuration file resolves dependencies at that time through data provided in the configuration file. For example, the DAO needs a data source, which it can query for a connection. The assembler reads the configuration file and creates a data source and a DAO, then wires them together simply by using Java reflection to set a parameter. You can see why many people prefer the term *dependency injection* to *inversion of control*.

Keep in mind that the inversion of control container does do some work for you, but your objects can live without it. This capability comes in handy as you build test cases. For example, to test the application in Figure 6-8, create a data source and provide it to your DAO manually. Your bean doesn't depend on an individual data source or on Spring. The end result is a decoupled object that's easy to code, test, extend, and use.

The Role of Interfaces

Interfaces play a critical role in this design philosophy. You can treat each service (or resource) as an interface. If a bean uses a resource, it relies on an interface rather than a base class with inheritance. You can then configure it to use any bean that implements that interface.

If this isn't clear to you, think of the metaphor that gave the plug-in its name—electrical appliances. A description of the plug is an interface (it has a positive and negative lead and a ground, for instance). You can build applications (appliances), or sockets (services), based on the interface. The application—such as an electric

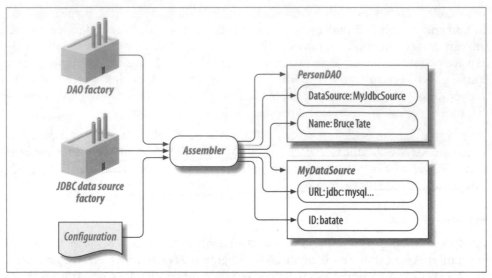

Figure 6-8. Lightweight inversion of control containers relieve applications of creation and assembly of objects.

drill—implements the interface as a plug. You can now use the appliance with any socket that supports that interface. In the same way, you can use a different service with any application that supports the interface.

To take it one step further, a skilled person can take:

- Appliances from around the world (like irons and hair driers)
- An adapter kit that works only with certain plugs and sockets
- The adapter kit's instruction manual
- Sockets in a hotel

Given these building blocks, that person could use the instruction manual to wire the appliances together for use in hotels around the world. That's the role of dependency injection. It takes a configuration file (the instruction manual) and inserts plugs (Java beans implementing interfaces) into sockets (typed fields of applications that code to that interface).

Who Is the Customer?

Usually, when a Java developer talks about extension, he's referring to ways that programmers can extend his application. That's only part of the total equation, though. Building an extensible API only lets your customer adapt your solution before build time. For some applications, the most useful extension happens after deployment! Your extension strategies for different customers will be different (Table 6-2). Understanding your options will allow you to accept an acceptable risk for your investment.

Table 6-2. Extension strategies

Customer	Strategy	Pros	Cons
All	No extension	Low startup cost Simplicity	Poor flexibility Expensive extension
Developer	Subclassing	Few lines of code Shared behavior	Reduced flexibility Code time only Can complicate designs
Developer	Interfaces	High flexibility	More lines of code Code time only
Admin	Plug-in	Best flexibility Post-deploy time Allows customization	Expensive to code
Admin	Standards + configuration	Allows replacement Post-deploy time	Limits choice

Table 6-2 shows how your customer affects extension. Although I haven't said it in this chapter yet, opting for simplicity over extension is perfectly valid. If you're coding a one-off solution that will be quickly replaced or has no possibility of changing in the future, extension is not a sound investment. Scaffolding code and quick interim solutions are but two examples of this type of application.

You should also understand your end customer. If you're building a custom application that has a very short, ongoing maintenance cycle, sophisticated configuration options have limited value, especially for services that are not likely to change—such as your RDBMS or your two million–class tax rules engine.

If your customer is not under your immediate control, or your cycle time is long enough to make coding changes painful, it pays to invest in extension. If you place hooks in the right places and think the configuration strategy through, your customers will surprise you. If you need evidence, look at projects that customers have extended well. James Duncan Davidson created the core of the Ant build tool on a five-hour flight to Europe. The core extension principles still exist, and now you see many thousands of Ant tasks. Consider your customers, your application, and the problem domain. Circumstances directly affect your decisions:

- The less you control your customer's requirements, the more you must consider extension.
- Commercial products usually need better configuration options than private IT projects.
- The longer the expected lifespan of a product, the more important post-deployment flexibility is.
- The longer your lifecycle, (specifically, the longer it takes you to respond to requirements), the more you've got to invest in post-deployment extension options.

Summary

Building an application that's easy to extend does not happen by accident. It takes patience, forethought, and effort. You've got to design your external interfaces well so programmers can extend your application. You've got to consider an effective configuration strategy and a plug-in model so administrators and users can extend your solution after deployment. You also have to make a deliberate decision about whether investing in extension makes sense at all.

You saw the basic toolkit for extension, including open standards, a configuration strategy, and class loading. I suggested three tools for configuration: Java Preferences, Apache Digester, and Spring. Each of these tools has strong support for the core features that you need, and each targets a different market. Preferences is the simplest configuration API, and is most appropriate on the client. Digester uses a SAX-based XML engine, and lets you specify patterns that fire rules. It's simple and you can understand it quickly. Spring is a framework with a unified configuration strategy. You need not use all of Spring to take advantage of its services. These basic tools combine nicely to support an extension model called the plug-in. You saw that plug-ins can use two different models: the service locator or dependency injection. I favor dependency injection, though some experts, including Martin Fowler, prefer the service locator. Each has strengths and weaknesses.

Finally, effective configuration and extension depends on an intimate knowledge of your customer. Your extension paradigm needs to reflect your cycle time and the needs of your end customer.

You've now seen each of the five principles for better, faster, lighter Java:

- Keep it simple
- Do one thing, and do it well
- Strive for transparency
- You are what you eat
- Allow for extension

I don't want to leave you hanging: in the next chapters, you'll see these principles in action. First, you'll see two of my favorite open source frameworks, written by third-party developers that I know and trust. Next, you'll see how to build a sophisticated open source service, using these principles. Along the way, we'll examine a fantastic variety of traditional enterprise web applications, a lightweight container, a persistence engine, and a web crawler. As you internalize these principles you'll see that they can be used for many different purposes.

CHAPTER 7

Hibernate

You have seen the basic principles. They may seem simplistic, but it's surprisingly difficult to be disciplined enough to follow them. One place where experienced programmers have continually broken these simple rules is in the area of persistence frameworks. Sometimes, persistence solutions like EJB CMP are too invasive, requiring extensive code changes to support. Other times, persistence frameworks do not allow for extension, so common legacy models like stored procedures cannot be supported. More often than not, though, they're simply overbuilt.

The Lie

As a kid, you probably heard the story of the three little pigs. In this story, there's a pig that "did it right the first time" by building a house out of brick. I'd like to suggest a more likely alternative. Once upon a time, there were three pigs that wanted to build houses. Two were reasonable and pragmatic. The third was an anal-retentive jerk. The first two pigs checked out the lay of the land and available resources. They built simple but functional houses with readily available, simple building materials. At the same time, the third pig decided to build a hardened mansion out of the world's hardest brick. He began to plan. The first two pigs completed their houses and happily moved in before their brother was half done with his new place.

The third pig was in over his head. He eventually ran out of money before he could finish and abandoned the project, leaving town in disgrace. When a wolf threatened, the two pragmatic pigs simply hardened their houses with adobe. The wolf left in frustration and eventually ate the third pig, putting him out of his misery. Of course, that's not what the full-color glossy brochures say.

Customer reference stories about overbuilt commercial technologies abound. Good companies meticulously plan those early successes. Be careful, though. If you're not one of the lucky few first customers, you'll likely do your homework and ask for references. It's hard to get the truth, especially in the earliest stages. Though the successes may be real, you will likely not have the massive support structures that the vendors put into such engagements to ensure successful reference stories. That's how we as an industry adopted EJB far before it was ready. In fact, EJB is only the latest in a line of a massive technologies that were adopted and lauded far before they provided mainstream value. At IBM, I lived through three in rapid succession in Open Doc, SOM, and CORBA. Big, reputable customers bought those solutions, and not because they were dumb. It's just harder to discern the truth when there's so much noise out there.

In this chapter, I'll show you an alternative to the mega-framework. First, you'll see a smaller, lighter persistence framework called Hibernate. It's a transparent persistence framework that you can use to keep to many of the principles in this book. Later, I'll go a step further and grade the Hibernate team on their observance of our five basic principles.

I'm going to assume that as a Java programmer, you've run across database problems often enough to know a little about relational databases such as the SQL query language. I don't assume that you know much more about persistence frameworks.

What Is Hibernate?

Hibernate is an open source project that lets you store plain Java objects to a database. Unlike JDO, Hibernate works only with relational databases, and only over JDBC. Hibernate's persistence strategy is known as *transparent persistence* because the model that you build contains no persistence code of any kind. By contrast, some other persistence strategies make you change your code (EJB), or deal with rows and columns instead of POJOs (JDBC). You don't always need a full persistence framework to do database programming but for some problems, it makes things easier in many ways:

- You'll be able to work with Java objects, instead of relational tables.
- Your whole application won't need to change if either the objects or database schema change.
- You won't have to worry about persistence details. Saving a whole object saves all of its fields and all of its attributes, even if they are objects or collections of objects.

The result is a cleaner, simpler application with a better separation of concerns. The details about the object model do not have to be muddied with the structure of your database.

Simple Example

The best way to learn Hibernate is by example. Here, I use a discussion board. Figure 7-1 shows the classes in our model and the relationship between each of them. The persistent classes are topics, which contain posts. Each post is associated with a user.

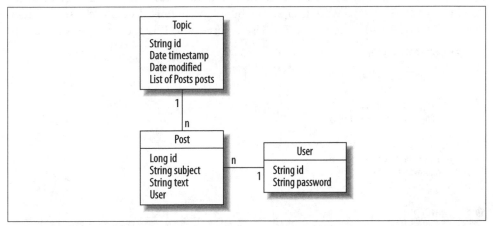

Figure 7-1. The object model for the message board application contains three classes

If you were to implement this application with JDBC, you'd have to maintain the relationship between topics and posts manually. Using Hibernate, you do most of the heavy lifting with simple configuration. You deal primarily in the Java space and let Hibernate manage the complexities of persistence. Follow these steps to build a Hibernate application:

1. Write your object model. Transparent persistence frameworks let you write an object model that has no specific database-aware code at all. By hiding the details from your application, you can better focus on what you want the object model to do.

2. Build your database schema. Your persistence model only affects your database schema in very small ways, if at all.

3. Configure your mapping file. The mapping file connects the pieces of the database schema, like tables and fields, with pieces of your application, like classes and attributes.

4. Configure Hibernate. You need to tell Hibernate some details about your application, such as where to find your JDBC driver and which relational database you're using.

5. Use the model. If your persistent object model is like the puppet, you need a puppeteer: an application that knows when to pull the right strings, saving and retrieving data from the model when your application needs it.

I'll show you how to write all of these by hand. In truth, you may use tools to generate your mapping, and possibly your schema.

Writing the Object Model

Let's start with the object model. Your object model deals only with your problem domain, while the persistence framework hides the details. I create classes for each part of the model shown in Figure 7-1 (User, Topic, and Post). First, here's the User:

```
package discussion;

public class User {

  String id = null;
  String password = null;

  User (String userID, String pw) {
    id = userID;
    password = pw;
  }
```

❶   `User () {}`

❷   ```
  public String getID () {
    return id;
  }
  public void setID(String newUser) {
    id = newUser;
  }

  public String getPassword () {
    return password;
  }
  public void setPassword (String pw) {
    password = pw;
  }
}
```

Notice that your object model has a couple of limitations:

❶ You need to allow a default constructor without parameters because Hibernate will create users. I also like to allow convenience constructors that set a user up in an acceptable state, but Hibernate will not use these to create its objects.

❷ Hibernate uses reflection to access properties. Even though the Java reflection API allows for field access without getters and setters, early versions of Hibernate required them. Hibernate has recently added support to directly access fields; most of the generators and existing code still use them..

Let's move on to a more complex class. Each topic has a series of posts it must maintain. You need to be able to add and delete posts.

```
package discussion;

import java.util.*;
```
```

```
public class Topic {

  Topic (String topicID) {
    id = topicID;
  }

  Topic () {
  }

  String id = "Unnamed Topic";
❶ List posts = new ArrayList();
  Date timestamp = new Date();
  Date modified = new Date();

❷ public String getID() {
    return id;
  }
  public void setID(String topic) {
    id = topic;
  }

  public List getPosts() {
    return posts;
  }
  public void setPosts(List p) {
    posts = p;
  }

  public Date getTimestamp() {
    return timestamp;
  }
  public void setTimestamp(Date t) {
    timestamp = t;
  }

  public Date getModified() {
    return timestamp;
  }
  public void setModified(Date t) {
    timestamp = t;
  }
}
```

Here's what the annotations mean:

❶ To manage our posts, I'm using a Java ArrayList. Rather than adding an API to Topic to add, delete, and update posts, I just provide public access to the Posts property and let my users access the list directly. Hibernate integrates with Java collections well, with explicit support for Sets, Bags, and Maps.

❷ Once again, you see the getters and setters for each property. In addition to the name of the topic and the list of posts, I've added timestamps: one to show when a user modifies a topic and one that indicates a topic's creation date.

The code for Post is the same. Once again, the class has properties, constructors, and accessors.

```
package discussion;

import java.util.*;

public class Post {
  Long id = null;
  String subject = "No subject";
  String body = "Empty post";
  User user = null;
```

❶
```
  Post (User u, String s, String b) {
    user = u;
    subject = s;
    body = b;
  }

  Post() {}
```

❷
```
  public Long getID () {
    return id;
  }
  public void setID(Long newPost) {
    id = newPost;
  }

  public String getSubject() {
    return subject;
  }
  public void setSubject(String s) {
    subject = s;
  }

  public String getBody() {
    return body;
  }
  public void setBody(String b) {
    body = b;
  }

  public User getUser() {
    return user;
  }
  public void setUser(String u) {
    user = u;
  }

  public String getBody() {
    return body;
  }
  public void setBody(String b) {
```

```
        body = b;
    }
}
```

Notice two special properties:

❶   User: as with most object models, this one has references to other objects. Later,
     I'll have a foreign key in the Posts table that maps to the User table.

❷   The ID is a unique identifier for a given post. I can choose to let Hibernate cre-
     ate the ID for me when it saves the object or I can choose to assign my own ID,
     as I did with User and Topic.

That's it. The clarity is marvelous. The model does one thing: represent the real-
world rules for a message board. It's not cluttered with persistence details like transactions, updates, or queries. You can easily tell what the object model does. You can
test your object model without testing the persistence. You can also stick to Java,
your native programming language, for expressing a model. Earlier, I mentioned that
Java developers built many persistence frameworks before they began to get them
right. Through all of the failures, the tantalizing level of simplicity that transparent
persistence promised motivated them to keep working to get it right.

Building the Schema

The next step for building a Hibernate application is to build your persistent schema.
I choose to create a script that accomplishes three tasks for each table: it drops the
table (and indices, if applicable), creates the table (and possibly indices), and adds
any special data.

Here's the script for the discussion application:

```
❶   drop table users;
❷   CREATE TABLE users (id       VARCHAR(20) NOT NULL,
                        password VARCHAR(20),
                        PRIMARY KEY(id)
    );

    drop table topics;
    CREATE TABLE topics  (id       VARCHAR(40) NOT NULL,
                          ts       TIMESTAMP,
                          modified TIMESTAMP,
                          PRIMARY KEY(id)

    );

    drop table posts;
    CREATE TABLE posts     (id       BIGINT NOT NULL,
                            subject  VARCHAR(80),
                            body     TEXT,
                            ts       TIMESTAMP,
                            poster   VARCHAR(20),
```

```
            topicID      VARCHAR(40),
            PRIMARY KEY (id)
    );

    drop table hilo;
    CREATE TABLE hilo (next BIGINT);
❸    insert into hilo values (1);
```

❶ Drop the table. If the table already exists, you want to drop it before creating it. This step seems trivial, but it's useful for situations when you're rapidly changing the schema in development. If your schema already exists and is fairly rigid, skip this step. In complex schemas where tables are related via foreign keys, it is optimal to have a script to drop them for you, as you have to drop them in reverse order.

❷ Create the table. The next step is to create the table. You'll want to specify primary keys for the Hibernate ID.

❸ Insert any data that the table needs to function. If you're creating a table to help assign identifiers, you need to seed it. Similarly, if you're building a read-only table of, say, Zip codes or states, you must seed those, too.

There's a table for each of the persistent classes. I've also added the *hilo* table, which supports one of Hibernate's unique ID-generating algorithms. You don't have to build your schemas this way. You can actually support multiple classes with each table. (As of the publish date of this book, you cannot assign multiple tables to the same class.) You can also generate your schema with the tool schemaexport, via Ant or the command line.

Configuring the Mapping

In Chapter 4, I emphasized using configuration rather than coding where possible. Like most persistence frameworks, Hibernate has the same philosophy. You'll build two types of configuration. In this section, you'll configure the mapping between your object model and your database schema.

With Hibernate, all mappings start with a class. Associate that class with a database table and then associate columns of the table with properties of your class. As you've learned, each property must have a getter and a setter. First, let's look at a simple mapping that maps *User.java* to the relational table users:

```
<hibernate-mapping>
  <class name="discussion.User" table="users">
    <id name="ID"
        column="id"
        type="string">
        <generator class="assigned"></generator>
    </id>
```

```
        <property name="password" column="password" type="string" />
    </class>
</hibernate-mapping>
```

This simple mapping associates the class `discussion.User` with the table `users`. To fully establish the relationship between domain objects and data tables, a mapping must also connect the properties of the class with individual fields in the table. In this example, the class property `ID` is mapped to the `id` column, and the `password` property maps to the `password` column. The ID property mapping is a special kind of mapping, described below.

Identifiers

I've chosen the `assigned` strategy for managing this identifier because a user will want to choose his ID. You already know that each Java object has a unique identifier, even if you don't specify one. The compiler virtual machine can uniquely identify an object by the memory address. That's why two objects containing the same string may not be equal: they may be stored at different memory addresses. In order to keep track of each unique object instance, Hibernate uses a special property called *identifier*. You can specify a strategy for the unique identifier. This identifier property uniquely identifies an object in the database table. Hibernate has several strategies for managing identifiers. These are some interesting ones:

increment
> Generates identifiers by incrementing a value.

hilo
> Uses values in a column of a specified table to seed a hilo algorithm.

native
> Relies on the underlying capabilities of the database server.

UUID
> Attaches a network adapter address to an identifier, making it globally unique across a cluster. May be overkill for lighter applications.

assigned
> The application assigns a unique identifier. Useful when your application already generates a unique identifier.

foreign
> Lets you choose an identifier from another object. (We discuss relationships in the next section.)

Each of these approaches has strengths and weaknesses. Some, like increment, are fast and simple, but won't work in a cluster because they would generate duplicate values. Others work well in a cluster (UUID uses the network adapter MAC address to form a globally unique identifier), but may be overkill for lighter applications. And some may not function well with container-managed JTA transactions because they would inject too much contention. Don't worry. The Hibernate documentation is outstanding; it walks you safely through the minefield.

Relationships

Of course, the User mapping is straightforward because Hibernate doesn't need to do anything special. The Topic mapping will be a little more complex. A topic must manage a collection of posts, like this:

```
<hibernate-mapping>
    <class name="discussion.Topic" table="topics">
        <id name="ID"
            column="id"
            type="string">
            <generator class="assigned"></generator>
        </id>

        <bag
            name="posts"
            order-by="ts"
            table="posts"
            cascade="all"
            inverse="false">
          <key column="topicID"/>
          <one-to-many class="discussion.Post"/>
        </bag>
        <property name="timestamp" column="ts"       type="timestamp" />
        <property name="modified"  column="modified" type="timestamp" />
    </class>
</hibernate-mapping>
```

Relational databases support all kinds of relationships. Wherever you've got two tables that have columns with compatible types, you can do a join and form a relationship on the fly. You manage relationships within object-oriented programs explicitly. In our case, we've got a managed many-to-one relationship between Post and Topic. Specifically, the application maintains a list of Posts within a Topic instance.

In this mapping, the magic occurs next to the *bag* tag. It defines a relationship that describes the interaction between Topic and Post. I specified the name of the Java property (name="posts"), and the ordering of the collection (order-by="ts"). In the mapping, I also tell Hibernate about the underlying database structure. I specify the associated table for posts (posts) and the foreign key that refers to a given topic (key column="topicID"). I tell Hibernate to also load or delete posts when I save or load a topic (cascade="all").

By defining a series of these managed relationships, you can let Hibernate load a very complex instance, such as a car or a corporation, by saving a single, top-level instance. You can also let Hibernate delete all children when you delete a parent. Here are some of the relationships supported by Hibernate:

One-to-one

Useful when two objects share an identifier; for example, a manager and a department may have a one-to-one relationship.

One-to-many

When an object has a collection property, Hibernate maps it as a many-to-one relationship. Hibernate has native support for several simple collections, including sets, lists, and bags.

Many-to-many

When many-to-one relationships occur in two directions, you've got a many-to-many relationship. For example, one person may work on many projects, and each project can have many people. Many-to-many relationships, on the relational database side, use an intermediate mapping table. In the object model in Figure 7-2, you see only Person and Project. Person has a collection of projects, and vice versa.

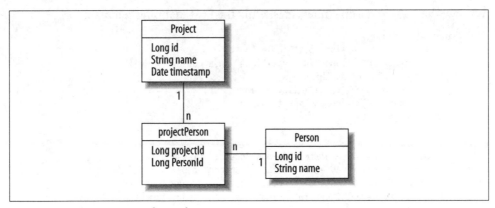

Figure 7-2. Many-to-many relationships

Inheritance

Inheritance relationships model one object that has an is-a relationship with another. Hibernate supports three basic mapping strategies. In the first, all subclasses go into the same table. In the second, each concrete class gets its own table. In the third, each subclass gets its own table. For example, an employee is-a person. Your database might have an employee table and a person table related by a foreign key, or all employees might live directly in the person table, mixed in with customers, vendors, and other types of people.

Maps

A collection of name-value pairs is known as a map. Hibernate supports several versions of maps, including hash maps.

Components

A component relationship collects several dependent properties with a first-class Hibernate mapping. For example, a user has an address. You can group the address elements together as a component.

Composites

Hibernate supports composite keys and indexes. For example, you might collect a timestamp and machine ID together to uniquely identify a log entry. You can then use this composite as a key or as an index into a map.

This list of relationships is not comprehensive. Extend Hibernate and form your own relationships as necessary in order to support your own relationships; you shouldn't need to do so very often. Relational database modelers tend to use a few well-known constructs over and over.

Types

We saw the User and Topic mappings. Only the Post mapping remains:

```
<hibernate-mapping>
  <class name="discussion.Post" table="posts">
    <id name="ID" column="id" type="long" unsaved-value="null">
      <generator class="hilo">
        <param name="table">hilo</param>
        <param name="column">next</param>
      </generator>
    </id>

    <many-to-one name="poster" column="poster" class="discussion.User"/>
    <property name="subject"   column="subject" type="string" />
    <property name="body"      column="body"    type="text" />
    <property name="timestamp" column="ts"      type="timestamp" />
  </class>
</hibernate-mapping>
```

Looking at these mappings, you may wonder why there's one type. After all, somewhere, you have to specify a type for the relational database table and a type for the Java object. Yet, in this mapping:

```
<property name="subject"   column="subject" type="string" />
```

I only specify a string, although we could actually build a persistence framework that specified two types. That architecture can be awkward to use because it's not always clear which types are compatible. Hibernate instead implements types as mappings. The Hibernate string type maps from *java.lang.string* to the SQL types VARCHAR and VARCHAR2. This strategy makes types easy to specify and leaves no ambiguity in the area of compatible types.

In addition, Hibernate lets you create new custom types. Further, a type can map onto more than one table of a database or onto complex objects. For example, you could map a coordinate bean with *x* and *y* properties onto two database columns with simple INTEGER types. In addition to types, you'll also see a number of other places where Hibernate provides access to classes that allow powerful and flexible extension.

Using Your Persistent Model

Within a Hibernate application, there are at least two types of code. You've already seen the model, which is completely independent of Hibernate. You also have the client that uses that model. This client can take a number of forms. It can be a J2EE application that uses EJB session beans, a lightweight container like Spring, a complex, non-EJB J2EE application that uses JTA to manage transactions, or a simple Java application.

In the previous section, I showed how to build a persistent model and map it to a relational database schema. That object model is completely transparent with respect to persistence. In this section, I show how to use that model. Of course, the code that accesses the persistent model must use Hibernate classes to load and save data, and possibly manage transactions.

Some simple persistence frameworks make each access to the database independent. If you're using such a framework, you can't manage transactions or cache in the persistence layer, and it places a heavier burden on the application, especially in a web environment. Like most of the more robust persistence frameworks, Hibernate uses sessions. Think of a session as a running conversation between your application and the persistent model, and through it, the database. A session factory provides a convenient attachment point for configuration options, and also caches and metadata related to a single Hibernate configuration.

Configuring Hibernate

You're going to need another type of configuration. If you were using EJB, you'd use a deployment descriptor to describe the configuration of your system. Hibernate has some of the same requirements. You're going to want to configure your JDBC drivers, connection pools, transaction strategy, security, and the like. Break configuration tasks into your configuration file and a few lines of code in order to load your configuration through the Hibernate API.

Recall that you configure the mapping between each persistent class and the database schema. The inventors of Hibernate had to decide how to organize the rest of the configuration. The main question is this: exactly what will the users be configuring: an application, a Hibernate instance, or all Hibernate instances? Some of those solutions—such as configuring an instance or all Hibernate instances—are simple, but they don't allow enough flexibility, for instance, for accessing two databases (with separate configurations) from the same application. One of the options (configuring every session) is too expensive. Instead, Hibernate lets you configure a session factory. Then, all of the sessions that you get from a factory are configured the same way.

Here's the configuration file for the discussion application, called *hibernate.properties*:

```
hibernate.connection.driver_class = com.mysql.jdbc.Driver
hibernate.connection.url = jdbc:mysql://localhost/disc
hibernate.connection.username = batate
hibernate.dialect=net.sf.hibernate.dialect.MySQLDialect
hibernate.show_sql=true
```

In this simple configuration, I've configured only the JDBC driver and one option that tells Hibernate to log all SQL statements that Hibernate generates. You can see the JDBC configuration parameters you'd expect, such as the URL, the driver's class name, and the connection credentials. The configuration file also has a *dialect*, a pluggable API that tells Hibernate the version of SQL to use. Very few SQL implementations actually meet the ANSII standard. In addition, you often want your framework to take advantage of extensions that aid performance or flexibility.

After you've built your model, mapped your model, and built your configuration file, load your configuration with a couple of lines of code at the beginning of each Hibernate client. You'll need a separate session factory for each configuration. Our discussion application only needs one session factory. Here's the code that loads our configuration:

```
class BoardManager {

    SessionFactory factory;
    Configuration cfg;

    BoardManager() {
      try {
        cfg = new Configuration()
          .addClass(discussion.User.class)
          .addClass(discussion.Topic.class)
          .addClass(discussion.Post.class);
          factory = cfg.buildSessionFactory();
      } catch (Exception e) {
        System.out.println("Hibernate configuration failed:" + e);
      }
    }
}
```

Notice that this code performs three discrete steps. First, it loads the configuration specified in the *hibernate.properties* file. Second, it adds the mapping for each class in your persistent model. If you've ever coded Smalltalk, you might have seen this coding style. All of the addClass() methods are chained together. If you prefer, and your coding standards permit, you can break out each addClass() method into a separate statement, like this:

```
cfg.addClass(discussion.User.class);
cfg.addClass(discussion.Topic.class);
cfg.addClass(discussion.Post.class);
```

Finally, build the factory. Keep in mind that the configuration file is very small; in a production environment, it's likely to be much larger. You're probably going to want to specify your own connection pool. You may want to configure a different transaction strategy (such as JTA), a cache manager, logging and debugging options, or even EJB sessions. A complete description of the entire configuration is beyond the scope of this book, but you can find out about each parameter in the excellent Hibernate documentation.

Using Your Model

Now you've got a model that's mapped onto a relational database. You also have a fully configured persistence framework in Hibernate to manage it. In keeping with our five principles for better Java, the model is completely transparent with respect to persistence. The concepts encapsulated by the business model are fully separated from all other aspects of the application. All that remains is to tell Hibernate how to move data to and from your model.

I like to have a class named xManager that manages persistence for a model. In this example, I've named the class that manages persistence for the discussion application BoardManager.

Loading data

The first task is to get Hibernate to populate your business objects. Like most persistence frameworks, you can ask Hibernate to populate your model in two ways. First, you can specify the ID of the root-level object that you wish to load. Second, you can issue a query in Hibernate Query Language, which is similar to SQL. Look at this code, which checks the password for a user:

```
public boolean checkPassword(String id, String password)
        throws Exception {

  User user = loadUser(id);
  if (user == null) {
    return false;
  }
  if (user.getPassword( ).equals(password)) {
    return true;
  }
  return false;
}
```

In this example, the method loads the user, given the user's identifier. Then, the method can access the user object directly, checking the value of the password property. In this method, exceptions bubble back up to the calling method. If you know the identifiers of the objects that you need, this is a convenient way to use the model.

Alternatively, you might need to use the SQL-like query language. For example, you might need to load all posts for a user. This code fragment does the trick:

```
List posts = session.find(
  "from posts as p where p.userID = ?",
  userID,
  Hibernate.string
);
```

The query language is nearly identical to SQL. You can specify parameters with the "?" character. The parameter list for the method specifies the values and types of the parameters. You don't see a SELECT statement, because usually you don't need one. You're usually going to return a list of objects of the type identified in the from clause.

Hibernate also supports some advanced SQL notions, such as aggregates. For example, to count the users in our table, issue the query:

```
SELECT count(*)
FROM users
```

Most query language for object-oriented persistence frameworks work only with true objects. SQL aggregate functions return a scalar type, not an object. Hibernate opts to keep a richer, more flexible query language by staying as close as possible to SQL. Other query languages, such as those for EJB and JDO, have had more limited success.

Updating the database

Now let's look at how you tell Hibernate to update the database. The discussion application must save new users to the database:

```
public void saveUser(User user) throws Exception {
  Session session = null;
  try {
    session = factory.openSession();
    session.save(user);

    session.flush();
    session.connection().commit();

    return;

  }
  finally {
    if(session.isOpen())
      session.close();
  }
}
```

For all the work that it does, the meat of the method is remarkably simple. I get a new session from the session factory and then call the save method on the session, passing in a new user. The rest of the method processes exceptions and cleans up the connection. The flush makes sure the cache is flushed, so the data will be in the database. The commit method commits the transaction, and we're done. In this case, User is a very simple object, but it might have been a complex object, and if I'd configured it to do so in the mapping, Hibernate would save each related object without any additional intervention from me.

Similarly, here's the code to delete a user from the database:

```
public User removeUser(String id) throws Exception {
  Session session = null;
  try {
    session = factory.openSession();
    User user = new User();     // object must first be loaded to be deleted
    session.load(user, id);
    session.delete(user);

    session.flush();
    session.connection().commit();
    return user;
  } catch (Exception e) {
    return null;               // not found condition should not force error
  }
    finally {
    if(session.isOpen()) {
        session.close();
    }

}
```

This code is similar to the saveUser method, with one difference: you must first load the User into the session in order to delete it. Once again, if you need to remove an object with relationships, such as a topic that contains other posts, you can choose to cascade the delete to all related objects, if you configure the mapping to do so. You can see that the persistence framework takes care of the tedious details of integrating a relational database and a persistent model. You didn't have to work with the JDBC connection and you didn't have to worry about coding the correct SQL. You simply tell Hibernate to save, remove, or update the object, and you're off to the races.

Evaluating Hibernate

We've covered some of the Hibernate basics. To recap, it's a persistence framework that allows transparent persistence from Java beans to relational databases over JDBC. So how does Hibernate stack up against our five principles?

Keep It Simple

It's easy to build simple solutions if you're solving simple problems. Complicated problems like persistence demand more thought and effort. If you want to understand how complex persistence frameworks can be, check out EJB entity beans. Compare that model with Hibernate. Hibernate's model code is fully transparent (except for the need to provide a default, parameter-less constructor). Configuration is a breeze. The mappings are simple when you're solving simple problems.

It's not just the Hibernate framework that benefits from a simpler mindset; Hibernate applications also reap the benefits. It's also easy to get started. I've learned that most students of my classes are able to get going in an hour or so, which is about how long it takes to get your first JDBC application off of the ground. After using Hibernate for some commercial applications, I've learned that they are easy to write and easy for my customers to understand. But simplicity does not mean Hibernate is too basic to solve difficult problems.

Do One Thing, and Do It Well

When you attack a big problem, it's tempting to just solve some smaller problems around the perimeter of your domain. With persistence frameworks, many designers try to build in transaction management, security, distribution, or other aspects. It's far better to layer your code, focusing each loosely coupled layer on just one aspect of the problem.

It's tough to solve every aspect of a problem domain like persistence. In order to focus on a difficult problem, you have to make simplifying assumptions. Hibernate creators wisely made some basic assumptions that let them simplify their implementation:

- Hibernate uses only JDBC. Some persistence frameworks support many types of data stores. By supporting only relational databases, Hibernate developers did not need to deal with nonrelational problems, thus simplifying their query language and focusing on JDBC.

- While some persistence frameworks support all types of Java classes, Hibernate supports only Java beans. The developers were therefore able to make use of the existing reflection API. To be fair, for many problems, reflection may be too simple. Hibernate has added CGLib in order to do byte code enhancement to support lazy loading, which may be a better overall technique for transparency, in this case.

- Hibernate punts on some of the peripheral problems, using other frameworks instead. Apache Commons handles logging, JTA provides a more robust transaction API, and JNDI provides a naming interface to help locate services.

By leaving these details to others, Hibernate creators were able to focus on building a fast, light persistence framework. Instead of wringing their hands over the performance of reflection, they wisely worked on creating efficient SQL first. That could only be done through loose coupling at the right places. As you'll see under the "Allow for Extension" section, the Hibernate extensions are loosely coupled and pluggable in the right places.

Strive for Transparency

For the most part, the Java community has had to wait a long time for transparent persistence. For a while, most of our attention was diverted as we tried to make the EJB experiment work. For persistence frameworks, transparency affects productivity more than any other feature. If you haven't used transparent persistence before, one look at our application will show you why you should. You're simply free to deal with the business domain independently of any other application concerns. This ability lets you break your programming down into manageable pieces with clearly defined roles. It also makes your domain easier to write and understand.

Allow for Extension

Too often, simple solutions are dead ends. They cannot be extended in the appropriate places. When you build simple software, it's got to be able to grow. The only constant in software development is change. You must anticipate the places your users will need to extend your frameworks and applications. The most successful open source projects are those that allow for extension. Apache allowed plug-ins to process many different types of web content. Ant allowed developers to plug in custom tasks, so they could use Ant for highly customized builds. Eclipse is an application development environment that's gathering momentum because of the vast array of compatible extensions. Hibernate also allows for smart extension in a number of important places:

SQL dialects

Hibernate users can switch between databases by simply configuring a different dialect. Users of a given dialect can choose to use proprietary extensions for added performance, or instead use a more generic dialect. The interface to create a dialect is open, so you can create new dialects as you need them in order to support the databases you need for a project.

The JDBC connection

Much of the OOP community frowns on the use of stored procedures but in the real world, they are a fact of life. Hibernate users can access the JDBC connection directly in order to use features that are not supported by Hibernate, such as stored procedures. By providing direct access to the level of abstraction immediately below, the architects allowed extension to areas completely outside of their realm.

Configurable transaction API

JDBC developers often like to manage their own transactions, but many advanced J2EE developers need more. Hibernate conveniently passes transaction responsibility through to the database for simple applications with explicit transaction support, and also lets the user configure the more advanced transactions through JTA.

I'd like to point out that standards play a role here, too. While you don't need to support every open standard, you can get significant leverage from standards in likely areas of extension. For example, the Hibernate inventors understood that JTA makes sense for transactions that may have a scope beyond the basic persistence framework. On the other hand, it clearly did not make sense to support earlier releases of JDO, since that specification forced byte code enhancement and had an awkward query language that might complicate and possibly confuse the API.

You Are What You Eat

Hibernate does a good job of integrating core standards where they exist, but it rarely forces you to use a complex standard. Instead, it provides an inexpensive default implementation. A good example is the JTA integration. You're free to configure JTA if you need it, but you're not bound to that approach. Where JTA is over-kill, you can easily delegate transaction management to the database without changing anything but configuration.

Hibernate also supports many lightweight solutions for logging and collections (Apache Commons), database access (JDBC), and enterprise containers (Spring). You can deploy with richer J2EE architectures, but Hibernate works perfectly well with Tomcat and MySQL.

Going against the grain

At some point, many of the more revolutionary successful frameworks reject conventional wisdom. For Hibernate, three crucial decisions played a significant role in its success:

Reflection is too slow

In fact, reflection is much slower than a direct method invocation. For a persistence framework, it's a price you're willing to pay because database access is inherently so expensive.

A query language must be fully object-oriented

Instead of starting with the premise that a query language for an object-oriented framework must return pure objects, the Hibernate query language started with

SQL. To use a query language as close to SQL as possible, it needed to support scalars and aggregates.

A persistence model must provide a shared, common object model

Instead of letting each application have a private cache with a private object model in each session, EJB applications share one major object model across all applications. This approach is a shared, common object model. EJB vendors theorize that such a design leads to better performance. In practice, a smaller, lighter persistence framework can share a common cache; even with a little extra object creation and destruction, it blows the doors off of EJB implementations.

The Down Side

Of course, no framework is perfect. Hibernate is young and largely unproven. Very few people provide the vision for the framework, and that's a dangerous, perhaps limiting model for growth.

As I write this book, the Hibernate team has fairly limited resources. That might be a good thing: such a situation works against unnecessary bloat. It also may hinder the team's ability to improve the framework in meaningful ways. As the project grows, additional programmers will naturally contribute. That's a double-edged sword; many open source projects do not manage growth well. Additionally, Hibernate has been subsumed into the JBoss suite of applications. The JBoss relationship will probably make better-paid support available, making it more attractive for some commercial applications.

Other commercial frameworks, such as Solarmetric's Kodo JDO, produce cleaner and faster SQL, if some of my DBA contacts are to be believed. It makes sense, because that product has been out longer and has a larger team of full-time programmers to help.

Earlier editions of Hibernate had aggressive marketing language criticizing JDO's use of byte code enhancement. Ironically, byte code enhancement may turn out to be a better method than reflection for implementing persistence. Hibernate had early success with reflection only to hit a wall when adding performance enhancements like lazy loading. The proven byte code enhancement techniques common in the JDO marketplace may yet provide a faster, more flexible means of achieving transparent persistence. Hibernate's inclusion of CGLib is an early indication of the limitations of reflection; CGLib provides more flexible lazy loading through, you guessed it, byte code enhancement. In addition, although byte code enhancement has taken some hits in recent years, it's the technology that powers many of the aspect-oriented frameworks.

Alternatives

Hibernate is not the only framework that supports transparent persistence. For many projects, it's not even the best way. If you're willing to pay for a persistence framework and you like open standards but abhor EJB, explore JDO. A number of good implementations exist. My favorite is Kodo JDO. It probably generates the cleanest, prettiest SQL. Even a DBA that I know was impressed. It's a framework that uses byte code enhancement to achieve better transparency, supporting more Java constructs than most other products.

Velocity is not a persistence framework, but you can use this code generator to generate data access objects and transparent models. Sometimes, persistence frameworks are simply overkill. Template-based technologies often give you better access to SQL than other alternatives.

OJB is another open source framework, under the umbrella of Apache. It's got a number of usage models, including ODMG, EJB, and JDO. I know many developers who use it and like it, although I haven't had much experience with it. If you're a pure Oracle shop, you may consider TopLink. It was once the top object-relational mapping tool. Interest has waned since the Oracle acquisition.

Summary

In this section, I introduced Hibernate. It's a transparent persistence framework for Java beans to relational databases over JDBC. The five basic steps for Hibernate applications are:

1. Create the model.
2. Create the database schema.
3. Map the model to the schema.
4. Configure a session factory.
5. Use the model.

The message board application that we built showed each of these five steps in action. You saw how to create a model with nothing but business logic, composed of pure Java beans. Then you saw how to save and load data from that model using simple Hibernate commands.

Hibernate upholds the five basic principles set out in Chapters 2 through 6. I showed that Hibernate provides a simple, transparent approach to persistence that some other persistence frameworks lack. I also demonstrated that the benefits of simplicity extend beyond the framework to applications that use Hibernate. Then I pointed out where Hibernate users can embrace and extend the framework in all of the right places, such as providing SQL dialects, JTA transactions, and allowing full access to the JDBC connection. I finally showed how Hibernate can improve and suggested some persistence alternatives. In the next chapter, I introduce Spring, a small, light container.

Spring

In this chapter, we look at an example of an enterprise web application using the Spring framework. While Hibernate provided a single service, the Spring framework provides an efficient way to build and assemble Java applications, with abstractions for many services. Although it supports many services, Spring stays focused and clean with excellent layering and encapsulation. Like EJB, the centerpiece for Spring is a container, and like EJB, the Spring framework provides access to core J2EE services. But that's about as far as any similarities go. Here's a metaphor.

I love to kayak and spend a lot of time teaching kayaking skills. One of my specialties is teaching students how to roll an upside-down kayak in whitewater. One day, I was teaching this skill to a muscle-bound hulk and a dainty little 97-lb woman. While I talked through the technique on dry land, Meathead stared into the distance, disinterested. The woman focused well and wanted to practice the foundational techniques over and over. Within a half an hour, she hit her first roll incredibly well while he was just thrashing about, whipping the calm water into fine white foam. He didn't come close until his third session. In sessions to come, she relied on her technique to improve quickly; he relied on strength, and floundered. When it was time to put the skills into practice, she rolled while he swam. Programmers, take note. It's usually better to solve problems with simplicity and finesse rather than muscle.

What Is Spring?

Spring is an open source framework intended to make J2EE development easier. It consists of a container, a framework for configuring and assembling components, and a set of snap-in services for transactions, persistence, and web user interfaces. The container itself is small—only 90 KB. The entire framework is much larger, but it does a marvelous job of shielding that size and complexity from you using many of the principles in this book. It's a mind-bending framework, but in a good way. You'll find that once you learn to give away a whole lot of control, you also lose a lot of tedious, repetitive detail, simultaneously gaining elegance and simplicity. Here's how to build something in Spring:

1. Code lower-level Java beans that will go into the container. Some of your beans will have dependencies on others. Omit some of the controlling code that you're used to; let the framework take care of those details.

2. Configure your beans. Most will use Spring's XML configuration service. Describe each bean, including primarily a name, your bean's class, its fields, and the initial values that you want to set for those fields. As you configure, you can refer to other beans by name.

3. Spring reads the XML files, creating and populating your objects with reflection to set initial values for your fields. Along the way, Spring satisfies some dependencies. For example, you might set a dataSource property to MyDataSource.

You'll see a concrete example shortly, but bear with me. Since Spring is so different from most J2EE programming styles, you need a firm foundation before you dive in.

The centerpiece of Spring is the XML bean factory, a framework that uses independent beans and configuration to assemble an application. Alternatively, Spring can make many connections without configuration information through the autowiring option. For example, if your application needs a data source and you only specified one kind of data source, you can let Spring autowire that connection.

Atop these factories and configuration services, Spring snaps in some services. Most of them are simple, high-level abstractions that rely on J2EE services or other lower-level frameworks to do the work. These are the major frameworks now supported by Spring:

- A *JDBC persistence framework* makes it easy to create basic JDBC applications. You get a meaningful exception hierarchy rather than the generic SQLE exception with an SQLState error code and you get unified, consistent code without managing the tedious details like JDBC connections and result set mapping.

- An *OR mapping framework* makes it easy to use other OR tools such as Hibernate and JDO with Spring. You get help managing singleton sessions and resources, consistent configuration, a flexible abstraction for transactions, and simplified exceptions.

- Spring offers *connection pooling* for any POJO. Spring's clean abstraction of services makes this possible and convenient.

- A *transaction framework*, because declarative transactions allow you to configure a transaction policy rather than writing a lot of supporting code. Contrary to popular belief, you don't need a monolithic container to support transactions, even declarative transactions. With Spring, you can provide transactional support to a POJO. You can also transparently change the underlying mechanism from JTA to JDBC or back simply through configuration.

- While Spring isn't a full-blown aspect-oriented language, it has good support for many critical *AOP concepts*. Spring offers method interception and introduction, among other AOP concepts. Rod Johnson, creator of Spring, has this to say about his AOP support:

  > Spring AOP is actually fairly capable. It's no AspectJ, but it compares well to other proxy-based frameworks such as Nanning. For example, it has a powerful point-cut model and supports before and after returning and throws advice.

- Like Struts, an *MVC web framework* lets you cleanly separate model, view, and controller for web applications. There are some differences from Struts, but mostly it provides an MVC framework that's consistent with the rest of Spring.

You don't have to adopt any of these services to use Spring. Further, unlike EJB, you can adopt them piecemeal or extend them as needed to accomplish your goals. For the most part, the authors of Spring relied on existing frameworks to snap into Spring. They provided the underpinnings and additional abstractions to simplify a few services as needed. The real power is in the approach. The single exception is the MVC web framework, which directly competes with a number of viable alternatives.

Spring is part of a growing trend toward lightweight containers. It's easy to see the contrast between this approach and heavier containers:

- Heavyweight containers accept components of a *predetermined type*. EJB components, for example, inherit directly from a number of base classes. OLE from Microsoft enforces a standard interface. Tomcat accepts only servlets. In contrast, lightweight containers accept Java objects, using reflection or constructors to configure objects.

- Heavyweight containers force more *dependencies* on components that go into the container. EJB containers must use a rigorous API to maintain the EJB lifecycle, and do just about anything of consequence. EJB components have stringent requirements for threading, inheritance, and even, in some cases, re-entrance. Spring forces no dependencies on its components, so they can be run and tested outside of the container or ported to other architectures with far less effort.

The contrast, on the surface, is staggering. Build applications with both models, and you'll find that lightweight containers do more than save you from tedious details. They change the way that you think; they change the way that you test. In short, they change the way that you program from the inside out. The "secret sauce" combines two ingredients, dependency injection (described in Chapter 6) and *inversion of control*.

Inversion of Control

Earlier in the book, we discussed how modern developers get tremendous benefit by changing who's in control. Most applications hardwire services to objects or components that use the service. If you choose to code this way, you're choosing to couple your code, with all of the inherent disadvantages. Certainly, sometimes, you'll still want to directly call a service. After all, what is a method call?

Sometimes, though, you want to break all dependencies between the caller and the service. In the passive domain models in Chapter 3, you saw how to get more power and flexibility from an architecture that changes who is in control: specifically, control passes from your application to the framework. This idea is not new. Older applications used to control the navigation between screens of an application. When I worked at IBM in the late 1980s, we had a team of four working full time on the navigation for a query report writer. When we started building graphical user interfaces, control passed from the application to the graphical user interface framework. We stripped out our navigator component and replaced the navigator team with one part-time developer. That's the power of inversion of control.

Although lightweight containers use inversion of control broadly, inversion of control alone is not what makes them different. Within a lightweight container, inversion of control focuses on one particular aspect of the application: configuration and assembly through dependency injection. Rely on configuration rather than a hard-wired method call and trust the framework to wire your application together. A single assembler reads your configuration file, creates the beans that you've defined, and then initializes them, wiring them together in the process.

Figure 8-1 repeats the dependency injection figure from Chapter 6 (Figure 6-8). The job of creating objects and setting the properties appropriately passes from the more traditional application to the framework provided by the lightweight container. In the process, the container satisfies two dependencies: the dependency of the data source on its configuration and the dependency of the DAO on a data source. The coupling moves from code to configuration. Singletons disappear. You simply write the class and configuration and the framework creates and assembles instances to form an application.

Pet Store: A Counter-Example

The J2EE Pet Store application is an infamous programming example gone bad. It taught thousands of J2EE developers to build poorly designed, poor-performing code. It was also the center of a benchmarking controversy. A respected consulting company called The Middleware Company worked on a benchmark comparing J2EE with Microsoft's .NET platform. As a foundation for the benchmark, they chose the J2EE version of Pet Store. Though they worked hard to tune it, the J2EE version lost badly to the Microsoft .NET version and many criticized the design. I don't intend to lay any blame for this fiasco. Instead, I offer a different interpretation. It's my firm opinion that J2EE, especially EJB, makes it hard to develop clean, high-performance code. Put another way, the Pet Store benchmark was a symptom of a larger problem.

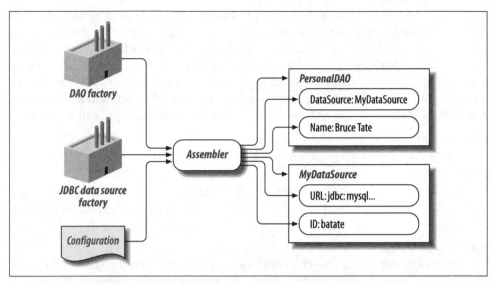

Figure 8-1. Lightweight inversion of control containers

After the benchmarking uproar, a number of people showed how to implement Pet Store with easier, simpler technologies. One of the strongest and simplest implementations, by Clinton Begin, used a DAO framework called iBatis instead of full entity beans. Rod Johnson's team converted that application to Spring, and now distributes it with the Spring framework. Here are some of the details:

- The Spring jPetStore application comes with Spring Versions M4 and beyond.
- It's a data-driven application with a JDBC DAO layer.
- It provides alternative frontends for Struts, and the Spring MVC framework.
- It provides two different models. The simplest uses a single database and simple JDBC transactions. The other uses JTA transaction management across multiple data stores.

In the following sections, I'll work through the version of the application with the MVC web frontend and simple transactions across one database. I'll focus on the domain model, the single-database DAO layer, simple transactions, and the Spring MVC frontend. Outstanding resources are available at the Spring web site for those who want to dive deeper.

The Configuration

When learning a Spring application, start with the configuration file; it shows you the major beans and how the application fits together. A Spring configuration file defines the beans in an application context. Think of the context as a convenient collection of named resources for an application.

Many J2EE applications keep track of application resources such as connections and the like with singletons. When you think about it, a singleton used in this way is not much different from a global variable; many Java developers lean on this crutch too often. J2EE's alternative is a directory service called JNDI, but it's overkill for many common uses. Spring, instead, uses an application context. Initially, you specify it in a simple XML file, although you can extend Spring to accept other kinds of configuration as well. Here are some of the things that might go into an application context:

Data sources
> A Java class that manages connections, usually in a pool.

DAO layers
> If your applications use a database, you probably want to isolate the database access to one layer, the DAO. You can access this layer through the application context.

Persistence managers
> Every persistence framework has an object or factory that the application uses to access its features. With Hibernate, it's the session and the session factory. With JDO, it's the persistence manager factory and persistence manager.

Transaction policies
> You can explicitly declare the methods that you want to participate in transactions and the transaction manager that you want to use to enforce that strategy.

Transaction managers
> There are many different transaction management strategies within J2EE. For single database applications, Spring lets you use the database's transaction management. For multiple databases or transaction sources, Spring allows JTA instead. You can keep the transaction manager in the application context.

Validation logic
> The Spring framework uses a validation framework similar to Struts. Spring lets you configure validation logic like any other business component.

Views and controllers
> The Spring framework lets you specify the controllers for a view and helps you configure the navigation path through them.

The jPetStore application uses the Spring application context for a data source, the DAO layer, and a transaction strategy. You define what goes into a context within an XML document that lists a series of beans. Each XML configuration file will have a <beans> heading, followed by a series of <bean> components, and a </beans> footer, like this:

```
<beans>

<bean id="MyFirstBean" class="package.MyFirstBeanClass">
  <property name="myField" ref local="MySecondBean"/>
</bean>
```

```
<bean id="MySecondBean" class="package.MySecondBeanClass">
</bean>

</beans>
```

These are the beans that make up an application context. They represent the top-level beans of an application. (They may create other objects or beans that do not appear in the configuration file.) In this case, you create two beans named MyFirstBean and MySecondBean. Then, you wire them together by specifying MySecondBean as the value for the field myField. When Spring starts, it creates both objects and sets the value of myField. You have access to both of these objects by name whenever you need them through the application context.

Let's look at a more concrete example. The jPetStore application has three configuration files for the business logic, the data layer, and the user interface, as in Figure 8-2. A separate Spring configuration file describes each one.

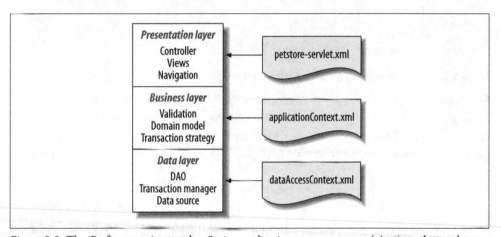

Figure 8-2. The jPetStore application has Spring application contexts to match its three distinct layers

These configuration files specify the context for the domain model, the data layer, and the presentation layer. Example 8-1 shows part of the application context for the business logic of the jPetStore application. Note that I've shortened the package name from org.springframework.samples.jpetstore... to jpetstore for simplicity.

Example 8-1. applicationContext.xml

```
<beans>
❶
    <bean id="accountValidator" class="jpetstore.domain.logic.AccountValidator"/>

❷   <bean id="orderValidator" class=" jpetstore.domain.logic.OrderValidator"/>

❸   <bean id="petStoreTarget" class=" jpetstore.domain.logic.PetStoreImpl">
❹   <property name="accountDao"><ref bean="accountDao"/></property>
```

Example 8-1. applicationContext.xml (continued)

```
            <property name="categoryDao"><ref bean="categoryDao"/></property>
            <property name="productDao"><ref bean="productDao"/></property>
            <property name="itemDao"><ref bean="itemDao"/></property>
            <property name="orderDao"><ref bean="orderDao"/></property>
        </bean>

❺     <bean id="petStore" class="org.springframework.transaction.interceptor.
    TransactionProxyFactoryBean">
            <property name="transactionManager"><ref bean="transactionManager"/></property>
            <property name="target"><ref bean="petStoreTarget"/></property>
            <property name="transactionAttributes">
                <props>
                    <prop key="insert*">PROPAGATION_REQUIRED</prop>
                    <prop key="update*">PROPAGATION_REQUIRED</prop>
                    <prop key="*">PROPAGATION_REQUIRED,readOnly</prop>
                </props>
            </property>
        </bean>

    </beans>
```

Here's an explanation of the annotated lines:

❶ *Business logic.* This section (which includes all bold code) has the core business logic. Validation and the domain model are both considered business components.

❷ *Validators.* This is the validator for Order. Spring calls it whenever a user submits the Order form and routes to the error page or an order completion page, as required.

❸ *Core business implementation.* This class contains the core implementation for the persistent domain model. It contains all of the DAO objects that you'll see below.

❹ *Properties.* Each of your beans has individual properties that may refer to beans you define elsewhere. In this case, the bean properties are individual DAO. Each of these beans is defined in another Spring configuration file.

❺ *Transaction declarations.* This bean specifies the transaction strategy for the application. In this case, the application uses a transaction manager specified in another Spring configuration file. It declares the methods that should be propagated as transactions. For example, all methods beginning with insert should be propagated as transactions.

In short, this configuration file serves as the glue that holds the business logic of the application together. In the file, you see some references to beans that are not in the configuration file itself, such as the DAO objects. Later on, you'll see two other configuration files that define some of the missing beans. One specifies the data access objects with the transaction manager. The other specifies the beans needed by the user interface. It's often better to break configuration files into separate layers, allowing you to configure individual layers as needed. For example, you may want to change strategies for your user interface (say, from Spring MVC web to Struts) or for data access (say, from DAO with one database to DAO spanning two databases with JTA transactions).

If you want to instantiate a bean from your XML context file, it's easy. For example, in order to access a bean called myCustomer of type Customer from a file called *context.xml*, take the following three steps:

1. Get an input stream for the XML file with your configuration:

   ```
   InputStream stream = getClass().getResourceAsStream("context.xml");
   ```

2. Create a new Spring bean factory using the input stream:

   ```
   XmlBeanFactory beanFactory = new XmlBeanFactory(stream);
   ```

3. Use the factory to create one of the objects defined in your *.xml* file:

   ```
   Customer cust = (Customer)beanFactory.getBean(myCustomer);
   ```

Or, if you want Spring to initialize a context and then grab, for example, your session façade, you'd use code like this:

```
protected static final String CONTEXT_FILE = "WEB-INF/applicationContext.xml";
Biz biz;  // session façade

FileSystemXmlApplicationContext ctx =
    new FileSystemXmlApplicationContext(CONTEXT_FILE);
biz = (Biz) ctx.getBean("biz");
```

It's often better to let go of that control. Usually, you won't have to access the application context directly. The framework does that for you. For example, if you're using servlets, the Spring framework provides a context for each servlet and a catch-all context for servlets. From there, you can usually get the appropriate context information, as you'll see later. Now that you've seen a configuration file representing the jPetStore application, it's time to see how to build the individual elements.

The Domain Model

In keeping with the principles in the book, the foundation of the application is the transparent domain model in Figure 8-3. The domain model contains the business relationships of objects that represent the real world. Pet Store is made up of carts and orders that contain items.

The application represents a simple pet store. It consists of a shopping cart containing cart items, which feeds an order containing line items. Items consist of products organized into categories. Each object is a transparent business object implemented as a Java bean with some properties and some business methods. Example 8-2 shows a CartItem. I've eliminated the imports and package detail, for brevity.

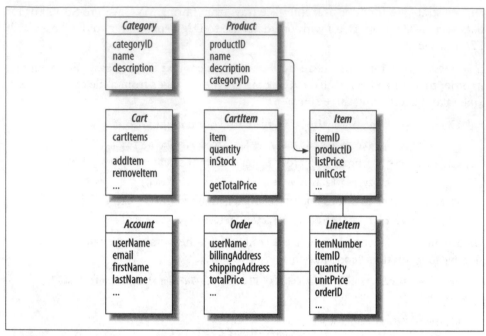

Figure 8-3. The center of an application is the domain model

Example 8-2. CartItem.java

```
❶  public class CartItem implements Serializable {

       /*Private Fields*/

       private Item item;
       private int quantity;
       private boolean inStock;

       /*JavaBeans Properties*/

❷  public boolean isInStock() { return inStock; }
       public void setInStock(boolean inStock) { this.inStock = inStock; }

       public Item getItem() { return item; }
       public void setItem(Item item) {
         this.item = item;
       }

       public int getQuantity() { return quantity; }
       public void setQuantity(int quantity) {
         this.quantity = quantity;
       }

❸  public double getTotalPrice() {
         if (item != null) {
           return item.getListPrice() * quantity;
```

Example 8-2. CartItem.java (continued)

```
    }
    else {
     return 0;
    }
  }

  /*Public methods*/

  public void incrementQuantity() {
    quantity++;
  }

  }
```

Here's what the annotations mean:

❶ The Spring framework does not force components to inherit from a Spring class.
    They are fully transparent, and can live outside of the container for testing pur-
    poses, or if Spring would some day prove inadequate.

❷ Each field is wrapped with get and set methods, so that Spring can configure
    them through Java reflection. (Spring can alternatively configure them through
    constructors.)

❸ Unlike many EJB applications, it's often helpful to include business domain logic
    within the domain model.

I call this model *passive*. It's invoked entirely by objects outside of its domain and has
coupling only to other objects within the domain. Notice that it is not merely a value
object, although it does have private properties and public fields It has business methods to calculate the total price and increment the quantity. This design makes this business object easy to understand and reuse, even though the overall design may evolve.
As we move into persistence, you'll see other parts of the model as well.

Adding Persistence

The CartItem object does not necessarily need to be persistent. On the other hand,
you'd expect to pull products and categories from a database. J2EE application
developers have long searched for a clean approach to persistence without much success. The best persistence frameworks allow transparency and do not invade the
domain model. Spring lets you separate your transparent object from the data access
layer. Spring then makes it easy to layer on persistence. You can use a JDBC abstraction layer, which abstracts away many of the tedious and error-prone aspects of
JDBC, such as connection management and error handling. The Spring JDBC layer
uses a feature called *callback templates* to pass control from your application to the
framework. With this strategy, Spring removes the need to manage connections,
result sets, and RDBMS-specific errors. This framework is useful when you want to
use JDBC directly to process relational queries.

Often, you'd rather deal with objects instead of relations. Spring also has an appropriate model for transparent persistence. The jPetStore uses Spring's OR mapping layer, which provides a variety of prepackaged choices. Spring now supports mapping layers for basic JDBC DAO, Hibernate, and JDO. This example uses a DAO framework called iBATIS SQL Maps to implement a Spring DAO layer.

The Model

Each of the Spring solutions starts with a transparent domain model. Example 8-3 starts with the transparent model object, a product.

Example 8-3. Product.java

```
public class Product implements Serializable {

  private String productId;
  private String categoryId;
  private String name;
  private String description;

  public String getProductId() { return productId; }
  public void setProductId(String productId) { this.productId = productId.trim(); }

  public String getCategoryId() { return categoryId; }
  public void setCategoryId(String categoryId) { this.categoryId = categoryId; }

  public String getName() { return name; }
  public void setName(String name) { this.name = name; }

  public String getDescription() { return description; }
  public void setDescription(String description) { this.description = description; }

  public String toString() {
    return getName();
  }

}
```

There's nothing special here. It consists purely of properties, accessed through getters and setters, and one utility method, toString. When you look into the jPetStore application, you'll find similar classes for each of the other persistent objects in the domain: Account, Order, Category, Item, and LineItem.

The Mapping

As with Hibernate, the iBATIS SQL Maps framework has a mapping file. In it, each persistent property in your Java bean maps onto a single database column. Using SQL Maps, create all of your SQL within that mapping file as well, isolating all SQL to your XML mapping files. Example 8-4 shows the XML mapping support for Product.

Example 8-4. Product.xml

❶ `<sql-map name="Product">`

❷ `<cache-model name="oneDayProduct" reference-type="WEAK">`
    `  <flush-interval hours="24"/>`
    `</cache-model>`

❸ `<result-map name="result" class="jpetstore.domain.Product">`
    `  <property name="productId" column="PRODUCTID" columnIndex="1"/>`
    `  <property name="name" column="NAME" columnIndex="2"/>`
    `  <property name="description" column="DESCN" columnIndex="3"/>`
    `  <property name="categoryId" column="CATEGORY" columnIndex="4"/>`
    `</result-map>`

❹ `<mapped-statement name="getProduct" result-map="result">`
    `  select PRODUCTID, NAME, DESCN, CATEGORY from PRODUCT where PRODUCTID = #value#`
    `</mapped-statement>`

❺ `<mapped-statement name="getProductListByCategory" result-map="result">`
    `  select PRODUCTID, NAME, DESCN, CATEGORY from PRODUCT where CATEGORY = #value#`
    `</mapped-statement>`

❻ `<dynamic-mapped-statement name="searchProductList" result-map="result">`
    `  select PRODUCTID, NAME, DESCN, CATEGORY from PRODUCT`
    `<dynamic prepend="WHERE">`
    `    <iterate property="keywordList" open="(" close=")" conjunction="OR">`
    `      lower(name) like #keywordList[]# OR lower(category) like #keywordList[]# OR`
    `lower(descn) like #keywordList[]#`
    `    </iterate>`
    `  </dynamic>`
    `</dynamic-mapped-statement>`

  `</sql-map>`

Here's what the annotations mean:

1. Each mapping file corresponds to a domain object. The domain object in this case relates to the return types of the queries specified for this DAO.

2. Other information about the DAO layer, like caching strategies, also belong in the mapping file. Here, iBatis maintains a cache for 24 hours and then flushes it.

3. Each of these queries returns, of course, a product. This mapping ties each column of the result set to one of the fields in product.

4. This SQL statement finds a product, given a productID.

5. This SQL statement finds all products in a category. It returns a list of products.

6. This SQL statement is dynamic. iBatis iterates over the keyword list and forms a dynamic query.

So far, you've seen the domain model for Product and its mapping, which contains queries. You're most of the way home.

The DAO Interface

Somehow, the application must integrate with both Spring and SQL Maps. The application ties the two concepts together with a DAO interface, and a concrete implementation. Example 8-5 is the interface.

Example 8-5. ProductDAO.java

```
public interface ProductDao {

  List getProductListByCategory(String categoryId) throws DataAccessException;

  List searchProductList(String keywords) throws DataAccessException;

  Product getProduct(String productId) throws DataAccessException;

}
```

That's simple enough. You can see an interface for each of the queries defined in the mapping. Specifically, you can see an interface getProduct that finds a product by ID, one for getProductListByCategory that returns all products in a category, and one for the dynamic query based on keywords. Now, the DAO throws Spring exceptions; any logic that uses the DAO will have consistent exceptions, even if you later decide to change implementations.

The DAO Implementation

All that remains is to implement the interface with SQL Map. Example 8-6 is the SQL Map implementation for Product.

Example 8-6. SqlMapProductDao.java

```
    public class SqlMapProductDao extends SqlMapDaoSupport implements ProductDao {

❶     public List getProductListByCategory(String categoryId) throws DataAccessException {
      return getSqlMapTemplate().executeQueryForList("getProductListByCategory",
        categoryId);
      }

❶     public Product getProduct(String productId) throws DataAccessException {
      return (Product) getSqlMapTemplate().executeQueryForObject("getProduct", productId);
      }

❶     public List searchProductList(String keywords) throws DataAccessException {
      Object parameterObject = new ProductSearch(keywords);
       return getSqlMapTemplate().executeQueryForList("searchProductList", parameterObject);
      }

      /* Inner Classes */
```

Example 8-6. SqlMapProductDao.java (continued)

❷   public static class ProductSearch {

```
    private List keywordList = new ArrayList();

    public ProductSearch(String keywords) {
      StringTokenizer splitter = new StringTokenizer(keywords, " ", false);
      while (splitter.hasMoreTokens()) {
        this.keywordList.add("%" + splitter.nextToken() + "%");
      }
    }

    public List getKeywordList() {
      return keywordList;
    }
  }

}
```

Here's what the annotations mean:

❶ These methods provide the SQL Map implementation of the interface. Other implementations might use Hibernate, JDO, or straight JDBC. In this case, the getTemplate call instructs Spring to get the template for iBATIS SQL Map support and execute the appropriate query using the framework.

❷ I'm not a big fan of inner classes, but that's what they used to implement the keyword search. In this case, the inner class supports the searchProductList method by implementing getKeywordList. The inner class helps to organize the code base, keeping all of the support in one location, with the rest of the DAO implementation.

Now you've seen the mapping, the model, and the DAO. You have a fully persistent model. Next, access the DAO layer with code. jPetStore funnels all DAO access through a façade layer.

Using the Model Through a Façade

Just as in Chapter 3, it often makes sense to have a higher-level interface for a model, called the *façade*. In this case, the jPetStore façade serves three purposes:

- Consolidates all of the clients of the data access layer.

- Presents a single, common user interface for the rest of the applications.

- Serves as an attachment point for other services, such as transaction support.

In this case, the façade is a very thin layer around all of the DAO. Through configuration and method interceptors, Spring attaches declarative transaction support to the façade. In this case, the façade is in two parts: the interface and the implementation. The interface allows you to change the implementation of the façade without impacting the rest of the code. Example 8-7 shows the interface.

Example 8-7. PetStoreFacade.java

```java
public interface PetStoreFacade {

    Account getAccount(String username);
    Account getAccount(String username, String password);
    void insertAccount(Account account);
    void updateAccount(Account account);

    List getUsernameList();

    List getCategoryList();
    Category getCategory(String categoryId);

    List getProductListByCategory(String categoryId);
    List searchProductList(String keywords);
    Product getProduct(String productId);

    List getItemListByProduct(String productId);
    Item getItem(String itemId);
    boolean isItemInStock(String itemId);

    void insertOrder(Order order);
    Order getOrder(int orderId);
    List getOrdersByUsername(String username);

}
```

Think of this interface as a consolidated list of every method that creates, reads, updates, or deletes any Pet Store object. Notice that you do not see every method from all of the DAO. You see only the methods that we wish to expose to the rest of the world. Also, notice the naming consistency within the interface. This is important because within our configuration file, you saw the transaction support configured to propagate methods beginning with get, search, update, or insert.

The implementation simply calls the underlying DAO to do the appropriate job. It must implement all of the methods in the interface. Example 8-8 is the implementation of the methods related to the ProductDAO.

Example 8-8. Excerpt fromPetStoreImpl.java

```java
❶   private ProductDao productDao;

    ...

    public void setProductDao(ProductDao productDao) {
        this.productDao = productDao;
    }

    ...
```

Example 8-8. Excerpt fromPetStoreImpl.java (continued)

❷   ```
      public List getProductListByCategory(String categoryId) {
        return this.productDao.getProductListByCategory(categoryId);
      }

      public List searchProductList(String keywords) {
        return this.productDao.searchProductList(keywords);
      }
    ...
    ```

Here's what the annotations mean:

❶   Shows the DAO access (includes the bold text). The Spring framework inserts the DAO into the façade using reflection. That means the façade must support a set method and a private member variable.

❷   The methods that provide data access use the underlying DAO to do the actual work (includes the bold text).

Of course, I haven't shown the implementation of all of the interface's methods. These are only the methods related to product. They come in two parts.

First, the application context wired each DAO to the façade. Spring uses reflection and the bean factory to create the product DAO and set it using the setProductDAO API. To support this, the façade needs a variable to hold the DAO and a set method to access it through reflection.

Second, the implementation is simple. The façade merely passes the request through to the model layer underneath. The ultimate implementation is much more powerful, though. The façade functions like an EJB session bean with respect to declarative transaction support. Through configuration, the POJO becomes a declarative transaction coordinator! It's also a central point of control for the entire database layer. All that remains is to configure the DAO layer.

## Configuration for the DAO Layer

Recall that you have seen only the configuration for the model. Example 8-9 shows the configuration of the data layer for a single database with simple transaction management. As you'd expect, you'll see the configuration of the JDBC driver and the declaration of all of the DAO beans.

*Example 8-9. dataAccessContext-local.xml*

```
<beans>
```

❶   ```
    <bean id="propertyConfigurer"
        class="org.springframework.beans.factory.
        config.PropertyPlaceholderConfigurer">
        <property name="location"><value>/WEB-INF/jdbc.properties</value></property>
    </bean>
    ```

Example 8-9. dataAccessContext-local.xml (continued)

❷
```
<bean id="dataSource" class="org.apache.commons.dbcp.BasicDataSource"
    destroy-method="close">
  <property
    name="driverClassName"><value>${jdbc.driverClassName}</value></property>
  <property name="url"><value>${jdbc.url}</value></property>
  <property name="username"><value>${jdbc.username}</value></property>
  <property name="password"><value>${jdbc.password}</value></property>
</bean>
```

❸
```
<bean id="transactionManager"
    class="org.springframework.jdbc.datasource.DataSourceTransactionManager">
    <property name="dataSource"><ref local="dataSource"/></property>
</bean>
```

❹
```
<bean id="sqlMap" class="org.springframework.orm.ibatis.SqlMapFactoryBean">
    <property name="configLocation">
      <value>classpath:/sql-map-config.xml</value></property>
</bean>
```

❺
```
<bean id="accountDao" class=" jpetstore.dao.ibatis.SqlMapAccountDao">
    <property name="dataSource"><ref local="dataSource"/></property>
    <property name="sqlMap"><ref local="sqlMap"/></property>
</bean>

<bean id="categoryDao" class="jpetstore.dao.ibatis.SqlMapCategoryDao">
    <property name="dataSource"><ref local="dataSource"/></property>
    <property name="sqlMap"><ref local="sqlMap"/></property>
</bean>

<bean id="productDao" class=" jpetstore.dao.ibatis.SqlMapProductDao">
    <property name="dataSource"><ref local="dataSource"/></property>
    <property name="sqlMap"><ref local="sqlMap"/></property>
</bean>

<bean id="itemDao" class=" jpetstore.dao.ibatis.SqlMapItemDao">
    <property name="dataSource"><ref local="dataSource"/></property>
    <property name="sqlMap"><ref local="sqlMap"/></property>
</bean>

<bean id="orderDao" class=" jpetstore.dao.ibatis.SqlMapOrderDao">
    <property name="dataSource"><ref local="dataSource"/></property>
    <property name="sqlMap"><ref local="sqlMap"/></property>
    <property name="sequenceDao"><ref local="sequenceDao"/></property>
</bean>

<bean id="sequenceDao" class="jpetstore.dao.ibatis.SqlMapSequenceDao">
    <property name="dataSource"><ref local="dataSource"/></property>
    <property name="sqlMap"><ref local="sqlMap"/></property>
</bean>

</beans>
```

Here's what the annotations mean:

❶ This bean handles the JDBC configuration. The JDBC configuration properties are in a standard JDBC configuration file, making them easier to maintain and read. Spring provides a configuring class that makes it easy to read property files without converting them to XML.

❷ Here you see the data source. It's a standard J2EE data source. Many J2EE applications and frameworks hard-wire an application or framework to a given data source. Configuring them instead makes it easy to choose your own source (and thus your pooling strategy).

❸ The *applicationContext.xml* configuration sets the transaction policy. This configuration specifies the implementation. This application uses the data source transaction manager, which delegates transaction management to the database via JDBC (using commit and rollback).

❹ The iBATIS SQL Map utility for building DAO must be configured. It's done here.

❺ Finally, you see the actual DAO configuration. As you may remember, the *applicationContext.xml* file referred to each of these beans by name.

This configuration accomplishes more than just decoupling the persistence tier from the model or the view. We've also decoupled transaction management from the persistence layer, separated the transaction policy from the implementation, and isolated the data source. Take a look at the broader benefits that have been gained beyond configuration.

The Benefits

That's all of the persistence code for the Product. The code for the rest of jPetStore is similar. The application effectively isolates the entire domain model within a single layer. The domain has no dependencies on any services, including the data layer. You've also encapsulated all data access into a clean and concise DAO layer, which is independent of data store. Notice what you don't see:

Data source configuration
Handled by the Spring framework. You don't have to manage a whole bunch of singletons, for session management, data sources, and the like. You can also delay key decisions such as the type of data source until deployment time.

Connection processing
The Spring framework manages all of the connection processing. One of the most common JDBC errors is a connection leak. If you're not very careful about closing your connections, especially within exception conditions, your application can easily lose stability and crash.

Specialized exceptions

Many frameworks pass SQL exceptions to the top. They frequently have SQL codes built in that may be specialized to your own RDBMS, making it difficult to code portable applications. Spring has its own exception hierarchy, which insulates you from these issues. Further, should you change approaches to Hibernate or JDO, you won't need to change any of your exception processing.

The end result of what we've done so far is pretty cool. We have a clean, transparent domain model and a low-maintenance service layer that's independent of our database. Each layer is neatly encapsulated. Now that we have looked at the backend logic, it's time to put a user interface on this application.

Presentation

In most places, the Spring framework doesn't reinvent working technologies. In the area of presentation logic, though, Spring introduces a simple model-view-controller framework called MVC Web that has many competing architectures, like Struts and Java Server Faces (JSF). Take solace, though. You don't have to use MVC Web to use Spring. But if you decide to do so, you will find a few advantages:

- MVC Web is based on interfaces rather than inheritance. As we discussed in Chapter 3, interfaces often give better flexibility and looser coupling than inheritance-based designs.

- MVC Web does not dictate your choice of view. Other frameworks tend to provide better support for favored view technologies, such as Velocity (proprietary) and Struts (JSP). For example, Struts exposes the model via request attributes. As a result, you need to build a bridge servlet to use a technology such as Velocity that doesn't understand the Servlet API. Spring exposes the model through a generic map, so it can work with any view technology.

- MVC Web provides consistent configuration across all aspects of a Spring application. It uses the same inversion-of-control paradigm that the other frameworks use.

- MVC Web makes testing easier. Since you don't have to extend another class (like Action or ActionForm in Struts), you can easily mock the request and response.

If you've ever used Struts, you're familiar with the basic paradigm of MVC Web. Figure 8-4 shows how it works. Controllers basically handle all incoming requests from input views. If the input request is a submitted form, the controller calls a business validation routine, created and configured by the programmer, and sends either the associated error view or success view back to the user, based on results.

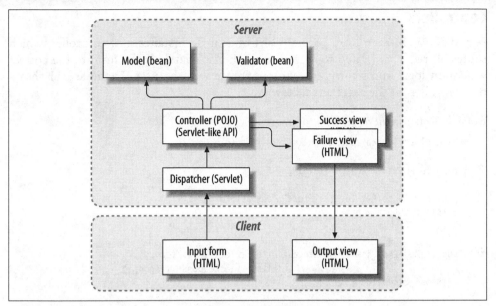

Figure 8-4. The MVC Web framework works much like Struts

Configuration

As with other elements of the Spring framework, when you're trying to understand a new application, start with the configuration files and drill down from there. In this example, the user interface is configured in the *petstore-servlet.xml* file.

Consider HTML pages that search for products in a category, and search for products based on keywords. The configuration file needs two controllers to the application context file. Each entry specifies a controller and the model object, like in Example 8-10.

Example 8-10. Excerpt from web.xml

```
<bean name="/shop/searchProducts.do"
  class="jpetstore.web.spring.SearchProductsController">
  <property name="petStore"><ref bean="petStore"/></property>
</bean>

<bean name="/shop/viewProduct.do" class="org.springframework.samples.jpetstore.web.
spring.ViewProductController">
  <property name="petStore"><ref bean="petStore"/></property>
</bean>
```

Recall that all access to our data layer goes through the façade. As you'd expect, these bean ID entries specify the façade, called *petstore*. Each form in the application works in the same way. Let's drill down further and look at the controller for searchProducts.

Controllers

For MVC Web, each form generally shares a single instance of a controller, which routes all requests related to a given form. It also marshals the form to the correct validation logic and returns the appropriate view to the user. Example 8-11 shows the controller for the searchProducts view.

Example 8-11. SearchProductsController.java

```
    public class SearchProductsController implements Controller {

❶  private PetStoreFacade petStore;

    public void setPetStore(PetStoreFacade petStore) {
      this.petStore = petStore;
    }

❷  public ModelAndView handleRequest(HttpServletRequest request,
                                      HttpServletResponse response)
     throws Exception {

❸  if (request.getParameter("search") != null) {
      String keyword = request.getParameter("keyword");
      if (keyword == null || keyword.length() == 0) {
        return new ModelAndView("Error",
                          "message",
    "Please enter a keyword to search for, then press the search button.");
      }
      else {
❹       PagedListHolder productList = new PagedListHolder(
                  this.petStore.searchProductList(keyword.toLowerCase()));
      productList.setPageSize(4);
      request.getSession().setAttribute(
                  "SearchProductsController_productList", productList);
❺     return new ModelAndView("SearchProducts", "productList", productList);
      }
    }
    else {
❻     String page = request.getParameter("page");
      PagedListHolder productList = (PagedListHolder) request.getSession().
        getAttribute("SearchProductsController_productList");
      if ("next".equals(page)) {
        productList.nextPage();
      }
      else if ("previous".equals(page)) {
        productList.previousPage();
      }
      return new ModelAndView("SearchProducts", "productList", productList);
    }
  }

}
```

Here's what the annotations mean:

❶ Each controller has access to the appropriate domain model. In this case, it's natural for the view to access the model through our façade.

❷ A controller has an interface like a servlet, but isn't actually a servlet. User requests instead come in through a single dispatcher servlet, which routes them to the appropriate controller, populating the request parameter. The controller merely responds to the appropriate request, invoking business data and routing control to the appropriate page.

❸ In this case, the request is to "search." The controller must parse out the appropriate keywords.

❹ The controller invokes the business logic with the keywords provided by the user.

❺ The controller routes the appropriate view back to the user (with the appropriate model).

❻ In this case, the request is "page." Our user interface supports more products than might fit on a single page.

Forms

Just like Struts, Spring can map HTML forms onto Java objects. Example 8-12 is the Java bean that's returned when a Pet Store user registers an account.

Example 8-12. AccountForm.java

```java
public class AccountForm {

  private Account account;

  private boolean newAccount;

  private String repeatedPassword;

  public AccountForm(Account account) {
    this.account = account;
    this.newAccount = false;
  }

  public AccountForm( ) {
    this.account = new Account( );
    this.newAccount = true;
  }

  public Account getAccount( ) {
    return account;
  }

  public boolean isNewAccount( ) {
```

Example 8-12. AccountForm.java (continued)

```
    return newAccount;
  }

  public void setRepeatedPassword(String repeatedPassword) {
    this.repeatedPassword = repeatedPassword;
  }

  public String getRepeatedPassword() {
    return repeatedPassword;
  }

}
```

Each of these bean fields corresponds directly to an HTML input field or control. The Spring framework translates a submit request to the form, which can then be accessed as a POJO for validation, mapping input data, or other purposes. With Spring, unlike Struts, form objects can be any Java bean. There's no need to extend ActionForm. That's important, because you don't need to copy properties from an ActionForm to a domain object or value object.

Validation

You may have noticed validation logic within the original *applciationContext.xml*. These beans are generally considered business logic, but they've got a tight relationship to the user interface and they're invoked directly by the Spring framework. When a user submits a form, Spring fires the validation logic. Based on the result, Spring routes control to the appropriate page. Example 8-13 shows the AccountValidator class, which validates the account form.

Example 8-13. AccountValidator.java

```
public class AccountValidator implements Validator {

    public boolean supports(Class clazz) {
        return Account.class.isAssignableFrom(clazz);
    }

    public void validate(Object obj, Errors errors) {
        ValidationUtils.rejectIfEmpty(errors, "firstName", "FIRST_NAME_REQUIRED",
            "First name is required.");
        ValidationUtils.rejectIfEmpty(errors, "lastName", "LAST_NAME_REQUIRED",
            "Last name is required.");
        ValidationUtils.rejectIfEmpty(errors, "email", "EMAIL_REQUIRED",
            "Email address is required.");
        ValidationUtils.rejectIfEmpty(errors, "phone", "PHONE_REQUIRED",
            "Phone number is required.");
        ValidationUtils.rejectIfEmpty(errors, "address1", "ADDRESS_REQUIRED",
            "Address (1) is required.");
```

Example 8-13. AccountValidator.java (continued)

```
        ValidationUtils.rejectIfEmpty(errors, "city", "CITY_REQUIRED",
            "City is required.");
        ValidationUtils.rejectIfEmpty(errors, "state", "STATE_REQUIRED",
            "State is required.");
        ValidationUtils.rejectIfEmpty(errors, "zip", "ZIP_REQUIRED", "ZIP is required.");
        ValidationUtils.rejectIfEmpty(errors, "country", "COUNTRY_REQUIRED",
            "Country is required.");
    }
}
```

In this example, the Spring framework makes life easier for developers in several ways. The developer does not need to write validation methods by hand. Also, many prepackaged methods exist. The framework takes care of validation and routing. The framework takes care of routing control based on success or failure.

One chapter on the Spring framework cannot do it justice, but you've seen the overall gist of it. The advantages of the framework—and more importantly, this coding style—should jump off the page at you if you haven't seen it before. In particular, notice the clarity and simplicity that a cleanly layered architecture provides. You can probably imagine how easy it is to incorporate business logic with a transparent framework like Spring.

Summary

I've chosen the jPetStore application for a variety of reasons. The biggest is that you can quickly see the difference between a simple, fast, light application and the alternative. If you are not yet a believer, I challenge you to look up the EJB version of Pet Store. If you've never seen it, you'll be blown away by the difference. Our version is transparent and independent; the EJB example is invasive and dependent on the container. Ours is easy to understand, whereas the J2EE counterpart was buried under the complexity of EJB best practices.

I haven't always been a believer. In fact, I didn't know who Rod Johnson was before we were introduced in Boston at a conference. I've since come to appreciate this simple framework as elegant and important. If you're new to Spring, you've seen only a single application. I hope that through it, you can see how it embraces the principles in this book:

Keep it simple

> Spring's easy to use and understand. In a single chapter, our example covers an application with transactions, persistence, a full web frontend, and a completely modular configuration engine.

Do one thing, and do it well

> Spring's framework has many different aspects and subframeworks. However, it separates each concept nicely. The fundamental value of Spring is the bean

factory and configuration service, which let you manage dependencies without coupling your code. Each additional layer of Spring is cleanly decoupled and independent.

Strive for transparency

Spring applications don't need to rely on the basic container at all. In fact, they can easily exist outside of the container. You need only create and configure them manually. This ability makes Spring applications a joy to test.

You are what you eat

Spring makes smart choices in the frameworks that it includes. The respected Apache projects for data sources and logging form a good foundation. Spring allows many configurable choices, letting you choose the best frameworks for a given solution.

Allow for extension

Spring may be the most open, extensible container in existence today. It allows effective and rapid extension with common configuration services and clean abstractions.

I haven't covered Spring in its entirety. My goal is only to show you that it's possible to build real-world applications that embrace the concepts set out in the first six chapters of this book. If you decide that you'd like to see more, make sure that you look into Spring's advanced features:

- Integration with Hibernate and JDO
- AOP concepts
- Transactional templates with JTA support

In the chapters to come, we continue to explore practical examples of the principles in this book. You'll see an implementation of a service called Simple Spider, and see that service integrated into Spring. Then, you'll be able to see the benefits of improved maintenance of a framework like this going forward.

Simple Spider

I once had the pleasure of building a house with a carpenter who was from Mexico; I learned a great deal in the process. Despite my broken Spanish (I once twisted the language so badly that I told him that I was going home to marry my sister), he was able to impart an incredible amount of wisdom. My observations were, shall we say... less wise. I told him that I was proud of my hammer. It had a sleek and heavy head, and a composite graphite handle that made it easy to swing. The head was waffled so it would grip the nails. He simply chuckled. At the end of the day, he had used his 10-year-old, plain-Jane hammer to drive in four times the nails as I did, with more accuracy and precision. He told me, "No esta el martillo:" it's not the hammer.

Luckily, I build code better than I build houses. In this chapter, I continue to put the five basic principles into action. I create a simple service with a light user interface to drive it. The service is an open source web indexer, primarily used to provide site search behavior for a single web site. It is called Simple Spider and is available at *http://www.relevancellc.com/halloway/SimpleSpider.html*.

I'll give you an insider's view of the real client requirements that spawned the application in the first place. The requirements were minimal and straightforward, but there was still a lot of work to do to understand the problem space. Notice large functionality areas that could be built for this application or reused from other tools; 'll walk you through the decision-making process that led us to use or discard each one. You'll also see the ways our desire for simplicity and our selection of the right tools led to the first iteration of the Spider. In the next chapter, I extend jPetStore to use the Spider. I do this while focusing on the use of transparency to enable extensibility.

Throughout both these chapters, I constantly apply the principle of focus: do one thing, and do it well. You want to build a simple hammer, one that fits like a glove in the hand of a skilled carpenter. That desire affects everything, from the requirements to the design to the individual lines of code you write. Along the way, I aim a spear at a variety of sacred cows, from over-burdensome frameworks and over-expensive data formats to notions about how technologies like JUnit and HTTPUnit should be used. In the end, you'll have an open source application and a greater appreciation for how good programming in Java can be if you just keep your wits about you.

What Is the Spider?

One of the most valuable features of any web site is the ability to search for what you need. Companies with web sites are constantly looking for the right tool to provide those features; they can write their own or purchase something from one of the big vendors. The problem with writing your own is mastering the tools. The problem with purchasing is usually vast expense. Google, the world's leading search provider, sells a boxed solution at $18,000 per unit—not including the yearly license.

Customized search engines are often built around the act of querying the database that sits behind a web site. Programmers immediately jump to this solution becausetools and libraries make querying a database simple. However, these customized search solutions often miss entire sections of a web site; no matter how stringently a company tries to build an all-dynamic, data-driven web site, they almost always end up with a few static HTML files mixed in. A data-driven query won't discover those pages.

Crawling a web site is usually the answer, but don't attack it naively. Let's look at what crawling means. When you crawl a web site, you start at some initial page. After cataloging the text of the page, you parse it, looking for and following any hyperlinks to other endpoints, where you repeat the process. If you aren't careful, crawling a web site invites the most ancient of programming errors: the infinite loop.

Take a look at Figure 9-1. The web site is only four pages, but no simple crawler will survive it. Given Page1 as a starting point, the crawler finds a link to Page2. After indexing Page1, the crawler moves on to Page2. There, it finds links to Page3 and Page4. Page4 is a nice little cul-de-sac on the site, and closes down one avenue of exploration. Page3 is the killer. Not only does it have a reference back to Page1, starting the whole cycle again, but it also has an off-site link (to Amazon.com). Anyone who wants a crawler to navigate this beast has more processor cycles than brain cells.

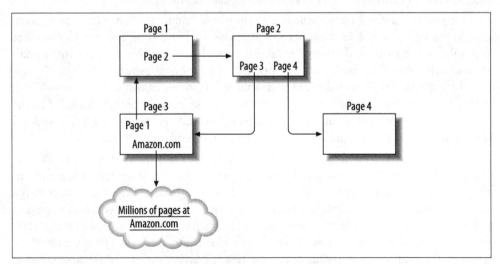

Figure 9-1. A simple, four-page web site that breaks any naïve crawler

I had a client who couldn't afford the $18,000 expense to buy search capabilities and didn't want to sit down and write something custom that might cost them the same amount in development dollars. They came to me and provided a set of straightforward requirements for an application that would enable them to search on their web site. Here's what they asked me to do:

1. Provide a service for crawling a web site, following all links from a provided starting point.

   a. The crawling service must ignore links to image files.

   b. The crawler must be configurable to only follow a maximum number of links.

2. Provide a service for indexing the resulting set of web pages. The indexing service should be schedulable; initially, it should run every night at midnight.

3. Each result of a search of the index should return a filename and a rank indicating the relative merit of each result.

4. Create two interfaces for accessing the spider:

   a. A console interface for local searches and testing.

   b. A web service that returns an XML document representing the results of all the searches.

My solution was to write an open source web site indexing and search engine. The goal was to have an application that could be pointed at any arbitrary web site, crawl it to create the domain of searchable pages, and allow a simple search language for querying the index. The crawler would be configurable to either allow or deny specific kinds of links, based on the link prefix (for example, ONLY follow links starting with *http:// www.yourdomain.com* or NEVER follow links starting with *http://www.amazon.com*). The indexer would operate on the results of the crawler and the search engine would query the index. Here are the advantages this engine would provide:

- No $18,000 to Google.
- No $18,000 to the IT department.
- General enough to work with any web site.
- A layered architecture that would allow it to easily be used in a variety of UI environments.

Examining the Requirements

The requirements for the Simple Spider leave a wide variety of design decisions open. Possible solutions might be based on hosted EJB solutions with XML-configurable indexing schedules, SOAP-encrusted web services with pass-through security, and any number of other combinations of buzz words, golden hammers, and time-wasting complexities. The first step in designing the Spider was to eliminate complexity and focus on the problem at hand. In this section, we will go through the decision-making steps together. The mantra for this part of the process: ignore what you think you need and examine what you know you need.

Breaking It Down

The first two services described by the requirements are the crawler and the indexer. They are listed as separate services in the requirements, but in examining the overall picture, we see no current need to separate them. There are no other services that rely on the crawler absent the indexer, and it doesn't make sense to run the indexer unless the crawler has provided a fresh look at the search domain. Therefore, in the name of simplicity, let's simplify the requirements to specify a single service that both crawls and indexes a web site.

The requirements next state that the crawler needs to ignore links to image files, since it would be meaningless to index them for textual search and doing so would take up valuable resources. This is a good place to apply the Inventor's Paradox. Think for a second about the Web: there are more kinds of links to ignore than just image files and, over time, the list is likely to grow. Let's allow for a configuration file that specifies what types of links to ignore.

After the link-type requirement comes a requirement for configuring the maximum number of links to follow. Since we have just decided to include a configuration option of some kind, this requirement fits our needs and we can leave it as-is.

Next, we have a requirement for making the indexer schedulable. Creating a scheduling service involves implementing a long-running process that sits dormant most of the time, waking up at specified intervals to fire up the indexing service. Writing such a process is not overly complex, but it is redundant and well outside the primary problem domain. In the spirit of choosing the right tools and doing one thing well, we can eliminate this entire requirement by relying on the deployment platform's own scheduling services. On Linux and Unix we have *cron* and on Windows we have *at*. In order to hook to these system services, we need only provide an entry point to the Spider that can be used to fire off the indexing service. System administrators can then configure their schedulers to perform the task at whatever intervals are required.

The final service requirement is the search service. Even though the requirements don't specify it as an individual service, it must be invoked independently of the index (we wouldn't want to re-run the indexer every time we wanted to search for something): it is obvious that it needs to be a separate service within the application. Unfortunately, the search service must be *somewhat* coupled to the indexing service, as the search service must be coupled to the format of the indexing service's data source. No global standard API currently exists for text index file formats. If and when such a standard comes into being, we'll upgrade the Spider to take advantage of the new standard and make the searching and indexing services completely decoupled from one another.

As for the user interfaces, a console interface is a fairly straightforward choice. However, the mere mention of web services often sends people into paroxysms of standards exuberance. Because of the voluminous and increasingly complex web services standards stack, actually implementing a web service is becoming more and more difficult. Looking at our requirements, however, we see that we can cut through most of the extraneous standards. Our service only needs to launch a search and return an XML result set. The default implementation of an axis web service can provide those capabilities without us messing around with either socket-level programming or high-level standards implementation.

Refining the Requirements

We can greatly improve on the initial requirements. Using the Inventor's Paradox, common sense, and available tools, we can eliminate a few others. Given this analysis, our new requirements are:

1. Provide a service to crawl and index a web site.
   a. Allow the user to pass a starting point for the search domain.
   b. Let the user configure the service to ignore certain types of links.
   c. Let the user configure the service to only follow a maximum number of links.
   d. Expose an invoke method to both an existing scheduler and humans.
2. Provide a search service over the results of the crawler/indexer.
   a. The search should collect a search word or phrase.
   b. Search results should include a full path to the file containing the search term.
   c. Search results should contain a relative rank for each result. The actual algorithm for determining the rank is unimportant.
3. Provide a console-based interface for invoking the indexer/crawler and search service.
4. Provide a web service interface for invoking the indexer/crawler and the search service. The web service interface does not need to explicitly provide authentication or authorization.

These requirements represent a cleaner design that allows future extensibility and focuses development on tasks that are essential to the problem domain. This is exactly what we need from requirements. They should provide a clear roadmap to success. If you get lost, take a deep breath. It's okay to ask for directions and clarify requirements with a customer.

Planning for Development

Once the requirements are clearly understood, the next step is to plan for development. Java is going to be our implementation technology because it easily provides both interfaces in our requirements (console and web service), has robust networking capabilities, and allows access to a variety of open source tools that might be useful for our project.

The principles of simplicity and sanity mandate that we provide thorough unit testing of the entire application. For this, we need JUnit. Since we are also talking about providing a web service frontend and making a lot of network calls, it behooves us to get a hold of HTTPUnit and the Jakarta Cactus tool as well. HTTPUnit is a tool that allows our unit tests to act like a browser, performing web requests and examining web responses. They model the end user's view of a web page or other HTTP endpoint. Cactus is a little different. It also exercises server code, but instead of examining it from the client's viewpoint, it does so from the *container's* viewpoint. If we write a servlet, Cactus can operate as the container for that servlet, and test its interaction with the container directly.

In addition to the unit-testing apparatus, we need a build tool. Ant is, of course, the answer. There really is no other choice when it comes to providing robust build support.

The Design

Our application is beginning to take shape. Figure 9-2 shows the entire design of the Simple Spider. It has layers that present a model, the service API, and two public interfaces. There is not yet a controller layer to separate the interfaces and logic. We'll integrate a controller in the next chapter.

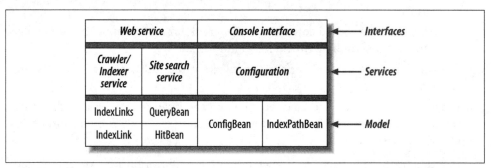

Figure 9-2. The Simple Spider design

We need to provide a configuration service to our application. I prefer to encapsulate the configuration into its own service to decouple the rest of the application from its details. This way, the application can switch configuration systems easily later without much editing of the code. For this version of the application, the Configuration service will consist of two class, `ConfigBean` and `IndexPathBean`, which will encapsulate returning configuration settings for the application as a whole (`ConfigBean`) and for getting the current path to the index files (`IndexPathBean`). The two are separate classes, as finding the path to the index is a more complex task than simply reading a configuration file (see the implementation details below). The configuration settings we will use are property files, accessed through `java.util.Properties`.

The crawler/indexer service is based on two classes: `IndexLinks`, which controls the configuration of the service in addition to managing the individual pages in the document domain, and `IndexLink`, a class modeling a single page in the search domain and allowing us to parse it looking for more links to other pages. We will use Lucene (*http://jakarta.apache.org/lucene*) as our indexer (and searcher) because it is fast, open source, and widely adopted in the industry today. The search service is provided through two more classes, `QueryBean` and `HitBean`. The former models the search input/output mechanisms, while the latter represents a single result from a larger result set. Sitting over top of the collection of services are the two specified user interfaces, the console version (`ConsoleSearch`) and a web service (`SearchImpl` and its WSDL file).

The Configuration Service

Let's start by looking at our configuration service, since it is used by all of the other services and interfaces. We need to provide a generic interface for retrieving our configuration options, separating the rest of the application from the details of how those values are stored or retrieved. We are going to use property files via *java.util. Properties* for the initial implementation.

Here is the class definition for `ConfigBean`:

```
package com.relevance.ss.config;

import java.util.Properties;

public class ConfigBean {

    Properties props = new Properties();
    int maxlinks;
    String[] allowedExtensions;
    String skippedLinksFile;

    public ConfigBean()
    {
        try
        {
            props.load(getClass().getResourceAsStream(
                "/com.relevance.ss.properties"));
```

```
        maxlinks = Integer.parseInt(props.getProperty("maxlinks"));
        allowedExtensions= props.getProperty("allowed.extensions").split(",");
        skippedLinksFile = props.getProperty("skipped.links.file");
    }
    catch(Exception ex)
    {
      //log the errors and populate with reasonable defaults, if necessary
    }
}

public String getSkippedLinksFile()
{
    return skippedLinksFile;
}
public int getMaxLinks()
{
    return maxlinks;
}
public String[] getAllowedExtensions()
{
    return allowedExtensions;
}

}
```

The class provides for the retrieval of three properties by name: MaxLinks, AllowedExtensions, and SkippedLinksFile. MaxLinks determines the maximum size of the searchable domain, AllowedExtensions is the file types the crawler should attempt to index, and the SkippedLinksFile is a logfile for keeping track of all the links skipped by a given indexing event.

Originally, I thought about adding an additional method to allow for future extension of the list of properties:

```
public String getPropertyByName(String propName)
{
    return props.getProperty(propName);
}
```

However, adding this method would be confusing and redundant. If the list of properties ever changes, we will have to make changes to the source code for whatever services use the new property; we might as well, then, also update ConfigBean at the same time to expose the new property explicitly. For the sake of simplicity, we'll leave this method out.

Getting the path to the index is not as simple as just reading the path from a file. If we were talking about only a console-based interface to the application, it would be okay. But since we are also going to expose a web service, we have to protect against multiple concurrent uses of the index. Specifically, we need to prevent a user from performing a search on the index while the indexer is updating it.

To ensure this, we implement a simple kind of *shadow copy*. The configuration file for the index path contains a root path (*index.fullpath*) and a property for a special extension to the index root path (*index.next*). *index.next* has a value at all times of either 0 or 1. Any attempt to use the index for a search should use the current value of *index.fullpath* + *index.next*. Any attempt to create a new index should use the alternate value of *index.next*, write the new index there, and update the value in the property file so future searches will use the new index.

Below is the implementation of IndexPathBean that allows for these behaviors:

```
package com.relevance.ss.config;

import java.io.IOException;
import java.io.File;
import java.io.FileInputStream;
import java.io.FileOutputStream;
import java.util.Properties;

public class IndexPathBean {

    private final String propFilePath = "index.properties";
    private String nextIndexPath;
    private String curIndexPath;
    private String nextIndex;
    private Properties props;

    private void getPaths() throws IOException
    {
        File f = new File(propFilePath);
        if (!f.exists()) {
          throw new IOException("properties path " + propFilePath
                                + " does not exist");
        }
        props = new Properties();
        props.load(new FileInputStream(propFilePath));
        String indexRelativePath = props.getProperty("index.next");
        if (indexRelativePath == null) {
          throw new IllegalArgumentException("indexRelativePath not set in "
                                + propFilePath);
        }
        nextIndex = Integer.toString(1 - Integer.parseInt(indexRelativePath));
        curIndexPath = props.getProperty("index.fullpath") + indexRelativePath;
        nextIndexPath = props.getProperty("index.fullpath") + nextIndex;
    }

    public String getFlippedIndexPath() throws IOException
    {
        getPaths();
        return nextIndexPath;
    }

    public String getIndexPath() throws IOException {
        getPaths();
```

```
        return curIndexPath;
    }

    public void flipIndexPath( ) throws IOException
    {
        getPaths( );
        props.setProperty("index.next", nextIndex);
        props.store(new FileOutputStream(propFilePath), "");
    }
```

The class exposes three public methods: getters for the current index path and next index path, and a method that flips them. Any class that needs to merely use the index can call getIndexPath( ) to get the current version. Any class that needs to modify the index can call getFlippedIndexPath( ) to get the version that isn't currently in use, and after modifying it, can call flipIndexPath( ) to reset the properties file to the new version. All three public methods rely on a private utility method called getPaths( ), which reads the current values from the property file.

From a simplicity standpoint—and, to a certain extent, transparency as well—we should probably expose the index path methods from ConfigBean, providing a single entry point into the application's configuration settings for the rest of the services. We'll leave the actual functionality separated for ease of maintenance and replacement (in case we have to modify the way the index path is stored over time). To do that, we add the following lines of code to ConfigBean:

```
IndexPathBean indexPathBean = new IndexPathBean( );
public String getCurIndexPath( )
    {
        String indexPath = "";
        try
        {
            indexPath = indexPathBean.getIndexPath( );
        }
        catch(Exception ex)
        {
        }
        return indexPath;
    }

    public String getNextIndexPath( )
    {
        String indexPath = "";
        try
        {
            indexPath = indexPathBean.getFlippedIndexPath( );
        }
        catch(Exception ex)
        {
        }
        return indexPath;
    }
```

```
public void flipIndexPath( )
{
    try
    {
        indexPathBean.flipIndexPath( );
    }
    catch(Exception ex)
    {
    }
}
```

Principles in Action

- Keep it simple: use existing Properties tools, not XML
- Choose the right tools: *java.util.Properties*
- Do one thing, and do it well: separate configuration details into separate service, keep simple properties and index path in separate classes
- Strive for transparency: one entry point for configuration settings, even though there are two implementations
- Allow for extension: expandable list of allowable link types

The Crawler/Indexer Service

The application needs a way to dynamically follow the links from a given URL and the links from those pages, ad infinitum, in order to create the full domain of searchable pages. Just thinking about writing all of the web-related code to do that work gives me the screaming heebie-jeebies. We would have to write methods to post web requests, listen for responses, parse those responses looking for links, and so on.

In light of the "keep it simple" chapter, it seems we are immediately faced with a buy-it-or-build-it question. This functionality must exist already, the question is, where? It turns out we already have a library at our disposal that contains everything we need: HTTPUnit. Because HTTPUnit's purpose in life is to imitate a browser, it can be used to make HTTP requests, examine the HTML results, and follow the links contained therein.

Using HTTPUnit to do the work for us is a fairly nonstandard approach. HTTPUnit is considered a testing framework, not an application development framework. However, since it accomplishes exactly what we need to do with regard to navigating web sites, it would be a waste of effort and resources to attempt to recreate that functionality on our own.

Our main entry point to the crawler/indexer service is IndexLinks. This class establishes the entry point for the indexable domain and all of the configuration settings for controlling the overall result set. The constructor for the class should accept as much of the configuration information as possible:

```
public IndexLinks(String indexPath, int maxLinks,
                  String skippedLinksOutputFileName)
{
  this.maxLinks = maxLinks;
  this.linksNotFollowedOutputFileName = skippedLinksOutputFileName;
  writer = new IndexWriter(indexPath, new StandardAnalyzer(), true);
}
```

The writer is an instance of org.apache.lucene.index.IndexWriter, which is initialized to point to the path where a new index should be created.

Our instance requires a series of collections to manage our links. Those collections are:

```
Set linksAlreadyFollowed = new HashSet();
Set linksNotFollowed = new HashSet();
Set linkPrefixesToFollow = new HashSet();
HashSet linkPrefixesToAvoid = new HashSet();
```

The first two are used to store the links as we discover and categorize them. The next two are configuration settings used to determine if we should follow the link based on its prefix. These settings allow us to eliminate subsites or certain external sites from the search set, thus giving us the ability to prevent the crawler from running all over the Internet, indexing everything.

The other object we need is a com.meterware.httpunit.WebConversation. HTTPUnit uses this class to model a browser-server session. It provides methods for making requests to web servers, retrieving responses, and manipulating the HTTP messages that result. We'll use it to retrieve our indexable pages.

```
WebConversation conversation = new WebConversation();
```

We must provide setter methods so the users of the indexer/crawler can add prefixes to these two collections:

```
public void setFollowPrefixes(String[] prefixesToFollow)
   throws MalformedURLException {
  for (int i = 0; i < prefixesToFollow.length; i++) {
    String s = prefixesToFollow[i];
    linkPrefixesToFollow.add(new URL(s));
  }
}
public void setAvoidPrefixes(String[] prefixesToAvoid) throws MalformedURLException
{
  for (int i = 0; i < prefixesToAvoid.length; i++) {
    String s = prefixesToAvoid[i];
    linkPrefixesToAvoid.add(new URL(s));
  }
}
```

In order to allow users of the application maximum flexibility, we also provide a way to store lists of common prefixes that they want to allow or avoid:

```
public void initFollowPrefixesFromSystemProperties() throws MalformedURLException {
  String followPrefixes = System.getProperty("com.relevance.ss.FollowLinks");
```

```
    if (followPrefixes == null || followPrefixes.length() == 0) return;
    String[] prefixes = followPrefixes.split(" ");
    if (prefixes != null && prefixes.length != 0) {
      setFollowPrefixes(prefixes);
    }
  }

  public void initAvoidPrefixesFromSystemProperties() throws MalformedURLException {
    String avoidPrefixes = System.getProperty("com.relevance.ss.AvoidLinks");
    if (avoidPrefixes == null || avoidPrefixes.length() == 0) return;
    String[] prefixes = avoidPrefixes.split(" ");
    if (prefixes != null && prefixes.length != 0) {
      setAvoidPrefixes(prefixes);
    }
  }
```

As links are considered for inclusion in the index, we'll be executing the same code
against each to determine its worth to the index. We need a few helper methods to
make those determinations:

```
boolean shouldFollowLink(URL newLink) {
  for (Iterator iterator = linkPrefixesToFollow.iterator(); iterator.hasNext();) {
    URL u = (URL) iterator.next();
    if (matchesDownToPathPrefix(u, newLink)) {
      return true;
    }
  }
  return false;
}

boolean shouldNotFollowLink(URL newLink) {
    for (Iterator iterator = linkPrefixesToAvoid.iterator(); iterator.hasNext();) {
    URL u = (URL) iterator.next();
    if (matchesDownToPathPrefix(u, newLink)) {
      return true;
    }
  }
  return false;
}

private boolean matchesDownToPathPrefix(URL matchBase, URL newLink) {
  return matchBase.getHost().equals(newLink.getHost()) &&
    matchBase.getPort() == newLink.getPort() &&
    matchBase.getProtocol().equals(newLink.getProtocol()) &&
    newLink.getPath().startsWith(matchBase.getPath());
}
```

The first two methods, shouldFollowLink and shouldNotFollowLink, compare the
URL to the collections for each. The third, matchesDownToPathPrefix, compares the
link to one from the collection, making sure the host, port, and protocol are all the
same.

The service needs a way to consider a link for inclusion in the index. It must accept the new link to consider and the page that contained the link (for record-keeping):

```
void considerNewLink(String linkFrom, WebLink newLink) throws MalformedURLException
{
    URL url = null;
    url = newLink.getRequest().getURL();
    if (shouldFollowLink(url)) {
        if (linksAlreadyFollowed.add(url.toExternalForm())) {
            if (linksAlreadyFollowed.size() > maxLinks) {
                linksAlreadyFollowed.remove(url.toExternalForm());
                throw new Error("Max links exceeded " + maxLinks);
            }
            if (shouldNotFollowLink(url)) {
                IndexLink.log.info("Not following " + url.toExternalForm()
                                    + " from " + linkFrom);
            } else {
                IndexLink.log.info("Following " + url.toExternalForm()
                                    + " from " + linkFrom);
                addLink(new IndexLink(url.toString(),conversation, this));
            }
        }
    } else {
        ignoreLink(url, linkFrom);
    }
}
```

newLink is an instance of com.meterware.httpunit.WebLink, which represents a single page in a web conversation. This method starts by determining whether the new URL is in our list of approved prefixes; if it isn't, newLink calls the helper method ignoreLink (which we'll see in a minute). If it is approved, we test to see if we have already followed this link; if we have, we just move on to the next link. Note that we verify whether the link as already been followed by attempting to add it to the linksAlreadyFollowed set. If the value already exists in the set, the set returns false. Otherwise, the set returns true and the value is added to the set.

We also determine if the addition of the link has caused the linksAlreadyFollwed set to grow past our configured maximum number of links. If it has, we remove the last link and throw an error.

Finally, the method checks to make sure the current URL is not in the collection of proscribed prefixes. If it isn't, we call the helper method addLink in order to add the link to the index:

```
private void ignoreLink(URL url, String linkFrom) {
    String status = "Ignoring " + url.toExternalForm() + " from " + linkFrom;
    linksNotFollowed.add(status);
    IndexLink.log.fine(status);
}
public void addLink(IndexLink link)
{
    try
    {
```

```
        link.runTest( );
      }
      catch(Exception ex)
      {
      // handle error...
      }
   }
```

Finally, we need an entry point to kick off the whole process. This method should take the root page of our site to index and begin processing URLs based on our configuration criteria:

```
public void setInitialLink(String initialLink) throws MalformedURLException {
  if ((initialLink == null) || (initialLink.length( ) == 0)) {
    throw new Error("Must specify a non-null initialLink");
  }
  linkPrefixesToFollow.add(new URL(initialLink));
  this.initialLink = initialLink;
  addLink(new IndexLink(initialLink,conversation,this));
}
```

Next, we define a class to model the links themselves and allow us access to their textual representations for inclusion in the index. That class is the IndexLink class. IndexLink needs three declarations:

```
private WebConversation conversation;
private IndexLinks suite;
private String name;
```

The WebConversation index again provides us the HTTPUnit framework's implementation of a browser-server session. The IndexLinks suite is the parent instance of IndexLinks that is managing this indexing session. The name variable stored the current link's full URL as a String.

Creating an instance of the IndexLink class should provide values for all three of these variables:

```
public IndexLink(String name, WebConversation conversation, IndexLinks suite) {
  this.name = name;
  if ((name == null) || (conversation == null) || (suite == null)) {
    throw new IllegalArgumentException(
      "LinkTest constructor requires non-null args");
  }
  this.conversation = conversation;
  this.suite = suite;
}
```

Each IndexLink exposes a method that navigates to the endpoint specified by the URL and checks to see if the result is an HTML page or other indexable text. If the page is indexable, it is added to the parent suite's index. Finally, we examine the current results to see if they contain links to other pages. For each such link, the process must start over:

```
public void checkLink( ) throws Exception {
  WebResponse response = null;
```

```
    try {
      response = conversation.getResponse(this.name);
    } catch (HttpNotFoundException hnfe) {
      // handle error
    }
    if (!isIndexable(response)) {
      return;
    }
    addToIndex(response);
    WebLink[] links = response.getLinks();
    for (int i = 0; i < links.length; i++) {
      WebLink link = links[i];
      suite.considerNewLink(this.name, link);
    }
  }
}
```

The isIndexable method simply verifies the content type of the returned result:

```
private boolean isIndexable(WebResponse response) {
    return response.getContentType().equals("text/html") || response.getContentType(
).equals("text/ascii");
}
```

whereas the addToIndex method actually retrieves the full textual result from the URL and adds it to the suite's index:

```
private void addToIndex(WebResponse response) throws SAXException, IOException,
InterruptedException {
    Document d = new Document();
    HTMLParser parser = new HTMLParser(response.getInputStream());
    d.add(Field.UnIndexed("url", response.getURL().toExternalForm()));
    d.add(Field.UnIndexed("summary", parser.getSummary()));
    d.add(Field.Text("title", parser.getTitle()));
    d.add(Field.Text("contents", parser.getReader()));
    suite.addToIndex(d);
}
```

The parser is an instance of org.apache.lucene.demo.html.HTMLParser, a freely available component from the Lucene team that takes an HTML document and supplies a collection-based interface to its constituent components. Note the final call to suite.addToIndex, a method on our IndexLinks class that takes the Document and adds it to the central index:

```
// note : method of IndexLinks
public void addToIndex(Document d)
  {
      try
      {
      writer.addDocument(d);
      }
      catch(Exception ex)
      {
      }
  }
```

That's it. Together, these two classes provide a single entry point for starting a crawling/indexing session. They ignore the concept of scheduling an indexing event; that task is left to the user interface layers. We only have two classes, making the model extremely simple to maintain. And we chose to take advantage of an unusual library (HTTPUnit) to keep us from writing code outside our problem domain (namely, web request/response processing).

Principles in Action

- Keep it simple: chooseHTTPUnit for web navigation code, minimum performance enhancements (maximumLinks, linksToAvoid collection)
- Choose the right tools: JUnit, HTTPUnit, Cactus,* Lucene
- Do one thing, and do it well: interface-free model, single entry-point to service, reliance on platform's scheduler; we also ignored this principle in deference to simplicity by combining the crawler and indexer
- Strive for transparency: none
- Allow for extension: configuration settings for links to ignore

The Search Service

The search service uses the same collected object pattern as the crawler/indexer. Our two classes this time are the QueryBean, which is the main entry point into the search service, and the HitBean, a representation of a single result from the result set. In order to perform a search, we need to know the location of the index to search, the search query itself, and which field of the indexed documents to search:

```
private String query;
private String index;
private String field;
```

We also need an extensible collection to store our search results:

```
private List results = new ArrayList();
```

We must provide a constructor for the class, which will take three values:

```
public QueryBean(String index, String query, String field)
    {
        this.field = field;
        this.index = index;
        this.query = query;
    }
```

* Unit tests elided for conciseness. Download the full version to see the tests.

The field variable contains the name of the field of an indexable document we want to search. We want this to be configurable so future versions might allow searching on any field in the document; for our first version, the only important field is "contents". We provide an overload of the constructor that only takes index and query and uses "contents" as the default for field:

```
public QueryBean(String index, String query)
{
    this(index, query, "contents");
}
```

The search feature itself is fairly straightforward:

```
public void execute() throws IOException, ParseException {
    results.clear();
    if (query == null) return;
    if (field == null) throw new IllegalArgumentException("field cannot be null");
    if (index == null) throw new IllegalArgumentException("index cannot be null");
    IndexSearcher indexSearcher = new IndexSearcher(index);
    try {
        Analyzer analyzer = new StandardAnalyzer();
        Query q = QueryParser.parse(query, field, analyzer);
        Hits hits = indexSearcher.search(q);
        for (int n=0; n<hits.length(); n++) {
            if (hits.score(n) < THRESHOLD_SCORE) {
                return;
            }
            Document d = hits.doc(n);
            String title = safeGetFieldString(d, "title");
            results.add(new HitBean(d.getField("url").stringValue(),
                        safeGetFieldString(d, "title"), hits.score(n)));
        }
    } finally {
        indexSearcher.close();
    }
}
```

First, we make sure our results collection is empty and all our arguments are within appropriate ranges. If they are, we create a new instance of Lucene's IndexSearcher, pointing it to the current version of the search index. Next, we invoke Lucene to do the actual search by creating an instance of Lucene's Query class, passing in our search term(s), the field we are searching, and a new instance of Lucene's StandardAnalyzer. The result of the IndexSearcher's search method is a collection of Lucene Hit objects, sorted in descending order by score. We grab the values we need from them in order to create instances of our own HitBean class. Notice we're using the helper method safeGetFieldString to retrieve values from the hit's document:

```
private String safeGetFieldString(Document d, String field) {
    Field f = d.getField(field);
    return (f == null) ? "" : f.stringValue();
}
```

This prevents us from adding a null instead of the empty string as our field value. Last, but certainly not least (it's in the finally block because it's important), we close the indexSearcher handle to the index. This step is vital when we start exposing the service via a web service: open handles to the index prevent other users from accessing it.

The HitBean is primarily for storing simple result data:

```
final String url;
final String title;
final float score;
private static NumberFormat nf;

static {
  nf = NumberFormat.getNumberInstance();
  nf.setMaximumFractionDigits(2);
}

public HitBean(String url, String summary, float score) {
  this.url = url;
  this.title = summary;
  this.score = score;
}

public String getScoreAsString() {
  return nf.format(getScore());
}
public String getUrl() {
  return url;
}

public String getTitle() {
  return title;
}

public float getScore() {
  return score;
}
```

Instances of the class store a full URL to the result file, the title of that file, and a relative rank score. We provide a series of getters to retrieve those values and a single constructor to initialize them. The only interesting part is the use of the java.text. NumberFormat class to create a formatter for our result score.

Once we chose Lucene as our search tool, our code became very straightforward. After a user supplies a search term, we simply verify that the query will run as provided and then execute it, compiling the results into a simple series of HitBean instances.

Principles in Action

- Keep it simple: simple objects representing query and results, unit tests for search results

- Choose the right tools: Lucene, JUnit

- Do one thing, and do it well: QueryBean focuses on search, ResultBean is simple data structure, and IndexPathBean encapsulates the configurable index property

- Strive for transparency: shadow-copied index so search and index can run simultaneously

- Allow for extension: none

The Console Interface

Console interfaces generally share a common usage idiom: provide a method for invoking the interface without arguments, but also allow for runtime decisions by providing for command flags. If the number of arguments does not match your expectations, return a usage statement.

If a user provides no command flags to our console interface, it launches into search mode. We'll allow users to enter search terms on the command line and return results. To quit, they just press Enter.

In order to launch an indexing event, the user passes in a flag in this format: */i: http://www.somedomain.com/*. This simply provides the starting URL from which the rest of the indexable pages are eventually discovered. If the user invokes the indexer, we'll bypass the search. If not, we go into search mode.

According to typical standards, we should allow the user to enter a help flag (we'll use /?) that produces the usage message. Any other number of or type of flag cause us to write out the usage message and quit.

Here are the utility methods:

```
private static void writeUsage()
{
    System.out.println("Usage: java ConsoleSearch");
    System.out.println(" -- /i:http://YOUR_INITIAL_INDEX_PATH");
    System.out.println(" -- /?:show this message");
}

private static boolean checkArgs(String[] args)
{
    if(args.length < 2 && args.length > 0 && args != null)
    {
        if(args[0].startsWith("/i") || args[0].startsWith("/?"))
        {
            return true;
        }
```

```
          }
      return false;
  }

  private static String getIndexFlag(String[] args)
  {
    for(int i=0;i<args.length;i++)
    {
        if(args[i].startsWith("/i:"))
        {
            return args[i].substring(3, args[i].length());
        }
    }
    return "";
  }
```

The last method, getIndexFlag, examines the args collection to see if the user passed in the /i flag. If so, it returns the URL that is passed in after the flag.

That only leaves the entry point to the application:

```
public static void main(String[] args)
    {
        // get configured index path from IndexPathBean
        ConfigBean config = new ConfigBean();
        String indexPath = config.getCurIndexPath();
        if(indexPath == "") return;

        // check args for index flag, retrieve initial page, execute index
        if(!checkArgs(args)) {
            writeUsage();
            return;
        }

        String indexInitialPage = getIndexFlag(args);
        if(indexInitialPage != "")
        {
            doIndex(indexInitialPage);
            return;
        }

        // Allow multiple queries from command line
        BufferedReader rdr = new BufferedReader(new InputStreamReader(System.in));
        try {
            while (true) {
              System.out.print("Query: ");
              String line = rdr.readLine();
                if (line.length() == 0) {
                  break;
                }
            QueryBean query = new QueryBean("contents", indexPath, line);
            query.execute();
            HitBean[] hits = query.getResults();
            for(int i = 0;i<hits.length;i++)
            {
```

```
                System.out.println(hits[i].getScoreAsString() + " " +
                    hits[i].getUrl());
            }
        }
    }
    catch(Exception e)
    {
        e.printStackTrace();
    }
}
```

This single method provides everything our human and machine users could want.
The live users can execute the main method and start interactively querying the
index. Conversely, they can pass in the /i: flag and operate just the indexing/crawl-
ing functionality.

First, make sure the arguments are correct; if they're not, call writeUsage and then
break. Check to see if the user is asking for an index instead of a search. If she is, call
doIndex, then return. If not, allow the user to enter a query and execute the search,
returning a simply-formatted result set. If anything goes wrong, print out the stack
trace.

Here's the doIndex method:

```
private static void doIndex(String indexflag)
{
    try
    {
        ConfigBean config = new ConfigBean();
        String nextIndex;
        try
        {
            nextIndex = config.getNextIndexPath();
        }
        catch(Exception ex)
        {
            return;
        }

        IndexLinks lts = new IndexLinks(nextIndex, config.getMaxLinks(),
                                config.getSkippedLinksFile());
        lts.initFollowPrefixesFromSystemProperties();
        lts.initAvoidPrefixesFromSystemProperties();
        lts.setInitialLink(indexflag);

        config.flipIndexPath();
    }
    catch(Exception e)
    {
        // handle error
    }
}
```

First, we retrieve the *alternate* index path from the ConfigBean. Remember, we need to create the index, but still allow other users to coninue to *search* it. Create a new instance of our IndexLinks class, passing in the alternate index path plus the MaxLinks and SkippedLinksFile values from our ConfigBean. Set up the avoid and follow link collections and kick off the index process. If everything succeeds, flip the indexes via the ConfigBean.flipIndexPath( ) method.

The console interface is simple enough that it doesn't need a controller layer between it and our business logic. In fact, the console interface looks a lot like a simple controller layer. It pieces together all three services without knowing anything about their internal configuration, demonstrating good interface separation. It is entirely focused on providing entry points to the application services to our users and returning results.

Principles in Action

- Keep it simple: no configurable schedule for invoking services, allow indexing output to show through to user
- Choose the right tools: JUnit
- Do one thing, and do it well: just read from command lines and return search results
- Strive for transparency: no internal knowledge of services
- Allow for extension: none

The Web Service Interface

The web service interface is even simpler to code than the console interface. The web service can provide two different access points: one for searching and one for indexing. The search method needs to return its entire result-set in a serializable format so that it can be returned across the wire via SOAP. The index method doesn't have to return any value at all; it only needs to accept the starting URL from the user to get the process rolling.

We must define this interface in WSDL in order for it to be available as a web service. WSDL (Web Services Description Language) files simply define the access methods and data types necessary for communicating with a given web service. WSDL files can contain much more: since we have narrowed our requirements down so much, we don't require most of those extra services.

The full WSDL file looks like this:

```
<definitions xmlns="http://schemas.xmlsoap.org/wsdl/"
             xmlns:xs="http://www.w3.org/2001/XMLSchema"
             xmlns:soap="http://schemas.xmlsoap.org/wsdl/soap/"
             name="SiteSearch"
```

```
              targetNamespace="http://www.halloway.net/SiteSearch"
              xmlns:tns="http://www.halloway.net/SiteSearch">
<types>
  <xs:schema>
    <xs:complexType name="queryType">
      <xs:sequence>
        <xs:element name="seachString" type="xs:string"/>
        <xs:element name="threshold" type="xs:float"/>
      </xs:sequence>
    </xs:complexType>
    <xs:complexType name="responseType">
      <xs:sequence minOccurs="0" maxOccurs="unbounded">
        <xs:element name="url" type="xs:anyURI"/>
        <xs:element name="score" type="xs:float"/>
      </xs:sequence>
    </xs:complexType>
    <xs:element name="query" type="tns:queryType"/>
    <xs:element name="queryResponse" type="tns:responseType" maxOccurs="unbounded"/>
    <xs:element name="index" type="xs:string"/>
  </xs:schema>
</types>

<message name="queryRequest">
  <part name="request" element="tns:query"/>
</message>

<message name="queryResponse">
  <part name="response" element="tns:queryResponse"/>
</message>

<message name="doIndex">
    <part name="request" element="tns:index"/>
</message>

<portType name="SiteSearch">
  <operation name="searchContents">
    <input message="tns:queryRequest" name="queryRequest"/>
    <output message="tns:queryResponse" name="queryResponse"/>
  </operation>
</portType>

<portType name="SiteSearch">
    <operation name="doIndex">
        <input message="tns:doIndex" name="doIndex"/>
    </operation>
</portType>

<binding name="SiteSearchSoapHttp" type="tns:SiteSearch">
  <soap:binding style="document" transport="http://schemas.xmlsoap.org/soap/http"/>
  <operation name="searchContents">
    <soap:operation soapAction="searchContents"/>
    <input name="queryRequest">
      <soap:body use="literal"/>
    </input>
```

```
            <output name="queryResponse">
              <soap:body use="literal"/>
            </output>
          </operation>
          <operation name="doIndex">
            <soap:operation soapAction="doIndex"/>
            <input name="doIndex">
                <soap:body use="literal"/>
            </input>
          </operation>
        </binding>

        <service name="SiteSearchService">
          <port name="SiteSearchSoap" binding="tns:SiteSearchSoapHttp">
            <soap:address location="http://localhost:8080/axis/services/SiteSearchSoap"/>
          </port>
        </service>

      </definitions>
```

The <types> section defines any datatypes that need to be exchanged by clients and servers; the <queryType> wraps the two inputs into a search query (search term and threshold for limiting results based on relative rank). <queryResponse> defines the sequence of individual results of a search operation.

After the datatypes, the individual messages are defined. Messages represent inputs to and outputs from individual web service endpoints. Three are defined here: <queryRequest> and <queryResponse> are the input message and output results of the search service, and <doIndex> is the input message to a return-less index service access point. After all these definitions, map the individual messages and datatypes to the methods of the implementation class. Note that the mapping of doIndex includes an input type but no output message.

The implementation is even simpler; it only defines methods that match the WSDL (one for searchContents and one for doIndex):

```
public ResponseType[] searchContents(QueryType request) throws RemoteException {
    try {
      ConfigBean config = new ConfigBean();
      ServletContext context = getServletContext();
      if (context == null) {
        throw new Error("null servlet context");
      }
      QueryBean query = new QueryBean(config.getCurIndexPath(),
                                      request.getSeachString());
      query.execute();
      HitBean[] fullResults = query.getResults();
      ArrayList result = new ArrayList();
      for (int n=0; n<fullResults.length; n++) {
        HitBean hit = fullResults[n];
        if (hit.getScore() >= request.getThreshold()) {
          ResponseType rt = new ResponseType();
```

```
            rt.setScore(hit.getScore());
            rt.setUrl(new URI(hit.getUrl()));
            result.add(rt);
      }
    }
    return (ResponseType[]) result.toArray(new ResponseType[result.size()]);
  } catch (Exception e) {
    getServletContext().log(e, "fail");
    throw new AxisFault(e.getMessage());
  }
}

public void doIndex(String indexUrl)
{
    try
      {

        ConfigBean config = new ConfigBean();
        String nextIndex;
        try
        {
            nextIndex = config.getNextIndexPath();
        }
        catch(Exception ex)
        {
            return;
        }

        IndexLinks lts = new IndexLinks(nextIndex,
            config.getMaxLinks(), config.getSkippedLinksFile());
        lts.initFollowPrefixesFromSystemProperties();
        lts.initAvoidPrefixesFromSystemProperties();
        lts.setInitialLink(indexUrl);

        config.flipIndexPath();

      }
      catch(Exception e)
      {
          //System.out.print(e.getStackTrace());
      }
}
```

These methods are similar to the methods defined in the console application, with minor differences in the types of exceptions thrown, as well as the creation of a the return value for searchContents.

Principles in Action

- Keep it simple: ignore the greater part of the web services stack; if you can't read it, don't automate it (the WSDL for this service was written by hand)
- Choose the right tools: Axis, JUnit, HTTPUnit

- Do one thing, and do it well: just invoke search and return response
- Strive for transparency: web service is the ultimate transparent layer to end users
- Allow for extension: none

Extending the Spider

So far, the Spider meets the needs the original client. We have provided all of the necessary functionality in a simple, efficient package. The user interfaces are nicely decoupled from the business logic, meaning we can extend the application into multiple other interface areas. Since we have designed the application with the idea of extensibility through transparency, we ought to be able to add other services fairly easily.

In the next chapter, we're going to see how easy it is to repurpose the spider for use in a different context. We'll replace the existing search functionality in the jPetStore sample application with the Simple Spider. This process demonstrates how following the principlels laid out in this book make it easy to reuse your code and make it work in new contexts. We'll layer our standalone application into a Spring framework with minimal changes to the original code.

Extending jPetStore

The previous chapter introduced the workhorse Simple Spider service with its console-based user interface and web service endpoint. In this chapter, we see how easy it is to add the Spider to an existing application, jPetStore. Some might argue the jPetStore already has a search tool; but that tool only searches the database of animals in the pet store, not all the pages on the site. Our customer needs to search the entire site; jPetStore has at least one page in the current version that isn't searchable at all (the Help page) and text describing the different animals that doesn't show up in a query.

We'll add the Spider to the jPetStore, paying careful attention to what we need to change in the code in order to enable the integration. In addition, we will replace the existing persistence layer with Hibernate. By carefully adhering to our core principles, our code will be reusable, and since the jPetStore is based on a lightweight framework (Spring), it doesn't make unreasonable demands on our code in order to incorporate the search capability or the new persistence layer. Coming and going, the inclusion will be simple and almost completely transparent.

A Brief Look at the Existing Search Feature

The search feature that comes with jPetStore takes one or more keywords separated by spaces and returns a list of animals with a name or category that includes the term. A search for "dog" turns up six results, while a search for "snake" nets one. However, a search for "venomless" gets no results, even though animal EST-11 is called the Venomless Rattlesnake. Even worse, none of the other pages (such as the Help page) shows up in the search at all; neither will any other pages you might add, unless they're an animal entry in the database.

The search feature has the following architecture (shown in Figure 10-1):

1. Any page of the jPetStore application may contain a search entry box with Search button.

2. Clicking the button fires a request (for */shop/searchProducts.do*) passing the keywords along as part of the request.

3. *petstore-servlet.xml*, the configuration file for the MVC portion of the jPetStore Spring application, has the following definition:

```
<bean name="/shop/searchProducts.do"
class="org.springframework.samples.jpetstore.web.spring.SearchProductsController">
    <property name="petStore"><ref bean="petStore"/></property>
</bean>
```

This creates a handler for the "/shop/searchProducts.do" request and maps it to an instance of SearchProductsController, passing along an instance of petStoreImpl called petStore.

4. SearchProductsController instantiates an instance of a class that implements the ProductsDao interface, asking it to search the database for the specified keywords.

5. ProductsDao queries the database and creates an instance of Product for each returned row.

6. ProductDao passes a HashMap containing all of the Product instances back to SearchProductsController.

7. SearchProductsController creates a new ModelAndView instance, passing in the name of the JSP page to display the results (SearchProducts) and the HashMap of values. The JSP page then renders the results using the PagedListHolder control (a list/table with built-in paging functionality).

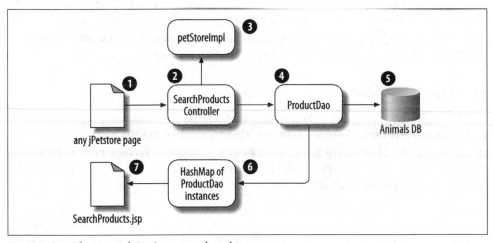

Figure 10-1. The original jPetStore search architecture

Only the ProductsDao knows how to interact with the underlying data. Product is a straightforward class with information about each product, and the view (*Search-Products.jsp*) simply iterates through the returned results to create the output page.

Deciding on the Spider

We've identified how the current search feature works and its limitations: the search feature only searches products in the database, not the site as a whole, and even then it doesn't search all available data about the products. The results it returns are extremely limited—though well-formatted.

The Simple Spider is a crawler-based search feature instead of focusing on the database: it searches everywhere on the site, not just the products table, and it treats any textual information visible to users as part of the search domain. The Spider does have a major limitation—since it is based on a web crawler, it can only catalog pages linked to other pages on the site. If a page is only accessible via some server-side logic (for instance, selecting a product from a drop-down list and submitting the form to the server, which returns a client-side or server-side redirect), the crawler never reaches that page and it won't be part of the search.

With a problem like this, in which a feature of the application is too limited to be of much service to our users, we have to decide between refining the existing service or replacing it entirely. The limitation of the jPetStore search is partly due to the fundamental nature of the service (it searches the database, not the site). Refining it to accomplish the full-site search would be horribly inefficient. The Spider is the obvious solution, but we must consider what we are already dealing with (remember, you are what you eat). If jPetStore uses a lot of server-side logic to handle navigation, the Spider simply won't be able to provide a complete catalog. In this case, though, all the navigation on the site is handled client-side, so the Spider is a perfect fit for solving our problem and coexisting with our current application.

Extending jPetStore

We have decided that an existing service layer of the application is unsuited to our current needs. Additionally, we have decided that replacing the service with a new one is the appropriate solution. This situation is a perfect test of extension: how easy will it be to replace this service? Will it involve new code? Changes to existing code? Or just changes to our configuration services?

In order to replace the existing functionality with the Simple Spider, we need to change the output formatting a little (our returns will display full URLs instead of product instances), write a new controller that knows to launch the Simple Spider instead of the ProductsDao object, and change our mapping layer to point to the new controller. Finally, we'll use Spider's configuration service so Spider works better with the new web site.

Looking at these requirements, we can already see we'll need to write fewer than 100 lines of code and make only minor configuration changes in order to get this to work. It's a reasonable price to pay for the end result we want. Because jPetStore

---

and the Simple Spider were designed to allow for extension in the first place, they fit together well with minimal work.

Conversely, we could write much less code and in fact do almost no work at all if we chose to connect to the Spider through the existing web service interface rather than integrating it directly with the jPetStore. Since the web service interface already exists, it might be construed as a violation of the "do one thing, and do it well" principle to add another, seemingly useless interface. In this instance, though, the added cost of sending a bloated message (XML/SOAP) over a slow transport mechanism (HTTP) is too heavy, especially given the minimal amount of work it will take to get a faster, more efficient integration.

Replacing the Controller

First, let's replace the SearchProductsController. Here's the main method of that class:

```
public ModelAndView handleRequest(HttpServletRequest request, HttpServletResponse
                            response) throws Exception {
    if (request.getParameter("search") != null) {
        String keyword = request.getParameter("keyword");
        if (keyword == null || keyword.length() == 0) {
            return new ModelAndView("Error", "message",
            "Please enter a keyword to search for,
            then press the search button.");
        }
        else {
            PagedListHolder productList = new PagedListHolder(
                this.petStore.searchProductList(keyword.toLowerCase()));
            productList.setPageSize(4);
                request.getSession().setAttribute(
            "SearchProductsController_productList", productList);
            return new ModelAndView("SearchProducts", "productList",
                productList);
        }
    }
    else {
        String page = request.getParameter("page");
        PagedListHolder productList = (PagedListHolder)
            request.getSession().getAttribute("SearchProductsController_productList");

        if ("next".equals(page)) {
            productList.nextPage();
        }
        else if ("previous".equals(page)) {
            productList.previousPage();
        }
        return new ModelAndView("SearchProducts", "productList", productList);
    }
}
```

The method returns a new instance of ModelAndView and Spring uses it to determine which JSP to load and how to wire data up to it. The method takes an HttpServletRequest and HttpServletResponse in order to interact directly with the HTTP messages.

The first thing the method does is make sure the user entered a search term. If not, it displays an error to the user; if so, it creates a PagedListHolder called productList with a maximum page size (number of rows per page) set to four. Finally, it calls the petStore instance's searchProductList method, which calls to ProductsDao and finally returns the HashMap of Product instances. The second clause is for when the user clicks the Next Page or Previous Page buttons on the paged list.

Rewrite or Replace?

The next question a conscientious programmer should ask is, does it make more sense to rewrite this class to make use of the Spider, or to write an entirely new controller? In order to answer that question, we need to consider three more-specific questions first:

1. Do we have access to the original source? Now that we have the jPetStore application, do we control the source, or is it all binary? If we don't control the source, we can short-circuit the rest of the decision. We can only replace the class; we can't rewrite it.

2. Will we ever need to use the original service again? Assuming we have the source and *can* rewrite the class, can we foresee ever needing to revert to or make use of the database-search functionality? For the sake of flexibility, we usually want to retain old functionality unchanged, which means we want to replace, not rewrite. However...

3. Does the current class implement an easily reused interface? If we are going to replace the class, how much work will we have to do to get the application to recognize and accept your new class? Think of this as an organ transplant; how much work and medication has to go into the host body to keep it from rejecting the new organ? Will our changes be localized around the new class or more systemic?

Here's the answer to these questions: yes, we have the source code; yes, we'll want access to retain the potential for using the old service; and yes, the controller implements a very simple interface. The controller only needs to implement a single method, handleRequest, which takes an HttpServletRequest and a HttpServletResponse and returns a ModelAndView. This means the jPetStore application doesn't need any systemic changes in order to use our new controller, as long as we support that interface.

Implementing the Interface

To replace this class, we're going to write our own controller class called SearchPagesController. It must implement the Controller interface, which defines our handleRequest method.

```
public class SearchPagesController implements Controller {
    ...
}
```

Here's our controller's handleRequest method:

```
public ModelAndView handleRequest(HttpServletRequest request,
                        HttpServletResponse response) throws Exception {
    if (request.getParameter("search") != null) {
        String keyword = request.getParameter("keyword");
        if (keyword == null || keyword.length() == 0) {
            return new ModelAndView("Error", "message", "Please enter a
            keyword to search for, then press the search button.");
        }
        else {
                ConfigBean cfg = new ConfigBean();
                    String indexpath = "";
                    try
                    {
                        indexpath = cfg.getCurIndexPath();
                    }
                    catch(Exception ex)
                    {
                      return new ModelAndView("Error", "message",
                                        "Could not find current index path.");
                    }

                    QueryBean qb = new QueryBean(indexpath, keyword, "contents");

                    qb.execute();

                    HashMap hits = new HashMap(qb.getResults().length);
                    for(int i =0;i<qb.getResults().length;i++)
                    {
                      hits.put("hits", qb.getResults()[i]);
                    }
                    return new ModelAndView("SearchProducts", hits);
        }
    }
}
```

For our search functionality, we won't use the paged results. We simply list all the results on a single page; as a result, we don't have to deal with the Next Page and Previous Page code. Our controller again checks for null keywords and returns an error if it finds them empty. Otherwise, the service is used almost identically as the console application in the Chapter 9 was used. First, create an instead of ConfigBean to find the most current index of the site, then create a `QueryBean` based on that index path. Finally, execute the query and put all the `HitBean` instances into a `HashMap` to return to the View.

The usage pattern is identical to that in the last chapter; the only difference is the format of our returned data. Instead of passing the native array of `HitBeans` back, the `ModelAndView` object requires a `HashMap`. It's easy enough to create the one from the other, and now we have an entirely new access point for the Spider application with almost no work.

There is one last detail we need to work out. The original `SearchProductsController` has a field called `petStore` of type `PetStoreFacade` that the Spring framework populates for it. In order to be a complete replacement for the original, our new controller needs to expose the same property and accessor methods, even though they aren't officially found on a standalone interface anywhere in the application. You will often find examples of this when you're extending or modifying an application.

```
private PetStoreFacade petStore;

public void setPetStore(PetStoreFacade petStore) {
    this.petStore = petStore;
}
```

Registering Our New Class with jPetStore

Finally, we alert `jPetStore` to the new controller's existence. If `jPetStore` is not coded for extensibility, we have to modify the application code in order to get it to work. For instance, if there are methods of `jPetStore` that create instances of `SearchProductsController` directly, we must change each of those lines to create a `SearchPagesController` instead.

It turns out, however, that `jPetStore` is quite ready for extensibility—partly because it is based on the Spring framework. In order to tell `jPetStore` about our new controller, we modify a single configuration file (*petstore-servlets.xml*). This file tells Spring what objects to create and how to wire them together to make a sensible application. Now, we just need to find the configuration setting used to launch the `SearchProductsController` and point it to our new `SearchPagesController` instead.

```
<bean name="/shop/searchProducts.do"
    class="org.springframework.samples.jpetstore.web.spring.SearchPagesController">
    <property name="petStore"><ref bean="petStore"/></property>
</bean>
```

We're telling the application to map requests for "/shop/searchProducts.do" to a new instance of `SearchPagesController`. At the same time, we tell it, provide the `SearchPagesController` with the current instance of `petStore` (in a property called `petStore`).

Principles in action

- Keep it simple: the controller logic is a simple invocation of Spider; the controller interface is *very* simple (one method)
- Choose the right tools: Spring and the Spider
- Do one thing and do it well: since the Spider is so well-encapsulated, it's easy to add to an existing service; the controller deals with invoking the Spider and the JSP only needs to display the results—MVC pattern well-demonstrated
- Strive for transparency: the site doesn't care how it is indexed; it can easily switch between data-driven and HTML-driven search technologies
- Allow for extension: we quickly expanded our search capabilities by adding a new tool with minimal code; the configuration abilities of jPetStore allow for no-code recognition of new service

The User Interface (JSP)

The user interface is fairly straightforward. Instead of just dumping our results to the console or creating an XML document of the results (as in the web service implementation from Chapter 9), this time we need to write a JSP that iterates over the results and displays them as hyperlinks in a table.

The original jPetStore search feature used a PagedListHolder for its results because it displayed the image associated with each returned product in the table. Since the images were arbitrary in size, jPetStore didn't want to display too many entries on a given page since it might result in a lot of vertical scrolling. Our results consist of a hyperlink to the returned URL and the relative rank of the given result; therefore, we'll use a simple table to display our results.

Again, we are faced with the rewrite-or-replace question. Just like last time, we have three questions to consider:

1. Do we have access to the original source? We must, since JSPs are just text files in both development and deployment mode.
2. Will we ever want to reuse the existing service? We do, but in this case, a JSP is so easy to recreate that it won't make much difference.
3. Does the current version implement some standard interface? Not as such, since JSPs are just mixes of static HTML and dynamic content.

Because of the rather trivial nature of the changes and because JSPs are easily edited in place (no compilation necessary), we'll just repurpose the existing *SearchProducts.jsp* file. This strategy saves us from having to change any more configuration settings:

```
<%@ include file="IncludeTop.jsp" %>

<table align="left" bgcolor="#008800" border="0" cellspacing="2" cellpadding="2">
<tr>
```

```
        <td bgcolor="#FFFF88">
        <a href="<c:url value="/shop/index.do"/>">
            <b><font color="BLACK" size="2"> &lt;&lt; Main Menu</font></b>
        </a>
        </td>
    </tr>
    </table>
    <table align="center" bgcolor="#008800" border="0" cellspacing="2"
        cellpadding="3">

        <tr bgcolor="#CCCCCC">  <td><b>URL</b></td>  <td><b>Rank</b></td> </tr>
        <c:forEach var="page" items="${hits}">
            <tr bgcolor="#FFFF88">
            <td><a href="<c:out value="${page.url}"/>">
                    <c:out value="${page.url}"/></a>
            </td>
            <td>
                <c:out value="${page.score}"/>
            </td>
            </tr>
        </c:forEach>
    </table>

    <%@ include file="IncludeBottom.jsp" %>
```

The JSP files in the application have a standard header and footer defined in *IncludeTop.jsp* and *IncludeBottom.jsp*. All we have to do is render the results in between the include directives. Start by creating a JSP-style forEach loop, with an enumerator called page pointing at each member of the HashMap called "hits." For each hit, we render a table row containing the URL (the value of which is both the text to display and the HREF to point it to) and the relative rank of the hit. JSP handles hooking up the variables and properties using reflection. However, when implementing this page, we come across the first (and only) reason to change some of the original Spider code.

Changes to the Original Code to Fit the JSP

JSP reflects on fields to hook up properties to <out> display tags instead of getters and setters. Unfortunately, our original implementation of HitBean marked all of its data private and only exposed getters and setters (normally, the appropriate strategy). Since we now have to have the fields exposed directly, we need to make a simple change to the Spider. The original class started with these declarations:

```
final String url;
final String title;
final float score;
```

It now has to become:

```
public final String url;
public final String title;
public final float score;
```

What if We Don't Have the Spider Source?

It is instructive to examine what happens when we aren't the original authors of either the application we are extending (jPetStore) or the service we are integrating (Simple Spider). If we don't have access to the source code of either project, we can still make the extension we've been working on. For the jPetStore, all we did was modify a configuration file and a JSP (which we always have the source for) and add a new class.

If we don't have access to the original source for the HitBean class, how can we make it work with the JSP? The answer is simple: write a wrapper class that exposes the correct properties (or just use the already exposed web service interface):

```
public class HitBeanWrapper {
    private HitBean _hitbean;
    public String url;
    public String title;
    public float score;

    public HitBeanWrapper(HitBean hitbean)
    {
        _hitbean = hitbean;
        url = hitbean.getUrl();
        title = hitbean.getTitle();
        score = hitbean.getScore();
    }
    public String getScoreAsString() {
            return _hitbean.getScoreAsString();
    }
}
```

This requires a change to the handleRequest method of the SearchPagesController, as well:

```
HashMap hits = new HashMap(qb.getResults().length);
for(int i =0;i<qb.getResults().length;i++)
{
        hits.put("hits", new HitBeanWrapper(qb.getResults()[i]));
}
return new ModelAndView("SearchProducts", hits);
```

That's it. We've edited the Spider all we need to in order to incorporate it into the jPetStore application.

Principles in Action

- Keep it simple: display the URL to result pages instead of complex rendering of product information; use simple table output instead of PagedListHolder (the need for it was gone)
- Choose the right tools: table, not PagedListHolder; JSP

- Do one thing, and do it well: JSP focuses on display of output, not search intricacies
- Strive for transparency: HitBean exposes simple data properties; use a wrapper for HitBean if the source is not available
- Allow for extension: none

Setting Up the Indexer

Now that the search service is integrated into the application, we'll configure the indexer to automatically update against the current version of the web site on a regular basis. If you recall from the previous chapter, both the console application and the web service have mechanisms that let you launch the indexer service instead of the search service. The question is, how should the indexer be integrated with jPetStore?

Embed in jPetStore or Launch Externally?

The first approach is to make the indexer part of the jPetStore application itself; in other words, to add code to jPetStore that invokes the indexer. jPetStore could invoke the indexer at the request of a user or on a schedule. Both methods have problems: if we expose a user interface for launching the indexer, we have to wrap it in some kind of secured section of the site for administrative users only. Currently, jPetStore has no such security built in. Building it just to wrap around the indexer seems like a major stretch—too much complexity, not enough payoff. Which means a manual access point is out.

The other option is to build a scheduler into the jPetStore application. Regardless of how the architecture, a scheduler would require the jPetStore application to be running for indexing to occur. Since jPetStore is a web- and container-based application, its lifecycle is entirely dependent on the external hosts. If the web server software is turned off for any reason, jPetStore shuts down as well. If the interval for the indexer falls in that window, the indexer doesn't run. In addition, writing scheduling code is completely outside of the problem domain for jPetStore, just as it was for the Simple Spider. The jPetStore application should do one thing: display animals in a web catalog.

We have no option but to invoke the indexer from some other location. A good strategy is to leverage an existing scheduler system: on Windows it's *schtasks* and on Linux it's *cron*. Let's implement the scheduled indexer on Windows.

Using the System Scheduler

For ease of use, we create a batch file for actually launching the service. We want to invoke the Java runtime to run our ConsoleSearch class's main method, passing in the starting point for jPetStore. The command (and, therefore, the contents of our batch file) looks like this:

```
java c:\the\path\to\ConsoleSearch /i:http://localhost/jpetstore
```

We store that in a file called *jpetstoreIndexer.bat*. For simplicity's sake, we'll store it in *c:\commands*.

In order to schedule the indexer to run every night at 2:00 a.m., issue the following command (whiled logged in as a local administrator):

```
c>schtasks /create /tn "jpetstore Indexer" /tr:c:\commands\jpetstoreIndexer.bat
       /sc daily /st 02:00:00
```

The /tn flag creates a unique name for the text; /tr points to the actual command to invoke; /sc is the time interval; and /st is the specific time to launch the indexer on that interval.

Similarly, on Linux, edit the *crontab* file and launch the *cron daemon* to accomplish the same thing.

Smell the Roses

The beauty of this solution is that our application, the Simple Spider, has been repurposed to run in both a container-based environment (Spring) and a direct runtime environment (via the scheduler calling the Java runtime directly) without any extra code whatsoever. Because of its simple architecture and loosely coupled services, the Spider itself can operate just fine in both environments simultaneously. We didn't have to write a new access point or code a new UI or even make any configuration changes. Even better, we were able to take a single application from our first chapter and repurpose its internal services to two different endpoints without much work. It's good to step back every now and again and smell the roses, just to realize what a little forethought and adherence to simple principles gets you.

Principles in Action

- Keep it simple: use system-provided scheduler and existing console-based access point to application
- Choose the right tools: *schtasks*, *cron*, ConsoleSearch
- Do one thing, and do it well: neither Spider nor jPetStore worry about the scheduling of the indexer; the scheduler only worries about the index, not the rest of the functionality
- Strive for transparency: the scheduler knows nothing about the implementation details of the indexer or even where the results of the indexing will end up: it's all handled in configuration files
- Allow for extension: none

Making Use of the Configuration Service

If we jump straight in and start using the search as it's currently configured, we'll notice a problem. Our searches are returning lots of results—more than can be possible given the number of products in the database. In fact, a search for "dog" returns over 20 results, even though there are only 6 dogs in the database.

This is happening because of the brute-force nature of the crawling service. Without extra help, the crawler finds every link on every page and follows it, adding the results to the index. The problem is that in addition to the links that allow users to browse animals in the catalog, there are also links that allow users to add the animals to their shopping carts, links to let them remove those items from their carts, links to a sign-in page (which, by default in jPetStore, loads with real credentials stored in the text-boxes), and a live link for "Login," which the crawler will happily follow—thus generating an entirely new set of links, with a session ID attached to them.

We need to make sure our crawler doesn't get suckered into following all the extraneous links and generate more results than are helpful for our users. In the first part of Chapter 9, we talked about the three major problems that turn up in a naïve approach to crawling a site:

Infinite loops
> Once a link has been followed, the crawler must ignore it.

Off-site jumps
> Since we are looking at *http://localhost/jpetstore*, we don't want links to external resources to be indexed: that would lead to indexing the entire Internet (or, at least, blowing up the application due to memory problems after hours of trying).

Pages that shouldn't be indexed
> In this case, that's pages like the sign-in page, any page with a session ID attached to it, and so on.

Our crawler/indexer service handles the first two issues for us automatically. Let's go back and look at the code. The IndexLinks class has three collections it consults every time it considers a new link:

```
Set linksAlreadyFollowed = new HashSet();
HashSet linkPrefixesToFollow = new HashSet();
HashSet linkPrefixesToAvoid = new HashSet();
```

Every time a link is followed, it gets added to linksAlreadyFollowed. The crawler never revisits a link stored here. The other two collections are a list of link prefixes that are allowed and a list of the ones that are denied. When we call IndexLinks. setInitialLink, we add the root link to the linkPrefixesToFollow set:

```
linkPrefixesToFollow.add(new URL(initialLink));
```

IndexLinks also exposes a method, initAvoidPrefixesFromSystemProperties, which tells the IndexLinks bean to read the configured system properties in order to initialize the list:

```
public void initAvoidPrefixesFromSystemProperties() throws MalformedURLException {
    String avoidPrefixes = System.getProperty("com.relevance.ss.AvoidLinks");
    if (avoidPrefixes == null || avoidPrefixes.length() == 0) return;
    String[] prefixes = avoidPrefixes.split(" ");
    if (prefixes != null && prefixes.length != 0) {
        setAvoidPrefixes(prefixes);
    }
}
```

First, the logic for considering a link checks to make sure the new link matches one of the prefixes in linkPrefixesToFollow. For us, the only value stored there is *http://localhost/jpetstore*. If it is a subpage of that prefix, we make sure the link doesn't match one of the prefixes in linkPrefixesToAvoid.

A special side note: good code documentation is an important part of maintainability and flexibility. Notice the rather severe lack of comments in the code for the Simple Spider. On the other hand, it has rather lengthy method and type names (like initAvoidPrefixesFromSystemProperties), which make comments redundant, since they clearly describe the entity at hand. Good naming, not strict commenting discipline, is often the key to code readability.

All we need to do is populate the linkPrefixesToAvoid collection. ConsoleSearch already calls initAvoidPrefixesFromSystemProperties for us, so all we have to do is add the necessary values to the *com.relevance.ss.properties* file:

```
AvoidLinks=http://localhost:8080/jpetstore/shop/signonForm.do http://localhost:8080/
jpetstore/shop/viewCart.do http://localhost:8080/jpetstore/shop/searchProducts.do
http://localhost:8080/jpetstore/shop/viewCategory.do;jsessionid= http://localhost:
8080/jpetstore/shop/addItemToCart.do http://localhost:8080/jpetstore/shop/
removeItemFromCart.do
```

These prefixes represent, in order, the sign-on form of the application, any links that show the current user's cart, the results of another search, any pages that are the result of a successful logon, pages that add items to a users cart, and pages that remove items from a users cart.

Principles in Action

- Keep it simple: use existing Properties tools, not XML
- Choose the right tools: java.util.Properties
- Do one thing, and do it well: the service worries about following provided links; the configuration files worry about deciding what links can be followed
- Strive for transparency: the service doesn't know ahead of time what kinds of links will be acceptable; configuration files make that decision transparent to the service
- Allow for extension: expandable list of allowable link types

Adding Hibernate

jPetStore uses a relatively straightforward architecture for providing database access. There is an interface layer that provides functional mapping to the DAOs themselves without worrying about actual implementation details. The specific DAOs vary based on the backend database; we'll be examining the ones targeting HSQLDB (Hypersonic SQL).

Existing Architecture

Let's look at how the Product class is managed. Product is the domain object that represents one item in the catalog.

```
package org.springframework.samples.jpetstore.domain;
import java.io.Serializable;
public class Product implements Serializable {

  private String productId;
  private String categoryId;
  private String name;
  private String description;

  public String getProductId() { return productId; }
  public void setProductId(String productId) { this.productId = productId.trim(); }

  public String getCategoryId() { return categoryId; }
  public void setCategoryId(String categoryId) { this.categoryId = categoryId; }

  public String getName() { return name; }
  public void setName(String name) { this.name = name; }

  public String getDescription() { return description; }
  public void setDescription(String description) { this.description = description;}

  public String toString() {
    return getName();
  }

}
```

Its persistence is managed through an object that implements the ProductDao interface. A ProductDao must be able to load a specific product given its ID, or load a list of products either from a category or from a set of keywords.

```
public interface ProductDao {

  List getProductListByCategory(String categoryId) throws DataAccessException;
  List searchProductList(String keywords) throws DataAccessException;
  Product getProduct(String productId) throws DataAccessException;

}
```

There currently exists a class called SqlMapProductDao that looks up product information in Hypersonic SQL through SQL mapping files.

Hibernate Mappings for Existing Domain Objects

To replace this architecture with one based on Hibernate, we first have to create mapping files that define the relationship between the domain objects and the database. Looking again at Product, we'll create a mapping file called *Product.hbm.xml* which looks like:

```
<?xml version="1.0"?>
<!DOCTYPE hibernate-mapping PUBLIC
    "-//Hibernate/Hibernate Mapping DTD 2.0//EN"
    "http://hibernate.sourceforge.net/hibernate-mapping-2.0.dtd">

<hibernate-mapping
    package="org.springframework.samples.jpetstore.domain">

    <class name="Product" table="product">
        <id name="productId"
            column="productId"
            type="string">
            <generator class="native"/>
        </id>
        <property name="categoryId" column="category" type="string"/>
        <property name="name" column="name" type="string"/>
        <property name="description" column="description" type="string"/>
    </class>

</hibernate-mapping>
```

In the mapping file, we first identify the package and particular class (org. springframework.samples.jpetstore.domain.Product) that we are mapping. We have to tell it what table to map to ("product", in this case) and then map the individual properties of the domain object to the columns in the table. This file needs to be saved somewhere on the class path; we'll create a new folder in the project structure called "hibernate" to hold our map files and our new DAOs.

Hibernate DAOs

The next step is to create a DAO that uses Hibernate as the persistence layer instead of the SQL mappings used in the original version. The new DAO needs to implement the ProductDao interface, just like the original DAO. However, the implementation of that interface will be totally different.

Here is the code for the new DAO:

```
public class HibernateProductDao implements ProductDao {
    SessionFactory factory;
    Configuration cfg;
```

```
public HibernateProductDao( ) {
    try {
        cfg = new Configuration( ).addClass(
            org.springframework.samples.jpetstore.domain.Product.class);
        factory = cfg.buildSessionFactory( );
    } catch (Exception ex) {
        System.out.println("Hibernate configuration failed: " + ex);
    }
}

public List getProductListByCategory(String categoryId)
    throws DataAccessException {
    List results = null;
    try {
        Session session = factory.openSession( );
        results = session.find("from product where product.category = ?",
                            categoryId, Hibernate.STRING);
        session.close( );
    } catch (Exception ex) {
        System.out.println("Failed to connect to database:" + ex);
    }
     return results;
}

public List searchProductList(String keywords) throws DataAccessException {
    return null;
}

public Product getProduct(String productId) throws DataAccessException {
    Product p = null;
    try {
        Session session = factory.openSession( );
        p = (Product)session.load(Product.class, productId);
        session.close( );
    } catch (Exception ex) {
        System.out.println("failed to connect to database: " + ex);
        p = null;
    }

    return p;
}

}
```

First, we need a way to interact with Hibernate. As shown in Chapter 7, we need to create a Hibernate SessionFactory and use it to get a Session with which to interact with the database. The DAO's constructor instantiates a new Hibernate configuration, loading the mapping file from the class path based on the name of the class added to the configuration. Then, it gets the SessionFactory from the Configuration.

Each method uses the SessionFactory to open a new Session with the database. The getProduct method is the most straightforward; first, we get the Session. Then, we ask the session to load an instance of the Product class, given its productId. Note that the result from the `session.load( )` call is of type `Object`, which we have to cast to Product. Finally, we close the Session. Hibernate handles all the SQL commands, looking up the mapping files, matching the productId to the right column in the table, populating all the fields, everything.

The `getProductListByCategory( )` method is less straightforward; it takes a `categoryId` and returns a List of all the products that match that category. In this case, we can't rely on the built-in SQL generation; we have to create our own query. Again, we first grab a `Session` from the `SessionFactory`, then use the `session.find( )` method, which returns a `List` of `Objects`. Find takes three parameters in this case: the HSQL query (which contains a placeholder for a query parameter, marked with a "?"), the value to fill into the query parameter, and the type of that parameter.

As shown in Chapter 7, HSQL (Hibernate SQL) queries look a lot like regular SQL statements, except here we left off the "SELECT [values]" part of the statement, since Hibernate will fill those in for us based on the mapping. This method will now look up all the rows in the Product table where `categoryId` equals the value passed in to the method, and create one instance of `Product` for each row in the resultset. All the product instances are placed in a `List` and returned.

The final method of the DAO, `searchProductList`, would be a lot more complex, but luckily, we don't have to implement it. Since we have already replaced the original search functionality with the Simple Spider, this method will never be called now, so we simply return `null` (we have to do something, since the `ProductDao` interface still mandates its inclusion).

To finish out the new architecture, we just repeat these steps for each of the remaining five domain objects. Each gets a mapping file and an implementation of the appropriate DAO interface.

Changing the Application Configuration

In order to get the new DAOs working with jPetStore, we need to modify some configuration files. First, we'll need to create the global *hibernate.properties* file, which tells Hibernate which database to use and how to use it. jPetStore is currently configured to use a local instance of Hypersonic SQL, with a username of "sa" and a blank password (NEVER do this in a production environment). The *hibernate.properties* file looks like this:

```
hibernate.connection.driver_class = org.hsqldb.jdbcDriver
hibernate.connection.url = jdbc:hsqldb:hsql://localhost:9002
hibernate.connection.username = sa
hibernate.connection.password =
hibernate.dialect=net.sf.hibernate.dialect.HSQLDialect
hibernate.show_sql=true
```

This file should be saved in the project root file, next to the other global configuration files. Hibernate will look for it by name.

Next, open up jPetStore's *dataAccessContext-*.xml* files (one is *dataAccessContext-jta.xml* and the other is *dataAccessContext-local.xml*). In each, there is a section that mapes the DAOs for the project. Change each mapping to point to the new DAO, and eliminate the now unnecessary properties. For example, the original mapping for ProductDao was:

```
<bean id="productDao" class="org.springframework.samples.jpetstore.dao.ibatis.
                   SqlMapProductDao">
        <property name="dataSource"><ref local="dataSource"/></property>
        <property name="sqlMap"><ref local="sqlMap"/></property>
</bean>
```

This now becomes:

```
<bean id="productDao" class="org.springframework.samples.jpetstore.dao.hibernate.
HibernateProductDao"/>
```

We can eliminate the properties because the Hibernate versions of the DAOs do not require any configuration information to be passed in by the controller; Hibernate manages those issues for us.

Once you have successfully changed all the DAO references, the last remaining piece is to include the necessary *jar* files in your class path. Hibernate requires the following *jars*: *hibernate2.jar*, *cglib2.jar*, *ehcache.jar*, *commons-collections.jar*, *dom4j.jar*, and *jta.jar* (all of which are included in the Hibernate download).

Spring's Built-In Hibernate Support

Now that you have seen the explicit way to do things, let's briefly take a look at the supporting infrastructure Spring provides for Hibernate. Spring, through its "inversion of control" architecture, can fully manage the creation of the SessionFactory for you. In addition, it provides a new class, HibernateDaoSupport, which allows your application-specific DAOs to reuse standard, template-derived calls for interacting with the datasource.

To set it up, you need to change your DAOs to extend HibernateDaoSupport. So, this:

```
public class HibernateProductDao implements ProductDao
```

becomes:

```
public class HibernateProductDao extends HibernateDaoSupport implements ProductDao
```

Then add the following code to enable Spring to pass in a SessionFactory:

```
private SessionFactory sessionFactory;
public void setSessionFactory(SessionFactory sessionFactory) {
    this.sessionFactory = sessionFactory;
}
```

After adding this, your DAOs can use an object provided by HibernateDaoSupport called HibernateTemplate. This new class, accessed through the new getHibernateTemplate() method inherited from HibernateDaoSupport, exposes a series of helper methods for interacting with the database, such as load, save, update, saveOrUpdate, get, and find. Our ProductDao becomes a lot simpler:

```
public class HibernateProductDao extends HibernateDaoSupport implements ProductDao {
    private SessionFactory sessionFactory;

    public void setSessionFactory(SessionFactory sessionFactory) {
        this.sessionFactory = sessionFactory;
    }

    public HibernateProductDao() {
    }

    public List getProductListByCategory(String categoryId) {
        return getHibernateTemplate().find("from product where product.category = ?",
                                           categoryId, Hibernate.STRING);
    }

    public List searchProductList(String keywords) throws DataAccessExcetption {
        return null;
    }

    public Product getProduct(String ProductID) throws DataAccessException {
        return (Product) getHibernateTemplate().load(Product.class, productId);
    }

}
```

To configure all of this, you'll have to make some changes to your configuration files. You now have to add a property for the SessionFactory where you defined the ProductDao bean:

```
<bean id="productDao"
 class="org.springframework.samples.jpetstore.dao.hibernate.HibernateProductDao">
    <property name="sessionFactory"/>
    <ref bean="mySessionFactory"/>
</bean>
```

Then add a definition of the mySessionFactory bean:

```
<bean id="mySessionFactory"
 class="org.springframework.orm.hibernate.LocalSessionFactoryBean">
<property name="mappingResources">
<list>
    <value>product.hbm.xml</value>
</list>
<!-- etc. -->
</property>
<property name="hibernateProperties">
<props>
<prop key="hibernate.dialect">net.sf.hibernate.dialect.HSQLDialect</prop>
</props>
</property>
<property name="dataSource">
```

```
    <ref bean="dataSource"/>
  </property>
</bean>
```

Add as many entries to the mappingResources property as you have *map* files, and make sure that the dataSource property refers to your already-configured dataSource bean. With these minimal changes, your DAOs become much more standardized and compacted, and Spring handles all your SessionFactory and Session implementation details for you. You are free to focus, yet again, on the problem at hand rather than the supporting framework.

That's it! Once again, we've managed to replace an entire swath of existing code without touching the original codebase itself. We have simply added new classes to the project and changed some configuration settings, and voila! Hibernate.

Principles in Action

- Keep it simple: domain objects remain unaware of persistence logic, Hibernate manages all configuration
- Choose the right tools: Hibernate
- Do one thing, and do it well: the domain model is focused on the business problem, the DAOs focus on data manipulation and are database-agnostic
- Strive for transparency: domain model is completely unaware of persistence layer
- Allow for extension: Spring configuration and IoC allow us to change persistence layers

Summary

Over the last two chapters, we have taken an initial customer's requirements for a generic, flexible web site search engine and refined them to meet our core principles. We then designed a simple, straightforward application that met those requirements—and then some—and made use of existing tools (however unorthodoxly) to accomplish a complex set of tasks. The result was a solution to the initial requirements that came in well below the $18,000 that Google charges for its search appliance, even if we had billed the customer not only for design and development, but also for all the time spent researching the included open source tools and writing these two chapters! And, frankly, we aren't cheap. Simplicity really does have its rewards.

We learned how easy it is to integrate two applications designed with our core principles in mind. Since the jPetStore sample is built on a lightweight framework (Spring) and makes good use of the world's most common design pattern (MVC), it was child's play to introduce a replacement service for the limited one provided.

Since the Spider is well factored and provides flexibility through its configuration service, it is easy to adapt it for use in a new context, in a container-based environment, and with an entirely new user interface, using only three changed lines of code to the original application (and those lines only added a new scoping keyword). And since Hibernate is also built on these same principles, it was incredibly easy to swap it into the project in place of the existing persistence mechanism.

These examples demonstrate that Java doesn't have to be hard. In fact, if you focus on the principles outlined in this book, Java can be downright fun.

CHAPTER 11
Where Do We Go from Here?

We've all come to crossroads in our lifetimes. One of the biggest for me was deciding where to live. After seeing Austin, Texas for the first time, I knew that my life would never be the same. A unique combination of place, opportunities, and people opened my eyes to a world that I never knew existed. Make no mistake: the Java platform is at a similar crossroads. I believe that Java developers will catch a similar glimpse of a new way of programming. It's my sincere hope that better experiences will lead us beyond J2EE as we know it, and into something simpler, cleaner, and much more effective.

In this chapter, I describe what that future might look like. I cover trends in technology and process that I believe will have profound significance in the near future, and some that might not hit the mainstream for years. I'll then speak directly to the leadership in the Java space, and make some suggestions that I believe are necessary for the long-term vitality of Java.

Technology

By now, you probably understand that I believe technology is only a small part of any given problem. Java is not the best programming language that's ever existed, although it's easily among the most successful. The tools are not nearly as important as the hands that wield them. That said, technology does lead any discussion about the future of a dominant platform.

Less Is More

By far the biggest challenge Java developers face is the issue of complexity. I'm starting to see more advanced customers scale down by strategically stepping back from traditional J2EE application models such as EJB with CMP to simpler models such as simple POJO deployed on Tomcat. It's difficult to estimate how well lightweight containers are doing, but the early buzz and adoption rates are promising. The trend toward simplicity is likely to pick up momentum in other places. Hibernate is wildly successful not because it's more powerful than TopLink or EJB CMP, but because it's simpler. JUnit has been more successful than any other testing framework, by far.

The success of these types of frameworks must trouble larger vendors. The top web application server vendors, BEA, Sun, Oracle, and IBM, must take notice of the simplicity trend. They've got no choice, because their customers are struggling with J2EE. You can already see those vendors start to embrace simpler, lighter frameworks:

- Most vendors are not selling EJB solutions as strongly as they once were. Vendors are especially backing off of EJB CMP for persistence solutions.

- Many vendors are quietly developing alternative persistence strategies. Oracle has acquired TopLink, Sun and JBoss have included JDO solutions with their application servers, and IBM is now co-marketing another persistence solution.

- Vendors are working to build better, simplified tools for their communities. IBM has worked with the Eclipse project to simplify and replace their massive VisualAge product suite, and BEA is increasing their investments in Work Bench, which simplifies development of web services applications.

Still, there's a long way to go. The current web services specification is spinning out of control and closing in on permanent bloat-ware status. XML is getting so complicated and awkward that some researchers are already seeking an alternative.

Open Source

I'm not convinced that the future direction of the Java platform could or even should come from the major J2EE vendors. You can see the results of committee-driven big-enterprise design:

EJB
> Vendors and customers alike spend too much time building on this dead-end technology.

Generics
> The implementation of generics in Java 1.5 is a solution without a problem. The current implementation forces an interface and increases the burden of the programmer, for very little benefit.

Web services
> Early versions of web services were light and simple. Later versions have patched a few holes and also dramatically increased the complexity.

Logging
> Log4j is a fantastic open source solution, but Sun decided to go it alone, creating a competing and many say inferior implementation.

As I said in Chapter 1, the pressure for larger companies to build bloated software is sometimes too difficult to resist. Some of the juggernauts are starting to understand this. IBM, for example, is showing interest in open source software. They know that embracing open source software makes good business sense and can bring innovations to light that may not have surfaced in other ways.

The open source community fills an important niche in the Java community. It allows software to evolve and improve based on usage patterns of its customers. Many of the revolutionary ideas in the Java community have come from open source projects:

- MVC template technologies such as Struts changed the way we integrate user interfaces.
- JUnit changed the way we integrate and test software.
- Ant changed the way we build software
- Eclipse and Tomcat changed the way big vendors approach open source software.
- Hibernate changed the way we think about reflection and transparent persistence.

The next generation of open source software is already making waves. You've seen Spring, one of the lightweight containers that dramatically improves integration and assembly. Lucene is a clean text search engine opening up applications to searches that go beyond the database. Velocity, WebWorks, and Tea are user-interface technologies that are challenging the state of the art. These projects have the potential to change the way we code in dramatic ways. Beyond individual projects, open source software has another affect on the industry. True, open source software is not right for every customer, but Linux and the Apache web server both have the market share and industry backing to be long-term players. Figure 11-1 shows the typical components and services of an enterprise application. Corporate shops are conservative with their adoption of open source solutions. Still, penetration of open source software, shown in darker colors in Figure 11-1, is increasing. Already, conservative customers, including banks and insurance companies, are deploying open source operating systems and web servers in increasing numbers. In the past five years, Tomcat and JBoss have also made inroads. It's only natural that the line between what's acceptable open source and what's proprietary is always moving further up. I believe that it will continue to do so. In particular, databases and persistence are services ripe for open source deployment.

I don't think it this trend will stop with the web server. While working at IBM, I never read one line of open source code, but that situation is changing quickly. For IBM, Eclipse is only the beginning. They are beginning to exert pressure on Sun to open up major pieces of the Java platform. They may not succeed, but it's hard to argue against the increasing roles that open source software can play. Oracle and BEA test their software for compatibility with key open source projects like Tomcat, and also generate Struts-compliant code.

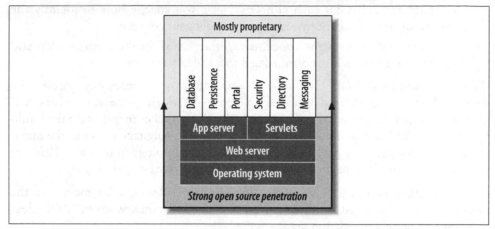

Figure 11-1. Open source penetration is increasing

Aspect-Oriented Programming (AOP)

Many a programmer has tried to design programming paradigms that make enterprise development easier. Object-oriented programming helps: you can make models with business rules that look and act much more like the real world. But OOP can only get you part of the way there.

Certain services called *crosscutting concerns* are difficult to add to an enterprise application because you need to apply them broadly, based on a changing policy. For example, many different objects might need to be persistent. You may want to add all methods to an audit log. You might also want a certain kind of method to participate in a transaction. You don't want to add this kind of service code to all of the classes in an application.

You've seen that object-oriented programmers tried to solve this problem with inheritance, interfaces, or programming models like containers. I've made a case that the best service implementation techniques preserve transparency with respect to the service.

AOP software is an attempt to make it easier to produce and consume far-reaching services (crosscutting concerns) while maintaining transparent models. Here's how it works:

- Break out core tasks, called concerns, from your requirements. The core concern is the business purpose of your application, such as making reservations in a reservation system. Other concerns (crosscutting concerns) should be separated from the requirements.

- Code individual aspects individually. This is where you'll notice the biggest productivity boost. You are free to think of each problem independently, allowing for better focus and better reuse.

- Configure the policy for each concern. Here, you specify how to identify the methods of your core concern and how to apply your concern.

- Your framework weaves the concerns together based on the configuration and implementation of each concern using a tool called a *weaver*.

That's the premise of AOP. Like most powerful ideas, it's remarkably simple. The details, though, can get tedious to implement Although some researchers and leading-edge developers are already using AOP, it's my belief that it will take a full-blown, successful aspect-oriented language to make the language thrive in the mainstream. We saw the same phenomenon with object technology in the early 1990s. It just takes time for the industry to move when it comes to major paradigms.

I do think that you'll start to see some aspect-oriented ideas quickly move into the mainstream well before AOP fully matures. In Chapter 8, you saw several AOP ideas in action in Spring's transaction management:

- Spring provides method interceptors to attach functionality to an existing method without changing the method.

- Spring provides a pointcut model to describe the methods that require a given concern, such as a transaction.

Other frameworks, such as JBoss, use core AOP ideas like method interceptors, and that's likely to continue. When enough developers use AOP ideas, it will be much easier for an aspect-oriented language to establish itself when the market conditions are right. Although you don't yet see AOP ideas in the mainstream, you do see several frameworks with an AOP flavor. The most common one is persistence.

Persistence

If you look closely at JDO, you can see several AOP ideas. Persistence is a crosscutting concern. JDO addresses it by implementing the concern independently of the core concern (your application). JDO then uses byte code enhancement to effectively intercept a Java thread of execution and inject calls to the JDO libraries—or, more generally, the persistence aspect. It's an effective solution. I've been impressed with the Kodo JDO product produced by SolarMetric. The performance, flexibility, and power of the framework is impressive, and big customers are starting to take notice. It warms my heart, because transparent persistence is important.

Nearly all enterprise applications have some persistence element. In some ways, the EJB CMP implementation has done us a disservice because it's made many gun-shy. The states of technology in persistence frameworks, RDBMS technology, and hardware have come far enough to make transparent persistence possible. While not all applications need persistence frameworks, many do. It's critically important for the Java community to establish an effective standard for transparent persistence. It looks like JDO 2.0 might be just what we need.

Containers

Most applications do not need EJB. It's just easier to build it all from scratch, adding in the occasional useful J2EE service as needed. I'll go even further: for the occasional application with true heavyweight enterprise requirements, there's a better way.

After reading Chapters 1 and 8, you know that I believe we're late in the era of the heavyweight J2EE container. They'll either wane or Java will die. They won't be killed by a technology so much as by an idea: that the idea of dependency injection has power. Right now, I've only coded minor applications in Spring, but after using Spring in the place of my J2EE container, I wondered what was missing.

Sooner or later, customers will notice that they're spending a lot of money without a lot of benefit. When that happens, vendors will respond. Whether they write their own or embrace open source containers doesn't make any difference. The idea of the lightweight container is what's important. The cat is out of the bag, and it will be tough to get it back in.

Process

After about a decade of stringent, heavyweight processes culminating in the rational unified process (RUP), the pendulum is finally swinging back in a more sane direction. While many larger IT shops are slow to adopt them, some of the ideas first collected in the Extreme Programming (XP) method are finally making it into the mainstream. Over the next couple of years, those ideas will gain momentum. I'm seeing customers who were hell-bent against agile development strongly consider it. It takes a long of time to turn a battleship, but it's happening. Continuous integration, automated unit testing, and simplicity are all getting more and more attention. Soon, you'll see full-blown test-driven development creep into conservative programming organizations. The ideas are powerful and sound.

The next important step is the reduction of tools. Right now, many developers spend too much time supporting formal documentation rather than concentrating on readable code. Formalized, full-blown UML-style modeling will not help a project as much as simpler temporary diagrams on a whiteboard. The role of a diagram is to improve understanding; if you are only producing it because you have to, and not because it adds value to the design, then don't bother. I also think model-driven architecture (MDA) is moving in the wrong direction. Generated code on such a scale is rarely legible, and visual languages have consequences on performance, reuse, and readability that we're only now coming to understand. You're better off writing simple, concise code from scratch that's easy to understand and maintain.

As that battleship comes around, some vendors will resist the simpler process. IBM's recent purchase of Rational gives more financial backing to the vendor supporting one of the heavier development processes, and they're starting to muddy the waters by labeling some of their own tools with the Agile label. Hopefully, independent consultants and academics will champion the lightweight development processes that are far more appropriate for most of the applications built today.

Even if you're not ready to adopt a whole new development process, take advantage of some of the principles. Automate your tests, value simplicity, and integrate continuously.

Challenges

Currently, the Java platform is the leading server-side development and deployment platform, but it's not beyond replacement. For continued success, leaders in the Java community must respond to a set of challenges:

Simplify
> Java development must get better for everyday developers. J2EE is not the ultimate answer; if it is not simplified, the average customer will no longer be able to afford the cost of developing and maintaining Java applications.

Leverage open source
> Most open source projects fail, and that's okay. The ones that succeed survive the withering test of everyday use. If an open source project works, standardize it and move forward.

Listen to developers
> Java's standardization process sometimes leads to many standards that have never been tried in the marketplace. A committee is a horrible place to design an API. No one is smart enough to understand all of the ways that things can break. Better adherence to successful open source APIs can help.

Deal with the albatross
> EJB is an albatross that is never fully going to take flight. It's important to modernize that architecture. Allowing pluggable persistence, separating services, allowing more transparent models, and lightening the container would go a long way toward a more successful EJB 3.0.

Conclusion

At one time, I usually traveled for business with two huge bags. They had fancy connectors and wheels, so I didn't need to bear any weight myself. I could carry the whole world with me, and I did. But getting through security got harder and harder, and I dreaded the sight of stairs. I've since learned to strip that pile down to one medium-sized bag for both my computer and clothes with only a shoulder strap for all but the longest trips. Life is much better.

Java has had an enormous impact on the way we write modern software. Yet for all the changes embodied by Java, it suffers from the same problems as every other development platform in history: namely, bloat. The bags are too full. We are at a turning point in the trajectory of Java. The community of programmers is starting to whittle those bags down, believing in their own power to write great software instead of relying on heavyweight, complex tools to do all their thinking for them.

This book is not intended to bash J2EE or any other technology. Designing any broad-based framework is a difficult process. But the state of the art is always moving. The tools we use are changing. The days when large-scale J2EE deployments were the only choice for enterprise development are over. In some ways, we need to take a few steps backward to move forward. We are taking advantage of lighter frameworks, like Spring, Tomcat, and Hibernate. We use better tools, like JUnit, Ant, Cactus, and HTTPUnit. We have lighter processes, like XP and agile development.

Just as the thought leaders are simplifying the core technologies that they deploy, you need to revisit and simplify the core principles that form the foundation of your development process, your thinking, and your code. You need to understand and use techniques that simplify and focus each individual layer of code.

Taken together, we have a roadmap to a better place where the code we write solves the problems we face instead of the problems brought on by our tools. By keeping to the path, remembering our principles, and using good old-fashioned common sense, we can beat back the bloat and write better, faster, lighter Java.

Bibliography

Books

- Beck, Kent. *Test-Driven Development*. Reading, MA: Addison-Wesley, November 2002.

- Bloch, Joshua. *Effective Java Programming Language Guide*. Reading, MA: Addison-Wesley, June 2001.

- Fowler, Martin, et al. *Refactoring: Improving the Design of Existing Code*. Reading, MA: Addison-Wesley, 1999.

- Gamma, Richard Helm, Ralph Johnson, and John Vlissides (The Gang of Four). *Design Patterns: Elements of Reusable Object-Oriented Software*. Reading, MA: Addison-Wesley, 1994.

- Hatcher, Erik, and Steve Loughran. *Java Development with Ant*. Greenwich, CT: Manning Publications Co., 2003.

- Hightower, Richard, and Nicholas Lesiecki. Java Tools for Extreme Programming: Mastering Open Source Tools, Including Ant, JUnit, and Cactus,New York: John Wiley and Sons, inc., November 2001.

- Hunt, Andrew, and David Thomas. *Pragmatic Unit Testing*. Raleigh, NC and Dallas, TX: The Pragmatic Bookshelf, 2003.

- Hunt, Andrew and David Thomas. *The Pragmatic Programmer: from Journeyman to Master*. Reading, MA: Addison-Wesley, 1999.

- Johnson, Rod. *Expert One-on-One J2EE Design and Development*. Wrox Press, October 2002.

- Poyla, George. *How to Solve It*. Princeton, NJ: Princeton University Press,1957.

- Martin, Robert C. *Agile Software Development, Principles, Patterns, and Practices*. Prentice Hall, October 2002.

- Seuss, Dr. *The Cat in the Hat*. New York: Random House, 1957.

- Tate, Bruce, et al. *Bitter EJB*. Greenwich, CT: Manning Publications Co., June 2003.

Referenced Internet Sources

- Fowler, Martin. "Inversion of Control Containers and the Dependency Injection." Pattern on martinfowler.com, January 2004 (*http://martinfowler.com/articles/injection.html*).

- Halloway, Stuart Dabbs. "Java Properties Purgatory, Part 1 and 2." InformIT August 23, 2002 (*http://www.informit.com*).

- Heudecker, Nick. "Introduction to Hibernate." theserverside.com, July 15, 2003.

- Johnson, Rod. "Introducing the Spring Framework." theserverside.com, September 4, 2003 (*http://www.theserverside.com/resources/article.jsp?l=SpringFramework*).

- Neward, Ted. "Understanding class.forName(): Loading Classes Dynamically from within Extensions." javageeks.com, May 24, 2001 (*http://www.javageeks.com/Papers/ClassForName/ClassForName.pdf*).

- Retting, Michael J. with Martin Fowler. "Reflection vs. Code Generation." javaworld.com, November 2, 2001 (*http://www.javaworld.com/javaworld/jw-11-2001/jw-1102-codegen.html*).

- Spolsky, Joel. "The Law of Leaky Abstractions." Joel on Software, November, 2002 (*http://www.joelonsoftware.com/articles/LeakyAbstractions.html*)

Helpful Internet Sources

- JUnit home page (*http://junit.org*)
- Hibernate home page (*http://hibernate.org*)
- Spring home page (*http://springframework.org*)
- The Agile alliance (*http://www.agilealliance.org*)

Other References

- Clark, Mike. "Test-Driven Development with JUnit." Technical presentation, developed by Denver, CO: Clarkware, LLC, 2004 (*http://www.clarkware.com*).

- Halloway, Stuart. "Java Reflection." Technical presentation at No Fluff, Just Stuff symposium series, produced by Denver, CO: Big Sky Technologies, 2003–2004 (*http://www.nofluffjuststuff.com*).

Index

We'd like to hear your suggestions for improving our indexes. Send email to *index@oreilly.com*.

I

identifiers, Hibernate configuration, 137
indexer service
    embedding, 214
    setup, 214–216
inheritance
    extension and, 108
    layers and, 54
inner questions, project planning, 104
installation of plug-ins, 123
interceptors, AOP and, 85
interfaces
    extension and, 108
    external, project planning and, 103
    implementation, 209
    Java, unplanned extension and, 111
    layers and, 47
    plug-ins, 123, 126
    Simple Spider
        console, 196–199
        web service interface, 199–203
    user (JSP), 211
Inventor's Paradox, Spider and, 180
inversion of control, 153
invoking methods, class loading and, 119

J

J2EE
    as golden hammer, 91
    Pet Store example, 154
Java
    as golden hammer, 91
    interfaces, unplanned extension and, 111
Java Preferences API, 114
    client-side configuration, 115
java.lang.reflection package, 71
JDBC
    Hibernate and, 147
    Spring and, 152
JDO enhancers, transparency and, 78
jPetstore
    class registration, 210
    configuration service, 216
    controller replacement, 207
    embedding indexer service, 214
    Hibernate and, 218–224
JSP user interface, 211
JUnit
    Ant and, 32
    assertions, 31
    as automated watchdog, 28

clean up, 30
coupling, 34
as developmental tool, 28
exceptions, 31
failure, intentional, 31
initialization, 30
refactoring, 33
test organization, 30
test reuse, 33
testability and, 33
unit testing automation and, 27
JUnitPerf, 34
JUnitReports, generating, 32

L

layers
    abstraction, 47
    applications and, 47
    in architecture, 46
    business domain models, 49
    common layers, 49
    communication, 50
    coupling
        configuration, 59
        databases, 59
        direct access and, 52
        facades, 57
        microcoupling, 52
        reducing, 52
        shared data, 58
        transitive, 55
        transparency and, 56
    creating, overview, 47
    data access objects and, 50
    facades, 50
    inheritance and, 54
    interfaces, 47
    peer layers, 47
    service and, 47
    simplicity and, 19
    user interfaces, 51
    value and, 19
learning curve, bloat and, 7
libraries
    bloat and, 7
    reflection, 71
lightweight containers, AOP and, 85

M

macrocoupling, 56
    communication model, 57
    databases, 59

subclassing, transparency and, 65
system scheduler, service launch and, 215

T

technology
    Java and, 226
    purchase considerations, 19
test unit automation, Ant and, 32
thin wrapper, EJB, 93
tools, extension and, 112
    class loading, 118
    configuration, 114
    plug-ins, 123
    standards, 113
transaction framework, Spring and, 152
transactions
    Hibernate, 148
    Spring, 156
transitive coupling, layers, 55
transparency
    alternatives, 64
        limiting, 69
    AOP and, 85
    benefits, 61
    bloat and, 13
    byte code enhancement, 77
    code generation and, 81
    code injection and, 77
    compromised, 65
    crosscutting concerns and, 68
    Hibernate, 147
    JDO enhancers, 78
    layers and, 56

models, 61
    adding code, 65
    metadata addition, 66
persistence frameworks and, 64
POJOs, 69
source code enhancement, 77
Spring, domain model, 162
subclassing and, 65
transparency persistence, Hibernate, 130
types, Hibernate configuration, 140

U

unit test automation, 26
    JUnit and, 27
unplanned extension, 111
user interfaces, layers and, 51
users, project planning and, 103

V

validation, Spring, 156, 174

W

Web services as golden hammer, 95
web services interface, Simple
    Spider, 199–203
web sites, crawling, 178
WSDL (Web Services Description
    Language), 199

X

XML as golden hammer, 93

About the Authors

Bruce A. Tate is a kayaker, mountain biker, and father of two. In his spare time, he is an independent consultant in Austin, TX. In 2001, he founded J2Life, LLC, a consulting firm that specializes in Java persistence frameworks and lightweight development methods. His customers have included FedEx, Great West Life, TheServerSide, and BEA. He speaks at conferences and Java user's groups around the nation. Before striking out on his own, Bruce spent 13 years at IBM working on database technologies, object-oriented infrastructure, and Java. He was recruited away from IBM to help launch the client services practice in an Austin startup called Pervado Systems. He later served a brief stint as CTO of IronGrid, which built nimble Java performance tools. Bruce is the author of four books, including best-selling *Bitter Java*.

Working as a professional programmer, instructor, speaker, and pundit since 1992, **Justin Gehtland** has developed real-world applications using VB, COM, .NET, Java, Perl and a slew of obscure technologies since relegated to the trash heap of technical history. His focus has historically been on "connected" applications, which of course has led him down the COM+, ASP/ASP.NET, and JSP roads.

Justin is the coauthor of *Effective Visual Basic* (Addison-Wesley) and *Windows Forms Programming in Visual Basic .NET* (Addison-Wesley). He is currently the regular Agility columnist on *The Server Side .NET* and works as a consultant through his company Relevance, LLC in addition to teaching for DevelopMentor.

Colophon

Our look is the result of reader comments, our own experimentation, and feedback from distribution channels. Distinctive covers complement our distinctive approach to technical topics, breathing personality and life into potentially dry subjects.

The animal on the cover of *Better, Faster, Lighter Java* is a hummingbird. There are over 300 hummingbird species, all found only in the New World. All these species are easily identifiable by their long, tubular bills and iridescent feathers. The iridescence is a refraction effect that can be seen only when light is shining on the feathers at certain angles. Hummingbirds range in size from the bee hummingbird, which, measuring 2 inches long and weighing less than an ounce, is the smallest of all birds, to the great hummingbird, which measures about 8.5 inches long.

Hummingbirds are so named because of the humming noise made by their rapidly moving wings. On average, hummingbirds flap their wings 50 times a second; some species can flap as many as 200 times per second. The wings are flexible at the shoulder and, unlike most birds, they are propelled on the upstroke as well as the downstroke. Because of this flexibility, hummingbirds can hover, fly right or left, backward, and upside down. Most hummingbirds have tiny feet that are used only for perching, never for walking. Hummingbirds will fly to travel even a few inches.

Hummingbirds expend a great deal of energy, and they need to feed every 10 minutes or so. They feed on nectar, for sugar, and small insects, for protein. Their long, tapered bills enable them to retrieve nectar from even the deepest flower. Pollen accumulates on the head and neck of hummingbirds while they gather nectar. They then transfer this pollen to other flowers and thus play an important role in plant reproduction.

Hummingbirds appear frequently in Native American legends and mythology, often as representatives of the sun. According to some folk beliefs, they can bring love. Since Europeans first spotted these beautiful, colorful little birds, they have often appeared in the art and literature of the Old World, as well.

Colleen Gorman was the production editor and the copyeditor for *Better, Faster, Lighter Java*. Jane Ellin was the proofreader. Matt Hutchinson and Mary Anne Weeks Mayo provided quality control. Johnna VanHoose Dinse wrote the index.

Ellie Volckhausen designed the cover of this book, based on a series design by Edie Freedman. The cover image is a 19th-century engraving from the Dover Pictorial Archive. Emma Colby produced the cover layout with QuarkXPress 4.1 using Adobe's ITC Garamond font.

Melanie Wang designed the interior layout, based on a series design by David Futato. This book was converted by Julie Hawks to FrameMaker 5.5.6 with a format conversion tool created by Erik Ray, Jason McIntosh, Neil Walls, and Mike Sierra that uses Perl and XML technologies. The text font is Linotype Birka; the heading font is Adobe Myriad Condensed; and the code font is LucasFont's TheSans Mono Condensed. The illustrations that appear in the book were produced by Robert Romano and Jessamyn Read using Macromedia FreeHand 9 and Adobe Photoshop 6. The tip and warning icons were drawn by Christopher Bing. This colophon was written by Clairemarie Fisher O'Leary.

Related Titles Available from O'Reilly

Java

Ant: The Definitive Guide

Eclipse: A Java Developer's Guide

Enterprise JavaBeans, *3rd Edition*

Hardcore Java

Head First Java

Head First Servlets & JSP

Head First EJB

J2EE Design Patterns

Java and SOAP

Java & XML Data Binding

Java & XML

Java Cookbook

Java Data Objects

Java Database Best Practices

Java Enterprise Best Practices

Java Enterprise in a Nutshell, *2nd Edition*

Java Examples in a Nutshell, *3rd Edition*

Java Extreme Programming Cookbook

Java in a Nutshell, *4th Edition*

Java Management Extensions

Java Message Service

Java Network Programming, *2nd Edition*

Java NIO

Java Performance Tuning, *2nd Edition*

Java RMI

Java Security, *2nd Edition*

Java ServerPages, *2nd Edition*

Java Serlet & JSP Cookbook

Java Servlet Programming, *2nd Edition*

Java Swing, *2nd Edition*

Java Web Services in a Nutshell

Learning Java, *2nd Edition*

Mac OS X for Java Geeks

NetBeans: The Definitive Guide

Programming Jakarta Struts

Tomcat: The Definitive Guide

WebLogic: The Definitive Guide

Keep in touch with O'Reilly

1. Download examples from our books

To find example files for a book, go to:

www.oreilly.com/catalog

select the book, and follow the "Examples" link.

2. Register your O'Reilly books

Register your book at *register.oreilly.com*

Why register your books?
Once you've registered your O'Reilly books you can:

* Win O'Reilly books, T-shirts or discount coupons in our monthly drawing.
* Get special offers available only to registered O'Reilly customers.
* Get catalogs announcing new books (US and UK only).
* Get email notification of new editions of the O'Reilly books you own.

3. Join our email lists

Sign up to get topic-specific email announcements of new books and conferences, special offers, and O'Reilly Network technology newsletters at:

elists.oreilly.com

It's easy to customize your free elists subscription so you'll get exactly the O'Reilly news you want.

4. Get the latest news, tips, and tools

www.oreilly.com

* "Top 100 Sites on the Web"—PC Magazine
* CIO Magazine's Web Business 50 Awards

Our web site contains a library of comprehensive product information (including book excerpts and tables of contents), downloadable software, background articles, interviews with technology leaders, links to relevant sites, book cover art, and more.

5. Work for O'Reilly

Check out our web site for current employment opportunities:

jobs.oreilly.com

6. Contact us

O'Reilly & Associates
1005 Gravenstein Hwy North
Sebastopol, CA 95472 USA

TEL: 707-827-7000 or 800-998-9938
        (6am to 5pm PST)

FAX: 707-829-0104

order@oreilly.com
For answers to problems regarding your order or our products. To place a book order online, visit:

www.oreilly.com/order_new

catalog@oreilly.com
To request a copy of our latest catalog.

booktech@oreilly.com
For book content technical questions or corrections.

corporate@oreilly.com
For educational, library, government, and corporate sales.

proposals@oreilly.com
To submit new book proposals to our editors and product managers.

international@oreilly.com
For information about our international distributors or translation queries. For a list of our distributors outside of North America check out:

international.oreilly.com/distributors.html

adoption@oreilly.com
For information about academic use of O'Reilly books, visit:

academic.oreilly.com

O'REILLY®

Our books are available at most retail and online bookstores.
To order direct: 1-800-998-9938 • *order@oreilly.com* • *www.oreilly.com*
Online editions of most O'Reilly titles are available by subscription at *safari.oreilly.com*